Pitching to the Corners

Pitching to the Corners
My Post–MLB Career Abroad

Don August
with Mark Knudson

Foreword by Dan Plesac

McFarland & Company, Inc., Publishers
Jefferson, North Carolina

All photos are from Don and Tami August
unless otherwise credited.

Library of Congress Cataloging-in-Publication Data

Names: August, Don, 1963– author. | Knudson, Mark, 1960– author.
Title: Pitching to the corners : my post-MLB career abroad / Don August with Mark Knudson ; foreword by Dan Plesac.
Description: Jefferson, North Carolina : McFarland & Company, Inc., Publishers, 2024. | Includes index.
Identifiers: LCCN 2024037435 | ISBN 9781476693071 (paperback : acid free paper) ∞
  ISBN 9781476653815 (ebook)
Subjects: LCSH: August, Don, 1963– | Baseball—Taiwan. | Baseball—Europe. | Pitchers (Baseball)—United States—Biography.
Classification: LCC GV865.A926 A3 2024 | DDC 796.357092 [B]—dc23/eng/20240903
LC record available at https://lccn.loc.gov/2024037435

British Library cataloguing data are available

ISBN (print) 978-1-4766-9307-1
ISBN (ebook) 978-1-4766-5381-5

© 2024 Don August and Mark Knudson. All rights reserved

No part of this book may be reproduced or transmitted in any form or by any means, electronic or mechanical, including photocopying or recording, or by any information storage and retrieval system, without permission in writing from the publisher.

Front cover image: Don August, 1987 (courtesy of Don and Tami August)

Printed in the United States of America

McFarland & Company, Inc., Publishers
  Box 611, Jefferson, North Carolina 28640
    www.mcfarlandpub.com

Table of Contents

Foreword by Dan Plesac 1
Introduction 3

ONE. Break on Through 5
TWO. Who'll Stop the Rain? 22
THREE. Travelin' Man 36
FOUR. Speaking in Tongues 57
FIVE. Cheeseburger in Paradise 73
SIX. Family of Man 90
SEVEN. The Replacements 106
EIGHT. Ramblin' Gamblin' Man 120
NINE. People Are Strange 135
TEN. Scenes from the Italian Restaurant 152
ELEVEN. The End 170
TWELVE. Glory Days 196

Epilogue: With a Little Help from My Friends 209
Index 217

Foreword

by Dan Plesac

The world of professional baseball is played and enjoyed by so many different personalities, nationalities ... but all have the same common goals: winning and having fun along the way. I played in Milwaukee with Don August ... just a fun-loving, upbeat and sometimes whacked-out guy! After playing for Team USA in the Olympics—what a thrill that would have been—Don made his big league debut in 1988 when I was already a Brewer. We were never roommates (I didn't have any sleepwalking adventures with him), but in June of 1989 we did team up to make some baseball history. Don started—and was the winning pitcher in—the first game ever played in the Toronto SkyDome (now the Rogers Center), then the brand-new home of the Blue Jays. I closed things out for the save.

Don always kept things light and funny. "Augie" had a great balance of being serious ... but he could also bring the locker room to tears with laughter! I can just imagine him telling the whole locker room a story about his first "squat toilet" experience.

None of us ever think we've reached the end of those great days ... even when we have. But Don's story is different because he wouldn't take "the end" for an answer. I played for six major league teams over my 18 years, but I can't imagine throwing my last big league pitch, and then staying on the path Don took ... through Mexico and back ... then the whole replacement player ordeal ... then to the Far East and finally Italy, just to try to throw one more big league pitch! And facing the kinds of obstacles—natural (like earthquakes and hurricanes) and man-made (like gangsters and warmongering)—and still going out there, sometimes hurt, and a lot of those times pitching just to keep your job, and becoming a league MVP.

Don traveled a lot of roads in baseball, but I'm 100 percent sure that every path he blazed, regardless of degree of difficulty, he did so with a smile and left a lasting impression on those who were fortunate enough to enjoy the ride with him!

Now you get to enjoy it too.

Dan Plesac pitched in the Major Leagues for 18 seasons and was a three-time All-Star selection while a member of the Milwaukee Brewers. He recorded 65 wins and 158 saves as a closer for seven different teams and remains the Milwaukee Brewers career leader in games pitched, saves and earned run average. Dan is a member of the North Carolina State University Hall of Fame, and since 2009, he has been a television broadcaster on the MLB Network.

Introduction

At the risk of sounding like a "get off my lawn" guy, back when I was playing college and professional baseball, pitching wasn't all about throwing as hard as you can every pitch, trying to strike out every hitter. Pitching was more of a craft, using your brain as well as your arm.

Counting college, I pitched like that for two decades. From high school, through college, as part of the U.S. Olympic team, into the minor and major leagues ... and then on to three foreign countries.

I was never a 95-mph guy. Didn't have to be, didn't want to be. I wanted to finish games that I started, which I did ... a lot. Starting pitchers today are happy if they go five innings throwing every pitch as hard as they can. For me, that was not how I viewed success.

As a kid, I basically taught myself how to pitch. I learned a curveball through trial and error. It became my "bread and butter" pitch. When I was in high school, it was fastball, big curve and not much else. I taught myself how to change speeds on my pitches and even throw them from different arm angles. My fastball was good enough, but my curveball got the attention of college scouts.

In college I learned a change up, another valuable weapon for pitchers who aren't just trying to overpower every batter. I learned a slider—sort of a cross between a fastball and a curve—during a summer in Alaska. Now I had four pitches—I could throw a fastball in the low 90s, but I had the excellent curve and good command of my change up and slider too. That got me drafted into professional baseball.

I threw hard enough and had enough movement on my fastball that I could set up my best pitch, the curveball. Knowing how to use all four pitches and out-think hitters got me to the big leagues. Once I was there, I had to continually make adjustments and alterations, because big league hitters are making adjustments to you all the time. When I landed in Taiwan, there were times when my slider became my best pitch.

After my Major League days were over, I used this same approach with great success in other leagues in other countries. Through it all, I had to maintain a great focus and remain fearless on the mound. You can't pitch any other way.

Playing internationally my stuff was good enough to succeed, but it wasn't about just having good pitches; it was the mental game, too … dealing with the culture shock, language, food, being very far away from home and family, and always having to be at your very best all of the time—or immediately face the prospect of getting released. I saw a lot of really good American players struggle because they couldn't handle being in a foreign country where everything was too different. In other parts of the world, the same abilities that were needed to succeed on the mound were needed just to handle life.

One

Break on Through

It was like being in a movie. And it was happening near Hollywood to boot.

Here's the setting: It's August of 1984, and this is the "XXIII Olympiad," otherwise known as the Los Angeles Summer Olympics. Baseball was not an official "medal" sport yet, but rather a "demonstration" sport for the first time. Even though there wasn't an *official* Olympic medal involved, it certainly wasn't meaningless to us—the members of Team USA. We had something to prove.

So I'm standing on the mound at Dodger Stadium. Our coach, the legendary Rod Dedeaux, had just called me in from the bullpen. It's the medal round, the winner plays the next day against Japan for the ceremonial Gold, the loser plays Chinese Taipei (Taiwan) for the Bronze. We're battling against Korea, it's the fifth inning, the score is 2–2, and the go-ahead run is on third with two outs. I enter the game and inherit not just the runner on third but a 2–0 count as well. Not ideal.

This is the same mound in the same stadium where I'd watched the Los Angeles Dodgers play pretty much my whole life. I glanced up into the stands at the seats I used to sit in. I was born near here and had lived my entire life in the greater LA area. I exhaled. As Dedeaux handed me the ball, he said only, "Get 'em, Tiger." Dedeaux called everyone "Tiger"; it didn't matter if you were eight years old or 78, everyone was "Tiger." I remember hearing him call legendary, white-haired Sparky Anderson, the Hall of Fame manager of the Detroit Tigers, "Tiger" while we were in Detroit on our pre–Olympics tour earlier that summer.

My first pitch to the Korean hitter was a 2–0 curveball that I threw for a strike. I followed that with another curveball for strike two, then another curveball that the hitter chopped into the ground weakly to third base, where future MLB All-Star Cory Snyder fielded it and threw across the diamond to future MLB superstar Mark McGwire at first for the final out of the inning. I'd held the runner at third, and the score held at 2–2. I went on to pitch the remaining 4⅓ innings—I went right at the Korean hitters, knowing that if I got in any trouble, I had future big leaguers Bobby Witt and Pat Pacillo in the bullpen. In the seventh inning, we scored three runs when Chris Gwynn (Tony's brother) drove in Oddibe McDowell with a single, followed by a Cory Snyder double, putting us up 5–2. I ended up giving up four hits, no runs, and no walks, with three strikeouts, and I got credited with the win.

Like I said, something out of a movie.

And the sequels got even better.

The Dodgers were still fairly new to California when I was born in nearby Inglewood in July of 1963. I grew up a big fan of the Big Blue, who swept the New York Yankees in the World Series the year I was born. I was brought up a big baseball fan, and everyone in my family loved the game. We always had the Dodgers or Angels games on the TV. I was four when my parents bought me a plastic bat and ball. I wanted to play every day. Like most boys, I played a lot of catch with my dad when he'd get home from working as a sheet metal worker. If he wasn't available, my mom would step in. Her participation ended when she missed a throw and the ball hit her in the face.

My dad didn't let me quit when I took a similar blow. I was around eight years old when we were practicing at Alondra Park in Lawndale. He was hitting me some ground balls and hit one I had to range far to my left to reach. I didn't see an old pitching rubber that was lying there. The ball hit the rubber and bounced directly into my face, hitting me in the mouth. I put my hand to my mouth immediately, and when I pulled it away I was holding two of my teeth and a handful of blood. I started crying, and I wanted to go home right then and there. My dad wiped away the blood, put my two teeth in his pocket, and walked back to home plate. He said we weren't done until I caught three more grounders. I think he wanted to instill some toughness in me, plus I think he wanted to make sure I wouldn't become afraid of the ball. Mission accomplished.

I couldn't be soft in my family, growing up with my three brothers, Brett, Lance, and Steve. We played baseball all the time with the neighborhood kids from sunrise to sunset. It was storybook: I began playing organized ball when I was seven years old, and that's when I decided I wanted to be a Major League baseball player. I never stopped believing that was what I was going to do.

After I played two years at Leuzinger High School, my parents got a divorce, and my mom moved me and my brothers an hour south to Mission Viejo. I had to start all over again and try out to make the varsity team as a junior at Capistrano Valley High School. I made that team too, and I played for the legendary high school baseball coach Bob Zamora. Coach Z had played a few years of minor league baseball. I was fortunate to be coached by him. He taught me a lot. When I came to Capo Valley, I considered myself a shortstop, since I only pitched in two games my last year at Leuzinger. But I told Coach Z that I pitched so I'd have a better chance at making his team. Smart move. He used me as a pitcher and allowed me to develop.

At the beginning of my senior year I had to undergo major back surgery. Fortunately, I didn't have to miss my senior year of high school baseball, and as I improved on the mound, I finished my senior year pitching three straight one-hit shutouts, the last one in a playoff game against Irvine High School. Things went so well that I got to pitch in the Orange County All-Star game. I was also invited to try out for the Southern California high school All-Star team that would go up to San Jose and play the Northern California All-Stars in a three-game series. The following week I played for the California All-Stars against Oklahoma.

I got some attention from area colleges, big ones like Stanford, San Diego State, and USC. I also got a phone call from Minnesota Twins scout Jesse Flores. I was excited there was a Major League team who knew who I was. The storybook ride just kept on getting better.

Then it didn't.

You learn to never overvalue what you're told by a single scout or college coach. They're telling a lot of guys the same stuff they're telling you. After I told Flores I was definitely interested in signing directly out of high school, I was convinced the Twins were going to draft me. We looked up where their rookie ball team played in rural Tennessee. I was ready to pack.

The draft took place on the same day as the Orange County All-Star game. During this event, whenever a player who was drafted came up to bat or came in to pitch, the public address announcer would say, "Congratulations to [so and so]. He was just drafted by the [MLB team] in the [blank] round." It was really cool! There were a lot of high school players drafted from Orange County. I was eager to hear my name since the Minnesota Twins were going to draft me. But when I came into the game to pitch? Nothing. I'd heard several other names but not mine. Maybe they missed it? For the next couple of days, I sat by the phone, waiting for my call from the Twins. It never rang.

Back then, Major League Baseball didn't publicize the names of guys picked in the late rounds. I may have been drafted and no one ever bothered to tell me. That's the way it worked sometimes. I waited by the phone for a call that never came.

I was going the college route. When I made contact with Stanford, they'd changed their mind too and said I should go to a junior college first. San Diego State didn't pursue me after showing initial interest, but I was excited that I still had USC, who had expressed a lot of interest. Their pitching coach had been calling me all the time, sometimes getting me called out of a class at school, telling me I would pitch as a freshman and talking about getting a full scholarship, etc. After he saw me pitch a one-hitter in a playoff game, he said he'd talk to me when my season ended.

I never heard back from him, either. When Coach Z got back to him? You guessed it. He changed his tune too. He said if I came to USC now, there'd be no scholarship money, and I would probably play for their JV team. I said, "See you later." The only school that I had left was Chapman College, a small Division II school. Chapman was only 20 miles from where I lived ... but I'd never heard of it, to be honest. But it was the same school Coach Zamora had attended. The Chapman coaches, Paul Deese and Mike Weathers, offered me a full scholarship and promised me I'd pitch 100 innings as a freshman. Finally, something that sounded good. They played all of the top Division I schools in Southern California: USC, UCLA, Cal State, Fullerton, Long Beach State ... and I saw a three-game series at Arizona State, too. I figured that if I got the chance to pitch against those schools, I could be seen by the scouts.

Chapman had a list of alums who had reached the big leagues, including Randy Jones, the 1976 National League Cy Young Award winner. John Young, Gary Lucas, Tim Flannery, Marty Castillo, and Jay Pettibone. I was hoping to add my name to that list.

After the disappointment of the draft and the schools that pulled back on me late, it was a relief when the coaches at Chapman did what they said they'd do: Give me the ball and let me pitch. I don't know if it was something subconscious after getting snubbed by those bigger schools or what, but during my three seasons at Chapman, I always seemed to pitch my best games against those bigger-name programs. After a solid freshman year, I spent the summer in Alaska, where I got a ton of great experience against dozens of future pros, including guys who would make multiple All-Star teams. I learned what it was like to be in "professional" circumstances, where if you didn't perform well, you got sent home.

Once, while I was a member of the Cook Inlet Bucs, based in Anchorage, our general manager, Dennis Mattingly, called a team meeting. This was the GM, mind you, not the manager. We'd lost about four of our last six and we weren't playing well. He was upset and flat-out told us, "We can't keep losing. You need to play better or else we'll send you home and get someone else here who can play. We're losing and not drawing fans." As I would learn the hard way over many years, baseball—even at these levels—remains a bottom line business.

I was young enough and stubborn enough to know I wasn't going to be sent home disgraced, with my tail between my legs, having to face my coaches and family. I ended up having a great summer. I won the ERA title and was the Pitcher of the Year. But the lesson was learned.

The next couple years at Chapman, I got a chance to beat powerhouses like Cal State, Fullerton, Wichita State, and the University of Arizona. Coach Weathers told me there was a very good chance I'd be a first-round draft pick after my junior season. He was right. I finished that spring with a 16-4 record and a 1.81 ERA, and the scouts were non-stop by this point, with the draft just a couple of weeks away. I'd been disappointed after high school, so I was sure not to take anything for granted this time around. Ironically, one of the scouts who called me was Jesse Flores from the Twins—the same guy who had told me a bunch of stuff that never ended up happening. When we spoke, Flores told me that since the Twins had drafted me out of high school in 1981, they needed me to sign some papers allowing them the chance to draft me again.

Really?

I told Flores that the Twins had never drafted me. I'd waited for three days for a phone call that never came. But he was insistent. "Yes, we did," he kept saying, never acknowledging that I never heard from anyone from the organization about being a Twins draft pick. It really didn't matter at this point. That was years ago. Time to turn the page. I agreed to sign the waiver—but had zero confidence that the Twins would actually be the team that drafted me. They had their chance three years ago.

I knew there was one team that *wasn't* going to draft me—my hometown California Angels. Their scout had brought me to a couple of Angels games before the draft. Anaheim Stadium is only a few miles away from Chapman College. He brought me up to the luxury boxes, where I got to eat from the great spread of food along with all of the other goodies they had. He told me the Angels were *not* going to draft me, that they were going to draft a catcher with their first-round pick. He said he brought me to these games to get this fine treatment and attention because I deserved it. I guess that's the good side of the business.

The night before the draft, I talked to four teams. Two told me that they had late picks in the first round, and that if I was still available, they were going to take me. Then I got a call from one of the few clubs I hadn't heard from before—the Houston Astros. Their scout told me they were interested in drafting me in the first or second round and asked how much money I'd be looking for to sign. Ah, the business part of the business again. Not my comfort zone. I didn't want to talk money, but I did tell the Astros that I was confident I'd be a first-round pick, considering all the teams that had called and told me so.

It took a while, but I finally fell asleep that night wondering which team was going to draft me and where I'd start my pro career. Then I reminded myself what had happened three years ago, that it was better to keep my expectations low.

When draft day arrived, I finally got the phone call I'd been waiting three years for. The Astros had made me their first-round pick.

Reggie Waller, the scout who drafted me—and with whom I'd end up having a long business relationship—showed up at my house a couple of days later to begin negotiating. I wasn't going to do this alone, sitting there trying to talk money with a professional negotiator. I think it surprised Reggie that I had my high school coach, Bob Zamora, and my college coach, Mike Weathers, there with me for support. He was surprised to see that I had an agent there too to negotiate. After the small talk, the negotiating began. Man, I was glad that I had an agent because when they began talking money, I got so nervous I literally couldn't speak. After the initial offers, my agent and Reggie said they would continue the negotiations later. Scouts and agents would be a big part of my life for the next two decades.

While all this was going on, I joined Team USA for the pre–Olympics tour. I'd been selected as one of 31 players invited to try out for the Olympic baseball team. After a week of training in Louisville, we embarked on a 32-game, 38-day tour of America. It was grueling, but obviously there was nowhere else I would rather have been.

After the first week, I survived the first cut reducing the team to 25 players. During the tour, we played in 12 Major League stadiums before the Major League game. We played five minor league teams, beating them

Don's brothers (from left) Lance, Brett, and Steve on the field at Anaheim Stadium with Don before a Team USA game in July 1984.

One. Break on Through

all; local college all-star teams; a Cape Cod League all-star team; Japan in a seven-games series; and Korea six times. Toward the end of the tour, we were playing Japan at the Astrodome in Houston. As fate would have it, I was scheduled to pitch there, in front of the Astros' brass who had recently drafted me. I hadn't given up an earned run all summer on the tour, and I had another strong outing, beating the Japanese team.

Before the game, my agent told me we had reached an agreement with the Astros, so after the game, I signed my first professional contract right there in the 'Dome. I was also informed that I'd made the final 20-man Olympic team roster and was going to represent the Stars and Stripes in LA. Maybe there would be a storybook ending after all.

Except this was just the opening chapter, as they say. We were coming up on the start of the LA Olympics, and after a final exhibition game in Anaheim, where I got to spend time with my family and friends, I was off to gain the experience of a lifetime as a member of Team USA.

The Olympic games were an amazing experience. We had a great team; it was called by many the greatest amateur baseball team ever put

Don (third from left) and Olympic teammate Bob Caffrey with other Team USA members before President Ronald Reagan's address to the Olympians at the Olympic Village, July 1984.

together. We had John Marzano, B.J. Surhoff, and Bob Caffrey as our catchers. Mark McGwire was at first base, Flavio Alfaro at second, Cory Snyder at third, and Gary Green at shortstop. Future Hall of Famer Barry Larkin was a backup infielder! In the outfield, we had Shane Mack, Oddibe McDowell, and Chris Gwynn … plus future All-Star Will Clark, who played outfield, first base, and DH. Our starting pitchers were John Hoover, Scott Bankhead, and Billy Swift. Our relievers were Bobby Witt, Pat Pacillo, Mike Dunne, Sid Akins, and me.

In 1984, that team could have held its own with any minor league outfit, and if we'd stayed together a few seasons, I think we could have won the World Series.

But it was much more than baseball. We participated in the Opening Ceremonies at the LA Coliseum. It was incredible entering with more than 100,000 people there, including President Reagan, who gave us a pep talk on the USC campus. Being there with all of the other countries' athletes, I had never been in front of a crowd that big, before or since.

After that, we were ready for Dodger Stadium.

There were eight teams competing for the gold medal: in Group One, the United States, Chinese Taipei (Taiwan), Italy, and the Dominican Republic; in Group Two, Japan, Korea, Canada, and Nicaragua. On the first day of the tournament, we played the feature game against Chinese Taipei. That followed the Italy vs Dominican Republic game. When the first game ended, we anxiously made our way out onto the field. There was still some time before our infield/outfield warm-up was to start, so a group of us went down the left field line to play catch and settle our nerves.

Don August's 1984 USA Olympic Baseball team trading card.

Our games at Dodger Stadium were all sell-outs, 54,000 people. As we played

One. Break on Through 13

catch, we noticed the growing crowd, when suddenly the PA announcer came on and said, "Ladies and gentlemen, I direct your attention to the left field line, the United States baseball team!" The crowd went absolutely crazy. It was so loud I couldn't believe it. On the field, you could yell and not be able to hear your own voice. I looked at my teammates' faces, and they all looked totally freaked out. It was hard to continue to play catch. I got such a surge of adrenaline that I was afraid I would throw the ball into the stands. I knew everyone's hearts were pounding full speed. The crowd broke out into a chant of "USA! USA! USA!" which put us all over the edge. We slowly regained our composure and got ready to play the game.

Our starting pitcher, John Hoover, pitched a complete game and beat Chinese Taipei, 2–1. We were trailing 1–0 in the seventh inning before John Marzano hit a home run to tie it. With a couple of base runners on, Will Clark hit a two-out RBI single to give us the 2–1 lead and eventual win. The Chinese Taipei team did give us a scare.

After an off day, we faced Italy. Scott Bankhead got the start, and in front of another sell-out crowd and in an incredible atmosphere, we blasted Italy, 16–1. Oddibe McDowell hit two home runs and had five RBI, and Shane Mack and Will Clark each hit a home run. The bullpen got into action in this one, with Mike Dunne, Sid Akins, and Pat Pacillo taking the mound before I got my shot. I entered in the ninth inning to try to hold that 15-run lead. I honestly didn't care, I was so happy that I got into the Olympics, pitched on the Dodger Stadium mound, and was in the books. I was thankful Coach Dedeaux got me in.

Two days later, we played the Dominican Republic. Through the first five innings, we were winning, 2–0, before our offense exploded, scoring 10 more times over the next three innings. Once again, Coach Dedeaux had me pitch the ninth inning, this time to hold onto our 12-run lead. Again, I was just happy that I got into another game. Now I'd gotten into two games! Will Clark hit two more home runs and had a double and single. Cory Snyder hit a home run and a double and had three RBI. This win put us into the medal rounds.

I seriously thought I was done for the tournament, and I was good with that: I'd gotten into two games.

Two days later, we were facing Korea, and the winner would play Japan for the gold medal. The loser would play Chinese Taipei for the bronze. I figured that I wasn't going to pitch since I'd pitched in two games already, and Bobby Witt and Pat Pacillo, two hard throwers, were available to relieve starter Scott Bankhead if necessary. I came into the dugout ready to watch and support our team, wearing my turf shoes, not my spikes, with no protective cup on, and having left my glove in the locker room. Coach Dedeaux and pitching coach John Scolinos probably noticed

Members of Team USA on the field at the Los Angeles Coliseum for the 1984 Olympic Games Opening Ceremonies.

my casual attire, came up to me, and said, "You're the first man up in relief tonight ... are you ready?!" Shocked, I quickly replied, "Yeah!" and after they turned around, I sprinted back up the tunnel into the locker room to prepare myself to pitch, not just watch. I did make it out to the bullpen before the game started, thankfully.

Bankhead had pitched great all summer long, but tonight he wasn't his usual self. During the first three innings, he wasn't sharp but worked himself out of jams. In the fourth inning, he finally gave up a run. Dedeaux had already gotten me up and ready twice. We kept battling. Oddibe McDowell responded with a two-run homer to give us a 2–1 lead. In the fifth inning, Bankhead got two quick outs before giving up a home run to tie the game. He gave up another double, then threw a wild pitch, allowing the go-ahead run to reach third base. That's when Coach Dedeaux came out and called me into the game. This is where I had watched all those Dodgers games in person and on TV. I was now on this mound to get the United States baseball team into the gold medal game in the Olympics. I was working with catcher B.J. Surhoff, who became a teammate in the Major Leagues with the Milwaukee Brewers four years later.

I got the first hitter I faced to end the inning, and a couple innings later, with the score still tied 2–2, Chris Gwynn delivered an RBI single to give us the lead. Cory Snyder followed with a two-run double that gave us a 5–2 lead. I pitched the final 4⅓ shutout innings and got the win. That sent us into the gold medal game against Japan—a team we'd beaten six out of the seven times we'd played them over the summer. We were very confident.

But you can't take anything for granted in this game. The Japanese team came out playing their best baseball. Our starting pitcher, John Hoover, struggled with his curveball, his best pitch. He was getting outs with his fastball, but he needed his best pitch. The Japanese ultimately took a 3–1 lead, and we were hoping Dedeaux would bring in Bobby Witt or Pat Pacillo, guys with overpowering fastballs. Didn't happen soon enough. Late in the game, a big Japanese hitter hit a three-run homer when Hoover hung a curveball, giving them a 6–1 lead. Cory Snyder hit a two-run shot in the ninth inning, making it a 6–3 game, but that's as close as we got.

None of us could believe it. We'd actually lost! We weren't supposed to lose. We had such great fans, we had a great tour, we'd won every previous Olympic game … but it all ended with a loss! We had to watch the Japanese team celebrate on our field. We had to watch Peter Ueberroth—the future commissioner of Major League Baseball—put *our* gold medals around the Japanese players' necks. We had to accept our silver medals even though most of us didn't want them … and then listen to the Japanese national anthem, not the Star Spangled Banner. It was heartbreaking.

We blew it. And it's a pain none of us will ever forget.

The next day I was stunned to see that almost all of my teammates had already gone home. Only Mike Dunne, B.J. Surhoff, and I remained. To be fair, I was already home, but the three of us really wanted to stick around and finish the Olympic experience. We stayed and watched some other Olympic events and then got to be a part of the closing ceremonies. All that was left was three players and our coaches on the field of the LA Coliseum.

It was a great laser show. The XXIII Summer Olympics were over. I spent one last night in the Olympic Village and the next day made the short trip home.

Seventeen of the 20 players on that USA Olympic roster would end up making it to the Major Leagues.

My professional career was now ready to start. I didn't get much time off before reporting to the Astros' Fall Instructional League in Arizona that September. It would last for six weeks. I got introduced to the organization's minor league coaches and several other first-year players. After a short winter, it was off to Spring Training in Kissimmee, Florida. This is where I met the Major League coaches and players. It was amazing to be out there doing the pitchers' fielding practice drills with Nolan Ryan, Bob Knepper, Joe Niekro, Mike Scott, and others. I was young, only 21 years old, and several of the big league players came by me during the drills and batting practice, making sure that I was okay. The two main guys were Craig Reynolds and Joe Sambito.

It was a lot of work, and there was plenty of rookie hazing—not the bad kind—going on too. During the first week, we were ready to do some drills when veteran pitcher Joe Niekro asked me to hurry up and play some catch to warm up. I gladly obliged. About his fifth throw, he tossed me one of his wicked knuckleballs without telling me. The ball fluttered through the Florida air, dancing in the breeze before it suddenly and abruptly darted down, missing my glove entirely and hitting me square in the chest. Instantly, I heard everyone laughing out loud and looking at me. I realized I'd been set up. Nothing to do but just laugh it off … because it was actually pretty funny. I think the big leaguers were just trying to see what kind of a guy I was. I suppose I passed that test.

I played my first professional season in AA Columbus, Georgia, in the Southern League. Before the 1986 season, I was invited back to Major League spring training. The Astros had a new manager, Hal Lanier, and a new bench coach, Yogi Berra, the legend himself. The big leaguers remembered me and congratulated me on having a good season. I was sent down to Tucson to play AAA in the Pacific Coast League.

Reaching Triple A in just two seasons was a solid achievement, but I had my sights set on reaching the big leagues. I started really well in Tucson, and by mid-season my ERA was at the top of the league. I had to be patient while I watched a few of the older pitchers get called up during the season.

On the morning of August 15, the phone in my apartment rang. I was sleeping on the couch because my visiting mother was sleeping in my bed. I answered while I was still half asleep. The voice on the other end said, "Hello, Don, this is Bill Wood calling." He was the Minor League director and assistant to the general manager. He said, "Don, there's no easy way to say this, but the Houston Astros have traded your contract to the Milwaukee Brewers."

I sat there for a few minutes, stunned and not sure if I really heard what he just said to me. Mr. Wood thanked me for my hard work and everything I did for the organization. I was able to spit out something, asking him who I'd been traded for. He told me that I and another player to be named later had been traded to the Brewers for veteran Major League pitcher Danny Darwin. At the time, the Astros were in first place in the National League Western Division, and it was the stretch drive to make the playoffs. I'd been part of a trade for a veteran pitcher for the pennant drive.

The Astros ended up winning the division and making the playoffs against the New York Mets, who would win the 1986 World Series. The player to be named later turned out to be my very good friend and roommate Mark Knudson. When Bill Wood was done talking, he said the Brewers would be calling me shortly. As I sat there on the couch, still half asleep and waiting for the Brewers to call, I couldn't tell my mom or my roommate, Chuck Jackson, because they were still asleep. A few minutes later, my phone rang, and it was Harry Dalton, the GM of the Brewers. He welcomed me to the team, telling me they really wanted me in this trade and that they remembered scouting me when I was at Chapman College. He told me I would be joining their AAA Vancouver team the next day in Phoenix, where they were currently playing. A few minutes later Bruce Manno, the Minor League director, called to welcome me and gave me my travel plans.

Good thing my mom and brothers were visiting. They helped me clean out my apartment and pack, then took most of it back to California since I was heading to Canada. Later that day, I went to Hi Corbett Field in Tucson to clear out my locker. I got there during batting practice. While I was cleaning out my locker, my now-former teammates came by to say goodbye and wish me luck. The last guy was Knudson. I was surprised to see him. He'd been with the Major League team in Houston until just that day, when he'd been sent back down. Mark came up to me and said, "Good luck.... I wish it was me who'd been traded." He hadn't been told yet that he was the player to be named later and he'd be going too.

Manager Carlos Alfonso told me he was proud of me, and pitching coach Eddie Watt told me that he'd told the Astros he was against trading me. I gathered my things, but before leaving I sat down behind home plate to watch a couple of innings with the season ticket holders. I'd gotten to know some of them pretty well. Back then, the starting pitcher for the next night's game would not be in uniform but instead would sit behind home plate in street clothes and chart pitches or operate the radar gun. The people sitting nearby would sometimes offer to buy me a beer during the game, but I couldn't accept, obviously … although a couple of times it was so hot that they put beer in a Pepsi cup and gave it to me. This time, there was no need to hide anything, and after enjoying a beer, I said goodbye and went back to my apartment.

The next day, I met my new team in Phoenix. I was sad I wasn't part of the Astros' organization anymore. I'd gotten very comfortable there. I knew everyone. I was a first-round pick doing well. But now I was a Brewer, a new guy in a new organization. I met my teammates, including B.J. Surhoff, my former Olympic teammate. I found out that the player to be named was Mark Knudson, and I chuckled, remembering how he told me he wished he was going too.

I finished the year strong but didn't get called up in September like I hoped. I had to look forward to spring training the following year.

One of the best things about being a young player is meeting and being teammates with some of the best players in the game. In Houston, I was with future Hall of Famer Nolan Ryan. Now, with the Brewers, I was with future Hall of Famers Robin Yount and Paul Molitor. I had another really good season at Triple A in 1987 but still didn't get called up. Frustration was setting in.

The following year, in early June of 1988, I finally got the call.

There are days and situations you never ever forget. When I arrived at the airport in Milwaukee, the Brewers had someone there to pick me up ... but two of my suitcases didn't make it. The guy told me we'd find them later, that we were in a hurry to get me to County Stadium for that night's game. It was definitely a weird feeling but great at the same time. I was getting settled at my locker when Mark Knudson came over and sat down. He'd been called up about a week earlier. He showed me around the stadium before the game. While we were talking, I said, "Please don't let me do anything stupid." I just didn't want to make any rookie mistakes my first day.

We were playing the California Angels that night, and the game was televised back to my home in Southern California, where my family and friends could watch. As fate would have it, in the fifth inning, our starter got into trouble. Manager Tom Trebelhorn called left-hander Paul Mirabella into the game. As he reached the mound, the bullpen phone rang again. Bullpen coach Larry Haney hung up and told me, "Get ready, you have the sixth inning."

The first big league hitter I faced was All-Star catcher Bob Boone. I got him to ground out to Paul Molitor at third base, I got the next batter, Dick Schofield, to ground out to short, and then Chico Walker grounded out to second. My first big league inning was three up, three down. In the seventh inning, I walked Wally Joyner on a 3-2 pitch but got Johnnie Ray and Brian Downing to fly out and Chili Davis on another grounder. In the bottom of the inning, we scored four runs to take a 7-4 lead. Trebelhorn brought in our All-Star closer, Dan Plesac, to pitch the last two innings and earn the save. We ended up winning, 9-4. My first day in the majors, and I got my first big league win.

Back in the clubhouse, I found a bunch of media guys ... and my missing suitcases.

I would find out later that I became the 13,081st player in history to make it to the Major Leagues.

I had a really good run the rest of the season as a starter. They even asked me if I wanted a "walk up song" for when I took the mound. I thought about it for a moment and chose a song from my all-time favorite rock

Don pitching against the Chicago White Sox at County Stadium in Milwaukee in April 1990.

band, The Doors. "Break on Through" seemed appropriate for what had finally happened.

I was off to a nice start to my Major League career. By the time September rolled around, we were 11 games out of first place with 31 games left to play. That month, I won six starts in a row, and as a team we won 22 out of those last 31 games. It was exciting to be in a pennant race. We ended up two games out of first place, behind the Boston Red Sox. I finished the season with a 13–7 record and a 3.09 ERA. I was named the Brewers' Rookie of the Year and finished fourth in the American League Rookie of the Year voting.

It was a great feeling going into spring training the following season, knowing that I was going to be part of the Major League team. Toward the end of spring training, with our top starter Teddy Higuera out due to injury, Trebelhorn named me our Opening Day starter in Cleveland. I pitched a complete game, but I lost, 2–1. That was the start of an up-and-down season. I finished the season with a 12–12 record.

The next year, 1990, was a struggle. I started the season in the bullpen, and after only three games in relief, I was sent down to AAA Denver, which is not the place a pitcher typically goes to regain his form or confidence. I ended up scuffling in Denver, both physically and mentally. I finally pulled myself back together in the month of August, and I was called back up on September 1. I got in just two games the rest of the season before I hurt my lower back.

In spring training of 1991, I was back in great shape and ready to fight for a spot in the Brewers' rotation. I had a great spring, pitching my last 12 innings without giving up a run, but still got sent down on the very last day of spring training. I was the Opening Day starter for Denver, but somehow it just didn't feel like any sort of honor. Fortune smiled on me again that day, however. After I threw five scoreless innings, manager Tony Muser told me I was done for the night. I didn't like coming out of games early, but when I started to argue with him, he told me that my next game was going to be in Toronto. The Brewers' Ron Robinson had gone on the disabled list, and I was getting called right back up to the big leagues.

Unfortunately, that season turned out to be a lot like the last time I was a regular in the Milwaukee rotation. I pitched a lot of good games, but some very bad outings killed me. I finished with a 9–8 record. Shortly after the season ended, general manager Harry Dalton was replaced by Sal Bando. The next day, Sal fired manager Tom Trebelhorn, and the next day Sal called me on the phone and told me I was being taken off the 40-man roster, which enabled me to become a free agent. Instead of accepting the assignment to the minor leagues, I chose to look for another team. I figured there had to be at least one team that liked me.

That December, I signed a minor league deal with the San Francisco Giants with a Major League spring training invite, with the chance at making the team for the 1992 season. Several front office people who were with the Houston organization when I was drafted were now with the Giants. Carlos Alfonso was their Major League pitching coach, so I felt like I would get a good shot. But right before spring training started, the Giants made a big trade, sending All-Star outfielder Kevin Mitchell to Seattle for three Major League pitchers, Billy Swift, Mike Jackson, and Dave Burba. This was a bad sign for me. I'd been told by Assistant GM Fred Nelson, who had signed me, that I would have a chance for the fifth starting spot and long relief.

I was throwing the ball very well in camp. I was scheduled to pitch in the second exhibition game against the California Angels. After our morning workout, one of the clubhouse workers told me that Roger Craig, the manager, wanted to see me in his office. It was way too early in camp to be sent down, I thought, plus I was scheduled to pitch that afternoon. When I walked in, general manager Al Rosen was there too, which surprised me. Rosen told me they were sending me down to minor league camp. I couldn't believe it. No one ever gets sent down before the games even start. When I was a brand-new, first-year rookie with Houston—with Rosen as the Astros' GM—I didn't get cut this early. I told them that I'd been told by Fred Nelson that I would compete for the fifth starting spot and long relief. Rosen quickly snapped back, "Fred Nelson isn't here anymore!"

Gulp.

After a few more futile words, I reminded them that I was scheduled to pitch in today's game. They asked me if I still wanted to pitch, and I said, "Hell yes!" They said okay. I left the office, feeling like I had one last shot to change their minds. I went out for the fourth and fifth innings focused and knowing I had to clutch up. Six up and six down with two strikeouts. I did what I had to do. Still, when I came off the field after my second inning, none of the coaches came up to say good job or anything. Not one word. I was hoping maybe I changed their minds. Instead, I sat in the dugout watching the rest of the game, and still nothing. I at least wished they had said get out of here.

I had to report to the minor league complex the next day. I was told by the Giants' secretary that I had to check out of the Major League hotel. When I asked her where the minor league hotel was, she told me that it was full, no rooms available. Where was I supposed to go? All of the hotels in Phoenix were full because of spring training. She offered zero help. I was stuck with nowhere to live. I ended up finding a place on my own at a trailer park on an Indian Reservation nearby. Needless to say, after pitching in only two games for the Giants' Triple A team, I was released.

That was basically the end to my big league career. I would never pitch in the Major Leagues again.

I had a lot of time to reflect. One thing—an odd thing—would stick in my mind and bother me for over 30 years. Did the Minnesota Twins draft me out of high school in 1981? Maybe things would have turned out differently? Back then, there wasn't the internet for me to find out. Since Jesse Flores told me they did in 1984, I kind of assumed I must have. Still, when people asked me if I was drafted out of high school, I had to tell them I didn't know, which got a strange look back. How could I not know? Over 30 years later, I was able to look up the 1981 MLB Draft on the internet. I went to the Minnesota Twins' selections, and my name was *not* there! Now I knew ... but I still kind of wished I had been.

Still, no regrets. Being a Major Leaguer gave me the chance to pitch in the minor leagues with four other organizations, but I never did get a real opportunity to get back. Being a former Major Leaguer also earned me the opportunity to play internationally in professional leagues around the world. For the next nine years, I traveled to a lot of different countries, starting out in Canada, then Mexico, Dominican Republic, Taiwan, Australia, Italy, San Marino, and Puerto Rico. I went to each of these places hoping to do well enough to earn another chance in the Major Leagues. Instead, I experienced different cultures, met fascinating people, and saw amazing things. A lot of crazy things would happen to me, and it would all be a part of the adventure.

Two

Who'll Stop the Rain?

Adventure is in the eye of the beholder, I guess. I didn't start out thinking about traveling the world. I wasn't looking for anything more than a chance to pitch in the big leagues again. While my abrupt release from the San Francisco Giants didn't put a damper on my dreams of returning to the show, other things did. Like weather. Bad weather. Lots of it.

And sometimes when important opportunities get postponed, they can't be rescheduled.

What can you do? Sometimes you just have to laugh.

I was probably the only person sitting in either dugout at Doubleday Field in Cooperstown, New York, on this particular summer afternoon in 1993 who actually *wanted* to play a baseball game that day. Pretty much every other player in uniform was happy to see the rain coming down, and even happier when the exhibition between the Los Angeles Dodgers—the team I grew up watching—and the Cleveland Indians—the team I was suited up and preparing to pitch for—was called off.

Me, I *really* wanted to play. I mean *really* wanted to. At that moment, I was on the Disabled List for the Indians Triple A team in Charlotte, North Carolina—even though I wasn't hurt at the time. This meaningless Hall of Fame exhibition game mattered to me because it would be my latest best chance to show the baseball world that I was still a big league pitcher, which I had been for the better part of the past half-decade.

But ... rain.

Then, déjà vu. I'd been right here in this very same spot before ... a decade earlier.

I had pitched pretty well the second half of that season for the Indians' Triple A team, which included future Hall of Famer Jim Thome and a host of future Cleveland stars like Manny Ramirez. There were a couple of other younger new AAA players on the team who would go up and play in the Major Leagues—Paul Byrd and Chad Ogea. Our team in Charlotte that year was mostly made up with players who played in the Majors

Two. Who'll Stop the Rain?

prior, a veteran minor league team with experience, we had at least four, maybe five guys who had previously played in the World Series. Sam Horn had such a great season in Charlotte with over 30 something home runs. But roster spots for an organization battling for an American League playoff spot are precious. When the Indians needed to make a move, it often involved their top minor league affiliate, and this time I was the odd man out. Fortunately, they chose to hang on to me by placing me on the DL, rather than just cutting me loose. Now, because the organization didn't want to use regular pitchers in a meaningless exhibition game, I was in the right place at the right time. I was being given the chance to put on a big-league uniform and pitch against the Dodgers, even if the results wouldn't be official. I think some of my Charlotte teammates were envious. I probably would have been, too, if I were in their spikes. I was given three days of big league meal money, a flight to Utica, New York, followed by a 40-mile trek to Cooperstown to try to jump-start my big league career again.

I arrived the day before, and the team had me spend the night in a hotel in Utica. The Indians' bus picked me up on the way to Cooperstown. It felt so good putting on a major league uniform again. I felt welcomed by the team, catching up with some of the players I'd competed against a couple seasons earlier when I was with the Brewers. I'd rejoined, if only temporarily, some of the guys I'd been teammates with in Charlotte who were now with the big league team. I felt like I belonged again.

We got to the ballpark, and the Dodgers were taking batting practice. As they were finishing up, we were coming onto the field, and everyone exchanged greetings with guys they knew on the Dodgers. I spent a few minutes with my old Olympic teammate Cory Snyder. A few steps away was rookie sensation Mike Piazza, and we were chatting with Dodgers manager Tommy Lasorda, the man in the middle of all the attention. This was "The Show" again.

As our batting practice began, ominous dark clouds approached. It began to rain very hard, and while it didn't last long, everyone had left the field. Major league teams aren't that interested in playing exhibition games in the first place, so it didn't take much for the teams to decide to cancel—not postpone—the game.

Me, I was so eager to pitch in front of the big league coaches and the big league front office people. Getting seen by the Dodgers, too. You never know whom you could impress.

But ... rain.

You just had to laugh.

It was a coping skill I'd learned earlier that same season.

No American kid grows up dreaming of playing professional baseball in a foreign country. But you make adjustments when your choices are limited. And mine were that season.

I had landed—literally—in Mexico in 1993 after not being able to find a job with a professional team in the states during a frustrating winter. In Mexico, I had two American teammates, Chris Bennett and Phil Harrison. We'd spend a lot of time griping to each other, frustrated with how things were being done—not in the "American" way. It was tough to accept not being in your home country. To keep that frustration from overtaking us, we'd look at each other and say, "You just have to laugh." We leaned heavily on the healing power of laughter, I suppose. The phrase would help us get by whenever we had difficulties. I'd stick with this phrase for years to come in my travels around the world. The idea was certainly in play that day in Cooperstown.

As I sat in the dugout, watching the rain come down, I thought back to 1984, the last time I'd been here, the home of the National Baseball Hall of Fame, and on this field. Back then I was wearing the red, white and blue as a member of the United States Olympic baseball team. Those memories were still fresh.

I remembered Mark McGwire—before he was a big league star. Mark was a guy you watched and admired. I knew him from Southern California and played against him in Alaska. To see him on a daily basis during the Olympic summer was something else. He was still learning all the nuances of being a full-time position player, since he'd been splitting his time between playing and pitching while he was a USC Trojan. As an Olympic teammate, I saw a side of Mark few others ever did. He took on this "mother hen" role with us, and when we were up a little late or something, he'd go around and tell us to get to bed, that we had a game tomorrow. He was super serious about the game, a very hard worker, and lived a very clean life.

Baseball autographed by President Ronald Reagan. Each member of Team USA received an autographed ball.

Back in the early 1980s, there were no tourist hotels in Cooperstown. The players stayed with "host families" during stops there, and the home I had stayed in was visible just over the center field fence. I wondered if that same family still lived there. I never did get a chance to find out.

Back then, our Olympic tour had us scheduled to play a game at Doubleday Field in Cooperstown. We were preparing to play Korea again after having just tied them, 2–2, at Shea Stadium in New York City. I was scheduled to pitch. At the time, I thought it would be special to pitch at Doubleday Field and in a town that had such an incredible place in baseball history. I went to bed ready to get my rest for the game tomorrow.

Don's 1984 Olympic Silver Medal.

But ... rain.

That game got rained out, and I missed out on a chance to pitch at Doubleday Field. Fast forward, and I was returning to Cooperstown years later with a makeup chance to finally pitch at Doubleday Field ... or so I thought.

When this rain-out became official, my time with the Indians came to a close. This ended up being the last time I put on a major league uniform. They let me keep the Indians hat as they dropped me off at the hotel in Utica before they flew off on their chartered plane. I spent the night in Utica and the next morning flew back to Charlotte to resume my unnecessary stint on the DL.

It had been a whirlwind season to that point. During the flight, I found myself wondering, just like the lyric in the Talking Heads song, "*Well ... how did I get here?*"

I'd been a first-round draft pick of the Astros; was traded to Milwaukee; met my wife, Tami, and got married there; and thought I had some roots. But unless you're a superstar, there are no "roots" in MLB...even though I won 34 games over four seasons for the Brewers. I still believed with all my heart that I could pitch and win in the big leagues.

After I got released by San Francisco during the spring of 1992, I signed with Detroit and bounced around within the Tigers' organization that season before being let go again.

That's when my *real* baseball odyssey began.

During the 1992 season, while I was transitioning between Double A in London, Ontario and Triple A Toledo, Ohio, Tami gave birth to our son, Logan.

It wasn't an easy adjustment going back to life in the minor leagues. I hadn't been on a Double A bus trip since 1985. Those things didn't come with meals served by flight attendants, and I didn't get my own row of seats. I felt like an old-timer around most of these kids. I did remember playing with guys like Len Barker (the former Cleveland standout pitcher) when I was coming up through the ranks, and he was on his way down, trying to hold on. Now the roles were reversed. But it didn't make me any less determined to get back.

I had set my ego off to the side and accepted an offer from the Tigers to start the season in Double A. I spent six weeks there and did well enough in Double A to get that call up to Triple A Toledo. There were about seven weeks left in the season—enough time, I felt, to impress the Tigers' brass and become part of their long-term plans.

I was wrong about that.

I only pitched in five games, with three starts, two of which came with two days' notice or less. My first start went very well, coming off the All-Star break. After that, there were times where I had basically no notice and was told, "Hey, you're starting tomorrow." I couldn't get in a routine and didn't have the chance to throw practice sessions in the bullpen. It's

Don in the stands doing the pitching chart the night before his start in London, Canada, in 1992.

hard for a pitcher to get the right touch when you aren't in a regular routine. I'll own my failings, but in all fairness, it wasn't much of a chance. But that's how baseball works.

After an unceremonious end to my 1992 season, I decided I needed to do something different. I decided to go to Puerto Rico to play winter ball. While it was supposed to be a great opportunity to show I could still pitch at a high level, Mother Nature had other ideas. Again. Yep … more rain. It was so heavy and so frequent—nearly every day for the five weeks I was there—that I was able to pitch in just *two* games, and the season was called off early. I got home on New Year's Eve.

Rain. Sometimes, you just have to laugh.

Of the four major sports, baseball is the one game you can't play in those adverse conditions. And as everyone knows, Mother Nature isn't always a baseball fan. Even in places like Puerto Rico with warmer climates, there can be major weather issues. I grew up in the amazing climate of Southern California, but I'd gotten used to dealing with the cold weather in the spring and fall in Milwaukee and other northern American cities. But that much rain I had never seen before. Or since.

But it can—and did—continue as I traveled the globe.

Fast forward to 1995. My first scheduled start in my first season in Taiwan really opened my eyes. It was the final game of a road trip, which required about a five-hour bus ride. We dressed at our team hotel—just like we always would (there were no locker rooms)—and then drove directly to the stadium to play. After that game, we'd bus back to our home city of Taichung.

Taipei, the capital of Taiwan, is at the very north end of this island country. Pingtung—where we were headed—is more to the south, and Taichung—my new home city—is in the middle of the country. From the north of Taiwan to the south is a seven-and-a-half-hour bus ride. Taiwan is less than 100 miles off the coast of mainland China, separated by the Strait of Taiwan.

I had just arrived and met the team during a road trip when the bus pulled up. I had to carry down my belongings—including two big suitcases, a travel bag, and my baseball bag—and put all of it on the bus. I hadn't been to my home city yet and had no idea how baseball in Taiwan worked. The bus ride wasn't so bad. After we got out of the big cities, I got to see the countryside, including some rice paddies. When we were about 30 minutes from Pingtung, it began to rain very hard. When we arrived and entered the stadium, it was still pouring, and the all-dirt infield was completely under water. In Taiwan, they didn't have tarps for their fields. My first start didn't look like it would happen that night after all.

I told one of the guys, "Guess we aren't playing tonight." A couple of my new American teammates, Tony Metoyer and Cecil Espy, replied, "Once it stops raining, they *will* get this field ready, and we'll play." I thought they were crazy. There was no way. Tony—whom I'd known from our days together in the Houston organization—had been in Taiwan for what was now his *sixth* season. He'd seen a lot of things. But this seemed nuts.

When the rain finally stopped, there was a big group of young boys, at least 15 of them, all wearing blue gym shorts, white t-shirts, and sandals. They had these little buckets and big sponges. Each of them dropped his sponge into a big puddle and then squeezed the water into the bucket. They did this over and over. I couldn't believe what I was seeing. Cecil came back up to me and said, "This field will be ready in an hour." There were men with rakes pushing the water, and a few others were turning their rakes sideways and making grooves in the dirt to guide the water to a drain. They had the drill down pat.

To my extreme amazement, they slowly but surely got the field ready. The game was on. When I went out onto the field to get ready to pitch, the field wasn't muddy—it was firm and ready for play. The fans were excited to have a game, and I was excited and ready to pitch in my first game since the spring. I pitched six innings, came out of the game behind ,and we wouldn't catch up. I took a loss in my first game, but I was shocked that we even played. I learned that it took a lot more than a typical rainstorm to postpone games in Taiwan. I wondered why they didn't do this in Puerto Rico. It was good to know that it wasn't just on me to adjust to the rain. Everyone had to deal with it. Most of the natives handled it okay. They seemed to be used to it. But just like America, there are those in the population who struggle mightily in difficult weather conditions.

Once when my brother Lance visited me in Taiwan in 1999 (he was there for a month, and it rained almost every day), we were arriving by train in Kaohsiung and it was pouring. We got out in front of the train station under a roof, and there were literally 200 people crammed together, trying to stay dry and each trying to get the next available taxi. Lance and I stood there watching the rain come down with no hope of getting a taxi any time soon. While we were waiting, we saw this young Taiwanese guy walking in the downpour soaking wet. His soaked pants had slid all the way down his legs, leaving him totally—and I mean *totally*—exposed as he tried to walk. He was walking aimlessly, looking for cover. It was a strange sight, and Lance and I felt bad for him, because it appeared that he may have had some mental issues too.

Regardless, life went on—rain or not—like that every day in Taiwan. But there *were* occasions that no one could just "play through…."

We don't get hurricanes in California or Wisconsin. I'd only seen

Two. Who'll Stop the Rain?

coverage of them on television before I heard about a weather alert the last week of July 1996, during my second season in Taiwan. A super typhoon had formed in the Pacific and was heading towards us. "Typhoon Herb" or—as it was known in the Philippines—"Typhoon Huaning" was coming our way. A typhoon is a hurricane in the Pacific Ocean.

The night before the typhoon hit, the weather was nice in Taichung, my home city that season. Tony Metoyer and I went out to one of our hangouts, and the weather was calm. We stayed out all night, and when the sun came up, we looked out the windows and saw that it was getting pretty windy. We jumped in a cab and headed back to our apartments to sleep off the long night. I fell right asleep, and when I woke up hours later, "Herb" had arrived in full force.

The wind was blowing really hard, so hard that it was pushing water through the cracks of my apartment's kitchen window and sliding glass door. There was a lot of water all over my tile floor. The wind made a whistling sound, similar to a teapot. The power went out, and we had no electricity. I had nowhere to go, and no power, no lights, no TV, nothing. All I could do was sit on my couch in the dark and wait it out. Strangely, my telephone still worked, so I called Tami and talked to her for a little bit. We couldn't talk long because it was too expensive to make calls around the world, and Tami was starting to worry because she could hear the loud whistling of the wind blowing through the cracks of the windows.

After the phone call, I sat around for a while longer, bored and a bit nervous, before I went back to bed. I wasn't tired. I was just lying there, listening to the sound of the wind whistling through my window all night.

This was what it was like to ride out a typhoon.

The bigger shock came the next morning. I woke up to my telephone ringing. It was one of our coaches, calling to tell me to get ready, that we were going to practice. Practice. Really. During a typhoon. The team bus would pick us up at the usual spot outside of our apartment complex. I thought he was joking. There was still heavy rain coming down, and the wind was still blowing hard. It was dangerous, with the storm still raging. This was no joke. Regardless, I'm a professional and I'm under contract, so a few minutes later, I'm in my uniform and running out to the bus in the middle of a typhoon.

People die in these kinds of storms when they get stupid, go outside, and get hit by debris flying at them at 100 miles per hour. Still, the bus drove us to our practice facility. We didn't go to our field; instead, they took us to the double-decker outdoor driving range building nearby that was owned by our team owner. The players jumped out of the bus and ran to the semi-shelter of the driving range, which had minimal cover under a tiny roof. We were still exposed to the elements, and it was still very windy.

We played catch and did some running in circles. I still couldn't believe we were actually doing this, but we survived. And I never did see any young boys in blue gym shorts with sponges. Guess a typhoon was too much even for them.

When we were done with our mini-practice, the bus drove us back to our apartments. I spent the rest of the day alone and bored again. Of course, we practiced outside again the next day. Herb would finally weaken as it passed over Taiwan and moved toward China. In all, 51 people died, and 22 people were missing in Taiwan … but we were lucky. All totaled, in China Typhoon Herb killed 284 people, and 306 were listed as missing. Herb—a Category 5 storm when it hit—was the eighth-largest storm of its kind to hit the country in the previous two decades, and the fourth-wettest known tropical cyclone to impact the country. It did $500 billion worth of damage.

But we still got our practices in.

You don't really see all this while it's going on; you just want it to pass over and have things get back to normal. But I won't forget seeing chunks of metal and other debris flying through the air. Roads were destroyed, there were mudslides, and more. And all those people died.

Two years later, another Category 5 storm, Typhoon Zeb, hit late in the season. We were spared the worst impact, but that storm still killed 31 people in Taiwan and another 100 in other places. We had 16 inches of rain, and the storm caused $125 million in damage … but we only missed a few days of game action.

Real game *or* exhibition, if the game was important enough in Taiwan, we'd play *in* the rain.

We had a game that didn't even count—it was an exhibition game pitting a group of celebrities against our Taichung team—that was played in a steady downpour, because, well … rain didn't stop big events in the Chinese Professional Baseball League.

This group of celebrities was made up of famous Taiwanese movie stars, TV actors, comedians, and singers. The game was staged as a promotion for our team, and it was televised live across the country. We were told the day before to bring extra clothes with us because after the game, we were going to a spa to shower, eat as a team, and then join in some festivities with the celebs. It sounded like a lot of fun.

But … more rain. When we got to the ballpark, a large number of fans were anxiously waiting to see this game. We *were* going to play, regardless. As the introductions began, the rain started. It got heavier and heavier.

The PA announcer was introducing the celebrities first as the rain began coming down *hard*. I was starting to feel bad for the ladies because their hair and makeup was getting messed up. And it took a while for the announcer to get all the way through because he had to read all of their long bios. By the time he began to introduce us, the rain was coming down even harder, and the celebrities who were standing along the first base line were soaking wet.

We were waiting for someone to step in and call things off. That didn't happen. When they called my name, I remember jogging out to the third base line and finding myself soaking wet by the time I got there. As they continued to introduce our team, I looked around and saw water pouring off players' hats.

This had to be a joke, I thought. They had to cancel this meaningless exhibition game. Someone could get hurt in these conditions. But after the intros, the game did indeed start in steady rain. I wondered if maybe we'd just play an inning or two to make the fans happy. Nope. We played the entire nine innings.

It never stopped raining.

The moral of the story: In Taiwan, you play in the rain, and the grounds crew, somehow, some way, keeps the field playable ... even for exhibition games. So ... where was that Taiwanese grounds crew when I needed them in Cooperstown?

There's more to the story. When the game ended, everyone hurried off the field and onto the bus. We went to the spa to shower. Now you'd think that the last thing any of us would want to do after playing a baseball game in a steady rain was to do another activity that involved water. But before we could move on to the team dinner, we had to get into a swimming pool. Nobody had swimming trunks. The Taiwanese guys jumped in the pool naked.

It was an odd ritual. (I got to see a lot of those while I was in Taiwan.) After swimming, we had to go get into three different small pools. One had really hot water, the next one was medium, and the last one had very cold water. You were supposed to dip into each of these pools for a few minutes each. They told me it was good for your body ... that it helped circulation. Now I'm all for helping my body recover properly, but ... well, I guess there's nothing like a bunch of guys swimming naked together to help improve team unity and camaraderie.

Finally, we were able to dry off and get dressed, eat a quick and tasty dinner at the spa's restaurant, and head to a nightclub to hang out with the big celebrities—each of whom had dried out, too. It was actually a lot of fun meeting and talking with them—most of them spoke English very well. The regular customers were thrilled to see these celebs and baseball players hanging out in their favorite night spot. One of the famous comedians had a few drinks, grabbed four lit cigarettes, and ate them.

The game was a mess, but the post-game made up for it.

Dealing with rain was a constant in Taiwan. It was always so hot and humid that even when it wasn't raining, it felt like it was. When I pitched, I would sweat *hard*, so I was constantly changing undershirts—about every other inning. I remember looking down at the ground while I was sitting in the dugout between innings and seeing the sweat pouring off my face and hat and making a puddle at my feet. When I pitched deep into a game, I probably went through at least four and maybe five undershirts and two game jerseys every time.

Mother Nature doesn't just rain on you, however. During my fifth and final season in Taiwan in 1999, one of the worst earthquakes in the nation's history hit the island. This one stopped play for more than two weeks. It was so bad we didn't even try to practice.

I was lying in bed, letting my mind wander after a late-September game in the early morning hours, and I was almost asleep. Suddenly, at 1:47 a.m., my apartment began to shake. After about five seconds, the shaking didn't stop, and I realized it was an earthquake. I'd never been in a hurricane before, but I had been through earthquakes growing up in southern California. I knew earthquakes usually didn't last all that long. So as this hard shaking kept going and going, I got worried. A couple of months earlier, an earthquake had hit in Turkey, and I recalled watching the news and seeing the leveled buildings, how people were trapped under the debris, how after several days they were still trying to rescue people, and how miraculous it was when they found someone alive.

I jumped out of my bed and turned on the light, and as quickly as I could I put on my pants and slipped on some shoes. The shaking was still so hard that it felt like my 26-story apartment building was about to collapse. I figured if it did collapse, and I survived, I wanted to be wearing pants. If I had to crawl out of the debris, I would need some protection for my feet. After I put my pants and shoes on, I stood in my bedroom doorway. I'd always heard as a kid that if you're in an earthquake, you should stand in the doorway because it was the strongest part of the house. I stood there as the powerful shaking continued, and as I looked down the hallway, I saw the bathroom door and the other bedroom door opening and closing back and forth. In the hallway was a light hanging down from the ceiling, swinging back and forth, hitting the ceiling, then swinging back the other way and hitting the ceiling again, over and over. There was a loud metal squeaking noise, as if the pipes and metal in the building were being stretched.

The earthquake had been going on for a while, and it wasn't stopping. I figured that if it didn't stop, the building was coming down. I was now praying to myself, thinking "please stop, please stop!" Finally, after more scary seconds, the shaking stopped. I went out and did a quick inspection of the

Two. Who'll Stop the Rain?

Looking out the window from Don's high-rise apartment building at the surrounding neighborhood in Kaohsiung, Taiwan, 1998.

rest of my apartment. I found big, long cracks down some walls throughout the apartment. Things on shelves had fallen. The shaking had lasted for 102 seconds, which is very long for an earthquake. It had seemed longer than that. My apartment was on the fourth floor of the 26-story building. I'd have been crushed if the apartment building went down. Altogether, there were four 26-story buildings in my apartment complex, and there was a 50-story building right next door to us. They all stayed up.

But this wasn't over.

I got on the phone, and I was surprised it was working. I called Corey, one of my American teammates, and his wife, Glory, to make certain they were all right. After I hung up, I turned on my TV (the electricity to our building was still working too, which was a shock) to see what was on the news. The earthquake was all over of course, and it didn't take long for images to start to come in. I wondered where the epicenter was. As I watched, I tried to call Tami. It was about 1:00 p.m. in Milwaukee. She didn't answer. "*Hello, we are not able to take your call right now....*" I left a message. "Tami, I just want to tell you that I'm all right. Not sure what you'll see if you turn on cable news right now, but Taiwan just got smoked by a major earthquake. I don't know how bad the destruction is." As I said this, a very strong aftershock started. As it got stronger, I continued with my message: "Oh no, we're getting hit by an aftershock right now, I have to hang up and take cover, I'll try to call you back later," click.

I can only imagine what she must have been thinking the first time she listened to that message. I hung up the phone and ran back to the doorway. The light was swinging back and forth again, and the metal was squeaking noisily. Again, I feared that the building could collapse. When it stopped, I grabbed a bunch of water bottles, boxes of crackers, a bag of chips, and other dry food, and I put them under my very sturdy dining room table. If the building were to collapse, the table would protect me some, and if I was still alive in the debris, I could survive for several days with this food and water right by me.

I still had those images from Turkey in my mind, of those collapsed buildings, and how they presumed people dead after a number of days because they would have died from thirst and hunger. When I went back to the TV news, they were showing collapsed buildings and fires. At first, I didn't know which part of Taiwan these pictures were coming from. The phone rang. It was Tami calling me back. She said she'd just listened to my message and asked if I was okay. I assured her I was fine. She said she had the news on TV, and they were showing the earthquake in Taiwan, saying it was hard to tell how much damage there was because it was still dark. My voice message freaked her out, especially when the aftershock hit, and I had to abruptly hang up the phone. We talked for a bit longer before we said goodnight. I went to bed, but it was really hard to try to fall back asleep.

The next morning, we had a team meeting at the apartments. The league had suspended all games indefinitely. This was much more serious than the typhoons. There was a state of emergency throughout Taiwan. The earthquake was a 7.6 on the Richter scale, with several more aftershocks over 6.0 over the next several days. The epicenter was off the coast, nearer Taichung, and it rocked the entire island. Five days later, there was a 6.8 aftershock. A couple days later, we all boarded our team bus and went to donate blood.

In the daylight, things were even more horrific. Hundreds of buildings had collapsed, mainly in the Taichung area, and some in Taipei. There were no buildings collapsed near us in Kaohsiung, but many were severely damaged. As the aftershocks continued, the news reports showed hundreds of people setting up tents in parks in Taichung and sleeping outside. When someone spoke to one of my former teammates who was now living in Taichung, we found out some players from other teams were sleeping in a park. Some people felt safer that way, fearing that they'd be trapped or crushed in a collapsed building. The day after the earthquake, I was talking to Tami on the phone, and she brought up something I needed to do at my end with a local bank. I had to tell her that nothing was getting done around here, the entire region was under a "Tsunami alert." She said,

"So what … just do it." I realized that a Midwestern girl had no idea what a Tsunami was. I told her it was a tidal wave, and if it hit and I was outside, I would very likely be killed. So the bank would have to wait.

All our senses were heightened. A couple of days after the earthquake, I was watching the news live and it was showing rescue workers going through a collapsed building, looking for survivors in Taipei. All of a sudden, an aftershock hit, and they showed the rescuers running out of and away from the building. It suddenly hit me: The seismic wave would be hitting us in Kaohsiung in just a few seconds! As I ran toward my doorway past my sturdy table, the aftershock hit, and my apartment began shaking hard again.

After a while, the aftershocks began to lessen, and their intensity went down. It was still hard to fall asleep because you were waiting for the next one to start. When it was finally over, it was determined that 2,415 people had been killed, with over 11,000 injuries. A total of 51,711 buildings were completely destroyed, with more than 100,000 damaged. It was discovered that some of the collapsed buildings fell largely due to shoddy construction by the contractors. I was fortunate that our building had been well built. Some of the contractors had put trash and other fillers in places that required reinforced cement in order to save money. They figured no one would ever know.

People died in those buildings.

Since I was a Californian by birth, earthquakes were not foreign to me like hurricanes were … but if you asked me to choose, riding out a hurricane was a lot easier than that massive earthquake. The event was unique and historical in Taiwan.

Natural disasters aside, playing baseball in places like the Caribbean, Mexico, Taiwan, Australia, and Italy offered me a chance to play in some of the most beautiful settings and nicest climates anywhere. But nowhere is immune from Mother Nature. Nothing drives that home like shoveling snow in Wisconsin.

Three

Travelin' Man

When you decide to play overseas, it's not because of the weather (unless you're talking about playing winter ball in the Caribbean), it's because you just want a chance to play. You don't know what the climates or cultures will be like until you experience them. But you *do* know you'll be doing a good amount of traveling.

As a college kid, I'd crossed the border into Mexico several times, but that was pretty much the extent of my "foreign" travel. Later I got to travel to Canada with my professional baseball teams, but that was in a group where all the traveling details were handled by someone else.

I was so unfamiliar with crossing borders by myself that when I got the opportunity to play my first season of winter baseball in Puerto Rico, I went out and got a passport.

As I quickly found out, I didn't need the passport to travel there. But that passport became really valuable. The time and energy spent getting it turned out to be a great investment. Getting to and from these places wasn't always the easiest proposition. And once you arrived, you found a lot of … bumpy roads, so to speak.

Getting to Puerto Rico and back was a lot like flying to and from LA. No big deal. Driving in the PR, on the other hand, was … adventurous. They weren't much for speed limits—and having an open beer bottle in my hand didn't stop me from being able to rent a car. I was living in Dorado, near San Juan, a really nice place, and I spent most of my time near the beach. I only used a car to drive to the stadium and into San Juan to have some fun.

That changed when I finally did officially leave the USA in the early spring of 1993. I landed in Puebla, Mexico, to begin my first stint in the Mexican League, and it was obvious I wasn't in America any more.

I was behind. My first day there, the team had already been training for nearly two weeks. I was told to eat breakfast in the team motel, and from there I had to find the team bus to go to my first workout. After eating, I followed some of the Mexican players out the door. I figured they were going to the bus. One of the guys came up to me and introduced himself. "Hi, I'm

Three. Travelin' Man

Roy ... from Texas. You must be the new guy." Roy Salinas was Mexican American. He pointed me to another guy from the States, Chris Bennett. It was easy to pick out Chris. He was the only "Gringo." I noticed an open seat next to him, so I sat down and introduced myself. Chris told me my seat was usually Phil's, but said, "Phil isn't here right now." I found out that Phil Harrison had gone AWOL after the first week. Chris figured Phil had experienced too much culture shock, so he packed up his stuff and left in the middle of the night. Apparently, Phil hitchhiked out of town without telling anyone, and somehow made it to the airport and back home to California. I was surprised to say the least, so I asked, "Wow ... how did the team feel about that?" Chris said Phil hadn't told them. When he got home, the team reached out and got in touch with him. Phil told them he had a family emergency and had to go home but would return. Chris wasn't buying that. He didn't expect Phil to come back.

A few days later, Phil did return to the team. So now we had our full complement of Americans. Once I got to know him a little, I finally asked Phil what happened. He said he just basically freaked out and had to get out of Mexico, and when he left, he wasn't planning on coming back. He told the team a story about a family emergency, but they kept on pressing him to return. Eventually he changed his mind and decided to come back.

(From left) Phil Harrison, Don, and Chris Bennett in Puebla, Mexico, prior to the 1993 season.

Puebla, Mexico, newspaper announcing Don August as the team's Opening Day starting pitcher.

As the token Americans and pitchers, it was natural that the three of us would start hanging together. We began trying to learn our surroundings. On the eve of the start of the season, we came upon an old man selling newspapers. On the front page was a color picture of me, Chris, and

Phil standing together in our uniforms from the day before on media day. We all looked down at the picture, and the old man saw us, so he looked down at it too. Then he looked back up at us ... and then down at the paper again. He smiled, pointed at the paper, then at us, realizing that we were the guys in the picture. I decided to buy that newspaper, which I still have. It was also great practice using the newspaper to learn more Spanish.

The Mexican League is spread out over the entirety of the country—yet all the teams traveled exclusively by bus. Oftentimes we drove on deserted, dusty old dirt roads that seemed to lead to nowhere. The bus rides were endless, sometimes 12, 18, 24, and even 32 hours long. You learn to sleep sitting up.

We traveled to small towns and huge cities like Mexico City. In some of the small towns, we'd encounter these little roads that would lead into the town. As we got into the outskirts of the town, the roads would become very narrow. On one occasion, the roads got so narrow that the team bus couldn't make the turns. We had to get out of the bus, unpack and collect our gear and equipment, and walk the rest of the way through the town. The streets of some of these towns had old buildings that were probably built before there were cars.

When we were on the bus—especially after the games—things could get ... festive. Depending on what had just happened in the game and the

Members of the Campeche, Mexico, baseball team before a game in 1994.

mood we brought with us onto the bus ride, there could be a lot of beer and whiskey flowing. We'd have music blasting on a boom box too.

Early in my first stint in Puebla, we took a bus ride to Libres for an exhibition game against their local team. After a predictable lopsided win and a post-game "fiesta" with the town folk, the bus ride back was lively. After some drinks, one of the Mexican players got up in the aisle and started dancing. All the guys were laughing and cheering him on. After he was done, he pointed to me to get up and dance. At this point, I'd been on the team for about five days and still didn't know most of these guys. I basically only knew the other three American players. It usually takes some kind of event like this, an early road trip that has a lot of alcohol involved, for team bonding to begin. When I was chosen to get up and dance, I did. Maybe they weren't expecting me to, or maybe they were trying to see what kind of a guy I was. Either way, I got up in the aisle and I went right at it, no shame. My new teammates were laughing, clapping, and cheering me on. I probably looked like a total fool, but I had enough alcohol in me that I didn't care. I went at it for a few minutes. Suddenly tired, I grabbed our team manager (affectionately known as our "grunt") by the head and kissed him on his face. He was stunned and didn't know what to do. It was funny because earlier on the trip, he'd been talking a lot of smack to the American players about Pancho Villa. As I was walking back to my seat, all of my new teammates were laughing so hard they couldn't talk.

On another road trip, we'd finished playing in the Yucatan region and had a 16-hour ride home ahead of us. But the bus wasn't leaving until late in the afternoon, so Phil and I decided to rent a car and go see the pyramids at Chichen Itza. This was where the ancient Mayans had lived. We climbed up to the top of the pyramids, and you could see their athletic fields, where legend has it, they played an ancient game of basketball where the rings were very high. It's said the losing team would be sacrificed to the gods. I took a lot of pictures and found myself liking the idea of being a tourist from time to time. During the long ride home, I had time to reflect on the trip. We lost more games than we won, but the team bonded. There were several bus rides like that.

There were a few trips that were memorable for reasons that didn't happen *on* the bus. Once we were leaving Monterrey, heading for Laredo. We were driving on the open highway out in the middle of nowhere. In the middle of the night, our bus suddenly slowed down to about 10 miles per hour, and the driver turned off the headlights and all lights inside the bus. I was told that we had to drive very slowly and be very quiet through this stretch of road because there were bandits in the nearby hills that would storm buses and force them off of the road. Armed with rifles and guns, they'd rob everyone on board. Didn't sound like much fun to me.

We drove like this for a very long time, and it was tense. I stared out toward the hills, into the moonlight, waiting and watching for bandits to come out of the hills. I was picturing guys on horseback wearing black sombreros with bandoliers of bullets crisscrossing their chests. Maybe I've seen too many movies. Maybe not.

We made it to Laredo without incident. I wondered why we didn't just avoid that particular stretch of highway.

There were times we had to take a road trip to play a home game. The following season, after I was released by Puebla, I signed with a better team in Campeche. That franchise had agreed to play some series of games at our "other" home field in Carmen, about 260 miles away. During our last homestand of the 1994 season, we were going there to play my old team, Puebla. We arrived in Carmen just before lunch. Our bus pulled up to the sidewalk right in front of our hotel. When I got off the bus, I saw a dead cat lying there on the sidewalk. It looked smashed, eyes squinched, and its tongue sticking out of its mouth. My teammates just stepped right over it and walked into the hotel like it was nothing. I began to wonder why nobody from the hotel had come out to remove something like that right in front of their business. I stared while I walked past it and checked in, and after we dropped our bags off into the room, my roommate and I went back downstairs to get lunch. As we left the hotel, the dead cat was still lying there. When we came back over an hour later ... it was still there. Pedestrians walking by would have to either step over or around this dead cat.

After the game we went back to the hotel ... and the dead cat was still there! I don't ever remember seeing any dead cats in front of any of the hotels I stayed in when I played in MLB. Finally, the next morning, the cat was gone. Hopefully it wasn't taken away by the hotel restaurant cook.

After my first season in Mexico (followed by time with Triple A Charlotte), my hopes of getting another shot at the big leagues were still very high. But with no offer in hand for the 1994 season, a second stint in winter ball would be required. One of my former coaches in Milwaukee, Bill Castro, got me set up with a team in the Dominican Republic. That meant some big league competition and some crazy travel stories.

On the day after Thanksgiving, I was on a plane headed for the Dominican Republic. I flew all day long before I arrived in Puerto Plata. I was a little nervous about going to the "DR." I'd heard a lot of crazy stories from other Americans who'd played there, but I figured I'd be able to handle it. When I arrived, the team had someone waiting to drive me to Santiago, my new home city.

While I waited for my luggage and my ride, I got several offers to help. I kept smiling and saying no thanks before they started asking me for things like the baseball hat I was wearing. This was a very poor country, and a lot of the residents didn't have much of anything. When my driver arrived, he spoke no English. It was a long, dark drive to Santiago, and when we arrived, I found myself booked in a very posh hotel for the night.

Part of traveling is getting acclimated to your new surroundings. That's pretty easy in the States. It's just a matter of meeting your new teammates. But in a foreign country, there's a lot more involved. The first guy you need to know is the clubhouse manager. Our guy in the Dominican spoke great English, fortunately. That wasn't always the case, I'd find out. One of the assistants was an older guy, maybe in his late 40s or early 50s, who was missing his front teeth. He started talking to me in Spanish, but he was really hard to understand due to his missing teeth. One of my new teammates came up and told me he was looking at my glove and my baseball shoes and asking if he could have them. I thought, "Really?" Weren't clubhouse attendants supposed to get things *for* us? I had to tell him nicely no, that I needed my baseball equipment.

It helps when you have teammates who have been there, done that, of course. I always seemed to get lucky in that department. One of my favorites was star catcher Tony Peña, who played 18 seasons and almost 2,000 games in the big leagues and won four Gold Glove Awards. In the Dominican, I was also reunited with Manny Ramirez, who was still on his way to superstardom with Cleveland. I'd played against several of the other guys in the minors and big leagues, so things weren't too different, at least on the field.

They certainly had their own unique way of approaching the game. On my first day, while still a little unsure about everything, I was hanging out in left field just shagging balls when I noticed the old clubhouse helper going around the outfield, handing each of the players something. It looked like he was holding a coffee dispenser of some kind. Eventually he got to me. He wanted to know if I wanted some coffee. I told him no thanks. I thought, "Drinking coffee during BP? Really?" Then he gave me two pieces of Bazooka gum and moved on to the next player. He did this every night—it was one of his jobs, passing out coffee and two pieces of gum. Finally, one night I took him up on his offer. He gave me a tiny plastic cup the size of a small shot glass and squirted some coffee into it. I thought, "That's it?" After I drank it, I learned why. That Dominican coffee was mighty potent! It was coffee—along with some other stuff—brewed to wake you up! I suddenly had a lot of extra energy.

That old guy was doing all he could to make things better for all of us. There were others who made international play a little tougher.

For example, there was Fernando. He worked for the team, and one of his jobs was to drive the American players around in a van, supplied by the

Three. Travelin' Man 43

team. His job was to take the players living in the hotel to and from the stadium every day. If it was during the day, we'd call him up, and he'd come and get us and take us wherever we needed to go. Still, Fernando pretty much took over that van as his own personal vehicle. Most times he'd be available, but sometimes it was hard to get a hold of him. Even when you made plans with him in advance, he wasn't always right there. Sometimes it was more of a hassle to reach him, and I ended up on foot. Walking around the neighborhood near the hotel, I found a few places where I could eat lunch.

One day I wanted to go to the post office, so I called Fernando for a ride. I had some postcards and letters I wrote to family and friends back home, and I needed stamps. Plus, I wanted to buy a few extra stamps to collect, just to keep from the different countries that I'd been to. Fernando was reluctant to take me. He tried to talk me out of it, saying it'd be crowded on the street and hard to find a place to park. He was right about that. The traffic was crazy. People drove like there weren't any traffic laws.

Fernando pulled the van off to the side of the road, saying he was parking illegally and that I'd better hurry back. I dropped my letters into a mail slot and asked someone working there how long it would take for these to get to the United States. About a month or so, I was told. I did a double take. A month? Then again, I wasn't *that* surprised.

When I got back to the van, Fernando was upset. A cop came by and was coming back to write us a ticket. As the cop approached our van, Fernando told me to bribe him with some money. "What? You want me to try to bribe a cop?!" He yelled back at me to just do it. A few seconds later the policeman was at the window, Fernando looked at me and I put a 20-peso bill into his hand. The exchange rate in the Dominican Republic was eight Dominican pesos to one U.S. dollar. I realized I just bribed a cop $2.50. Fernando said I bribed the cop *too much*.

Other times, dealing with Fernando and his lack of dependability wasn't quite so funny.

The contract we'd negotiated with the Dominican team provided a flight home for the Christmas break, and then back for the remainder of the season. Teams are reluctant to do this because they're afraid of—and have been burned by—American players going home for the break and not coming back at a very crucial time, the last few games of the regular season, with the playoffs right after that. They didn't have to worry about that with me. I needed to be seen by every Major League scout possible, and the only way to do that was to pitch more.

I'd been in the Dominican Republic for about a month, and I was excited to go home for Christmas and be with my family. Our break arrived, and I got Fernando to take me to the airport in Puerto Plata. I told him several times, over and over, to confirm what day and time I was returning, and to make 100 percent certain he'd be at the airport, waiting to take me back to Santiago. I felt like I was nagging, and he was like "yea, yea, I know." Still, I had him repeat to me the day and time. When he dropped me off at the airport, I said, "You better be here," he said "Okay...," and I was on an airplane home.

It was nice to be home, even though it was cold. Tami noticed that I'd lost some weight ... largely because I wasn't eating much and my bouts with the diarrhea. Christmas was nice, lots of good food and a little down time. I called my agent to see if anything was happening with getting me a contract for next season. Nothing.

On the flight back to the DR, I found myself thinking about my upcoming start, and how there were only a few more games left in the regular season. After landing in Puerto Plata, I grabbed my two suitcases and was already holding my carry-on bag.

I looked around and didn't see any sign of Fernando.

At this point, I'm figuring he must be running late because I made *sure* he knew what day and time I was returning. That was just three days ago! He promised he'd be here. I waited. The usual people were hanging around the baggage claim and where the taxis waited. People were asking me for my hat again, and if I needed a ride. I told them no thanks; my ride would be here soon. I was tired and I wanted to get on the van, take the hour and a half drive through the mountain at night, and get to my room in Santiago.

More time passed, and still no Fernando.

Confidence in "my ride" was waning, and I started to look for a buses to Santiago. The last one had already left. I didn't know how much it would cost for a cab to Santiago, plus I didn't have that much money on me after leaving a lot at home in Milwaukee. Payday was just in a few days anyway. People kept asking me if I needed a ride or a place to stay. I kept on telling them no. Turned out to be my mistake.

An hour passed and still no Fernando.

I finally relented. I asked one of the guys hanging around if he could find me a place to stay in Puerto Plata. He said he could ... but this got complicated. A cab driver would take me to this bar, then I was supposed to go inside and ask for a guy named Freddy. Freddy would have a place for me to spend the night. I had no other choice at this point. I had my luggage and my travel bag, and I got inside this cab to go to this strange bar to find someone named Freddy that I was instantly supposed to trust.

I began wondering if I was being set up. The cab driver pulled up to this bar on a regular looking side street, and he told me this was the place. I paid him, and now I was carrying my three bags inside this bar to find this Freddy character. I didn't know what to expect. It wasn't that big of a place, but it was mostly full. I made my way up to the bar to speak to the bartender. When I got there, he started speaking to me in what I thought was German. In Spanish, I told him I didn't understand what he was saying. Then he asked me if I spoke English, and I said yes. He said he thought I was a German tourist. Slightly relieved, I told him I needed to speak to Freddy. I wouldn't have been surprised if he said he didn't know a Freddy, but he said, "Ya, I'll go try and find him." It was a relief that this was looking legit.

As I stood there waiting for Freddy, I looked around the bar and noticed that practically everybody in the place *was* German ... speaking German to each other. About 10 minutes later, a guy came up to me and introduced himself as Freddy. I told him the name of the guy at the airport who said I could find him here, and that he could find me a place to stay for the night. He said he thought he could, but he'd have to go and see for certain. He told me to wait here for a while and he would return.

Off he went, so I ordered a beer. I started talking to the bartender, who told me he learned to speak German because they got so many German tourists in the place. He thought I was another German coming to order a drink. After what seemed like forever, Freddy finally returned. He said he had a place for me three or four blocks away, and it would cost $15 American. It was all good. We left the bar and began walking down a very dark street. No streetlights, and I couldn't see a thing. We went a little further and turned down another street. I was hoping that nobody was going to jump out, rob me, and leave me for dead. I was really trusting this Freddy guy, whom I just met.

We walked a little more, and off to the right there was a group of buildings that looked like they were under construction. The place looked like an apartment. Freddy pulled out a key and opened the door, and we went inside. I saw right in front of me a cot, but the rest of the apartment was completely empty, still under construction. No problem, I just needed a place to sleep. I told Freddy I needed to take a bus back to Santiago in the morning. I asked him if he could show me how to get to the bus station. He told me to meet him back at the bar tomorrow morning. I hoped nobody would be coming through the door at daybreak while I was still asleep to start working on it. When I lay down, I think I fell asleep in seconds.

I woke up the next morning with the sun coming through the window. I looked at my watch, and it was close to 8:00 a.m. I jumped up, dressed, got my bags situated, and headed out the door to go back to the bar and meet Freddy. When I got outside, I didn't recognize a thing. With the sun out, there were things I hadn't seen the previous night because it was so dark. There was now construction work going on across and down the street. I didn't remember which way I'd come from; there were no landmarks to go by. I actually stood in the middle of the street with both of my suitcases in my hands, wondering which way to go. I was clueless. I decided to go left, hoping this was the right choice. As I began walking, this old man from the construction across the street asked me in Spanish where I was going. I told him a bar; he said which one? I told him I didn't know the name, and I asked if he knew Freddy. He didn't. As I began to walk, he started grabbing at my suitcase. I told him no, that I was fine carrying it myself. He wanted to help me carry it, so I finally let him. I figured he was looking for some money by helping me. Now the two of us were walking down the middle of the street, not knowing where to go. I was lost, but I knew the bar was close by. When we got to the end of that street, I decided we'd turn left. It was a coin flip at that point.

As we were approaching the next street, I saw Freddy flying by on a moped. As he passed, I yelled "Freddy.... Freddy!" He kept going, but he suddenly stopped and turned around. When he circled back, it seemed like he didn't know who I was. I told him I was supposed to meet him at the bar and that he'd promised to take me to the bus station. Fortunately, I jogged his memory. He told me to go back to the bar and wait for him; he had an errand to run and would be back at the bar shortly. Before he took off, I had to ask him which way the bar was. We were about three blocks away. The old man and I walked the three blocks and found it off to the left. The old man stuck his hand out for his gratuity, and I gave him 20 pesos. I figured if that amount was good enough to bribe a cop, then it would be good enough for him.

I went into the bar, and nobody was inside, except a lone guy working there. It was, after all, early in the morning. I told the guy I was waiting for Freddy. He asked me if I was hungry and surprised me by giving me a breakfast menu. After I finished some bacon and eggs, finally Freddy walked in. I lugged my bags to his car, but when he tried to start the car, it wouldn't turn over. Go figure. We got out of the car and Freddy walked over to his little moped. A joke? I thought there was no way we'd both fit on this thing, and how was I going to hold on to my two suitcases? At that point, there was no choice. I got on the back, strapped my carry-on bag around my neck and shoulder, and I held my suitcases off to each side of the moped. Off we went down the street.

We must have been quite a sight as we turned onto a busy street, with the traffic as crazy as ever. People in the DR pretty much make up their own traffic rules. There were cars going in all directions. I closed my eyes to prepare for the crash I felt was sure to come any second. I saw donkeys pulling carts right down the main street. We drove around a curve and started up a big hill. I heard the moped's engine straining ... we were too heavy. About halfway up this hill, the moped just gave out. Freddy pulled off to the side of the road and tried to restart it, over and over, but no luck. We'd walk the rest of the way. We left his moped on the side of the road and began on foot.

We made it up the hill, passing shops and stores and other little buildings. My bags felt heavier by the minute walking up that hill. I think we walked about a mile, it was hot and humid, and I was sweating pretty good when he finally told me, "There it is." I looked up, and I didn't see a bus station. "Where?" I asked. We walked a little further up to this small shack that had a tin roof. From outside, we stood at the window opening, and he asked the lady for a bus ticket to Santiago. She gave me the ticket, and I paid her. I felt a sudden burst of relief. Next to the building were some benches outside by the sidewalk. I sat down as Freddy told me the bus number. It was over a two-hour wait. I thanked Freddy for helping me, we shook hands, and off he went back down the street, I presumed, to try to start his moped.

I sat there daydreaming and nearly falling asleep until finally the bus arrived. I was off to Santiago. We had an away game that night, which I was going to be a no-show for. I never had a chance to find a phone to call the team. I knew they'd think I skipped out on them and wasn't coming back. It was a long ride, but after the two days I'd been through, I wasn't taking any chances. Before getting off the bus, I asked the driver if this was actually Santiago, just to make sure. All I needed was to get off in the wrong place.

When I finally—mercifully—arrived at my hotel and got up to my room, the first thing I did was call the general manager at his office. He answered the phone, and I told him that I just now arrived, that Fernando forgot to pick me up at the airport last night, and the rest of the amazing story. He told me not to worry, even though I had missed the bus to Santo Domingo. I wasn't pitching anyway, and I should just relax and meet the team tomorrow. He reminded me that I had better call my wife immediately, that she was worried to death.

I hadn't thought about Tami. As soon as I hung up with him, I called her. She answered the phone and was frantic, asking what happened to me! She said the team called her when I missed the bus, thinking I had skipped out on them, and they wanted to talk to me. She promised them that I had arrived in the Dominican Republic last night, that she had taken me to the airport in Milwaukee herself. At first, they weren't sure if she was lying. Now that I'd been missing for nearly a day, everyone was worried that something bad had happened. I would have thought the same thing. Tami even called my brother Lance in Las Vegas to have him call my hotel to ask what they knew, because he could speak a little Spanish. Lance later told me he called the hotel, and when he started speaking Spanish, they quickly told him they could speak English. I told Tami my whole story, I was okay, and everything turned out all right. We could all exhale.

The next day I saw Fernando.

I was still pretty pissed off. I got up in his face and shouted at him, "*Where the fuck were you! Do you have any idea what I had to do to get back here?*" He gave me some bogus answer, like I had given him the wrong day. It took all I had not to punch him right in the face. I finally said, "You lying asshole, I told you over and over again what day and time I was arriving! I even made you say it back to me!" He offered a weak apology, still trying to claim it wasn't his fault.

When we got to the game, my teammates told me they thought I wasn't coming back. I guess they didn't understand what lengths I was willing to go to make sure I got to pitch in front of big leagues scouts.

I'd been told I was being moved into the starting rotation after the break, so even after my adventurous trip back to the DR, I had to get ready to go. It was New Year's Day, and I needed to get a bullpen session in. Our manager told me I could throw at the stadium that morning. When we arrived, I wasn't expecting to see anyone, I just hoped there'd be a catcher available for me. When teammate Tom Marsh and I walked out onto the field, we were astonished to see a lot of people. I didn't know this, but during the day our field was used for a baseball school. There was instruction going on everywhere. I was impressed.

After we got our work in, Tom and I spent the day hanging out with a couple of wealthy businessmen we met while eating lunch. Our plans to watch college football bowl games all day went by the wayside when we drank with them for several hours before going to a casino. I ended up winning about $200 that night ... but missed all the football games. Not a terrible tradeoff, I suppose.

None of this—my wild trip back to the DR or my fun New Year's Day—was going to distract me from my starting assignment. It went well, and I felt like what I'd done during the winter should have gotten me a shot with another big-league team. For whatever reason, it didn't. But I was still ready and willing to travel to make my return to The Show happen. I was ready to go 7,500 miles. That's roughly how far it is from Milwaukee to Taipei, Taiwan.

Winter ball ended, and I didn't get a job in the States, even after putting up really good stats in the DR. After a second solid season back in the Mexican League, I got a chance to sign a minor league deal with the Pittsburgh Pirates for the 1995 season. Yes, this was the season that started late due to a players' union strike and a long battle between the owners and players that had wiped out the 1994 World Series the previous fall. That was the time when teams were looking to sign players in my situation as "replacement players." What a farce that turned out to be.

I wasn't going to be a replacement player under ANY circumstances, and my stint in the Pirates' minor league system was short-lived. After beginning the regular season in the starting rotation for Triple A Calgary, I was allowed to make exactly two starts before they released me.

A few weeks earlier, I'd gotten a call from Reggie Waller—the Astros scout who signed me 11 years earlier. After being let go from his role as the Assistant GM of the San Diego Padres the previous season, Reggie was now working with a group that was signing American players to contracts in the seven-year-old Chinese Professional Baseball League. Taiwan was still considered part of mainland China.

I didn't want to go back to Mexico, but I wasn't ready to give up on getting back to the big leagues, either. I'd been close with Pittsburgh, I felt. The players' strike and the addition of replacement players crowded the rosters and put up some roadblocks, but I know I could have made that team if I'd gotten the chance. Maybe going to Taiwan would be the jump-start my career needed. Tami and I agreed that I had to find out. Plus, the money was *really* good.

Passport in hand, I left Milwaukee and arrived 26 hours later in Taipei, Taiwan. I was nervous, going to the other side of the planet, and I didn't speak a word of Chinese. At least in Mexico I knew how to speak some Spanish, but this would be totally different. It was also a little unnerving to get a written warning with your travel visa that says, "Do not bring drugs into the Republic of China. This is punishable by *death*." I don't do drugs ... but it made me wonder what kind of penalties came with slightly lesser offenses?

I didn't know how long I'd be gone. The CPBL season goes into mid-October, and then there are the playoffs. My flight schedule was from Milwaukee to Detroit to Tokyo to Taipei. I left Milwaukee on May 4, and I arrived in Taipei on May 5. The flight from Detroit to Tokyo was so long that they showed three movies.

When you get off the airplane and get outside of the airport, you instantly know you're in a different part of the world. I was told that my contact would be a guy named Jeffrey Wilson. He took me to the hotel where my team was staying and helped me check in. He started speaking fluent Chinese to the people working at the front desk, and I was very impressed. He helped me get my bags up to my room and gave me his business card so I could call him if I needed anything. Jeffrey told me our team translator and coach would come by my room the next day to welcome me and to let me know what was going on from there.

Getting acclimated was a *huge* part of making this long trip. I arrived late at night, and I was very tired. I realized I was somewhere different, but figured I'd use my experience from Mexico, Puerto Rico, and the Dominican Republic to help me get by. Imagine how tired you get on a flight that literally takes two days.

Getting settled into my new surroundings wasn't all that easy, either. When I arrived in Taiwan, I was bounced from a hotel to an apartment with little or no understanding of the language and culture. After my first road trip, we got back to our home city around 3:30 a.m. When we got off the bus, the street was pretty empty, except for the stray dogs roaming around. I was supposed to be moving into a new apartment, but I had no idea where I was or where I was supposed to go. We were entering a group of four 26-floor apartment buildings that our team owned and operated on the outskirts of Taichung. He wasn't going to be there of course ... all I knew was I was supposed to meet a guy named Chan.

We arrived, and I began looking for this guy—I had no idea what he looked like since we had never met. I was dragging around five pieces of luggage, so I was eager to find my new apartment and get to bed. The players entered the complex through an automatic door that needed a card to open. I stopped in the middle of the square, surrounded by the four buildings, to wait for Chan to arrive and help me. I was alone. I waited five minutes. Then 10. Then 15. Still no Chan.

It's 3:30 in the morning, mind you. But what else could I do? I started yelling out loud: "Chan! Chan!" I was hoping maybe he dozed off and would hear me and come to my rescue. I yelled some more. I'm sure there were some mighty pissed-off residents by this point. Probably a few that wanted to kick my ass. They started looking down at me from their windows because I kept on yelling.

Eventually, a man arrived and identified himself as Chan. He didn't speak a word of English. But he did lead me to the elevators, to a third-floor room in the East tower. When we went inside, I couldn't believe my eyes. The room was a small rectangle, about 10' × 12'. It was more of a cell than a room. It wasn't even finished being built, and it was dirty. One sink, one twin bed, a dirty floor. No windows.

Chan handed me two sheets and a pillow. Then he led me down the hall and showed me an open door where there were two toilets, two showers, and a washer and dryer. This room was shared by everyone on the floor. It was like being a freshman in college all over again ... except my room at Chapman College was bigger and cleaner.

These dorm-style rooms were for younger players and team "grunts" to live in. All the foreign players and the older Taiwanese players lived in regular apartments throughout the four towers. Apparently, mine wasn't ready for me to move into yet. At least that's what I was told.

After Chan waved goodbye, I went back to my jail cell. I swept the floor and pushed the trash off to the side. There was no closet, no dresser. I dropped my suitcases on the floor and went to sleep.

Getting acclimated isn't always smooth and easy.

Three. Travelin' Man

Getting *to* Taiwan was the easy part, as it turned out. Getting around *in* Taiwan was a whole different adventure. The sight my first day there, when we walked outside of the hotel, was overwhelming. I'd arrived late at night, it was dark, and now in the daylight, all I could see was insane traffic with cars, taxis, and scooters everywhere. There are thousands of scooters parked everywhere on the sidewalks, which made it hard for the many people walking to navigate around. Scooters—they're a lot like "Mopeds" in the states—would be a big part of the rest of my time in Taiwan.

On the streets, it seemed like there were no rules. Red lights didn't mean anything, cars just turned in front of other cars; you had to stop or crash into them. They make their own new lanes. There's constant traffic everywhere. Drivers are literally making up their own laws. Right of way? No such thing.

Sometimes I'd just stand off to the side, in a safe place, and watch this crazy traffic go by. It was entertaining. I was waiting to see the inevitable accident, but I never saw anything bad happen. I learned to think of it as "controlled chaos." Nevertheless, while walking on the sidewalks near the streets, you did have to be careful. You literally could get killed.

It was no better inside a taxicab. Most of the time, they get you where you want to go, even if it's a scary ride. There was a time when I wanted to go home early during a night out with my teammates in our home city of Taichung. This would be my first time taking a cab home late at night by

Don outside a Buddhist temple in Kaohsiung, Taiwan, 1997.

myself. We weren't at one of our usual places, and my teammates asked me if I was okay doing this alone. I said sure. I was feeling confident in myself. I left the bar and flagged down a taxi. In my version of Chinese, I told the cab driver where to go, and I asked him if he knew where that was. He said yes.

So off we went, and everything seemed fine. We made a couple of turns ... and things didn't look familiar. Then again, at night nothing usually does, especially when the signs are in Chinese. I thought once the driver got on a main street, I'd recognize something, but that didn't happen. In my basic Chinese, I asked the driver again if he knew where he was going. Again, he said yes. He started to make a lot of turns, and I saw that he was looking around from side to side. Finally, he pulled over and began to speak to someone on the street. I had no idea what they were talking about, but I think he was asking for directions.

Now we're having a language barrier problem. It's late and I'm tired, and I just want to get home to my tiny room and go to sleep. Clearly, he didn't know where he was going ... and all the while the meter kept running. I felt like we were driving in circles. I finally told the driver to stop and let me out, even though I had no idea where I was. I was lost. The damn cab driver lied to me when he said he knew where he was going. He just didn't want to lose the fare and thought he could figure it out. I decided I'd walk around on my own until I saw something familiar. It was late, there weren't many people on the street to ask for help, and there weren't any other cabs around. I didn't even know which direction I was walking. I didn't know where to go, which is a terrible feeling.

I walked a number of blocks, and I still didn't know where I was. I was taking up time and getting nowhere. Finally, I saw a taxi and flagged it down. I told the driver my destination, he didn't seem sure, maybe it was my bad Chinese, but off we went. He was driving around and making turns, and still nothing looked familiar to me. Then he made another turn, and finally a street looked familiar. I told him to keep going straight ahead. I finally got to my apartment complex. The drive should have taken 15–20 minutes, but it took over two hours. I was never so happy to get back to my tiny little jail cell of a room. I thought back to one of my teammates telling me to carry around a business card from the apartment complex or hotel you're at on the road to show cab drivers who need directions. I wish I'd remembered to do that.

In my second year, it was the middle of May, and we had a short three-day trip in Taipei. My American roommate, Kevin Morton, and I checked into our hotel room. As we sat there chatting, I noticed that he had two big suitcases and another small bag along with his baseball bag. I asked him why he had so many bags for this three-day trip. He replied,

Three. Travelin' Man

"I'm leaving." There was a pause. I stammered, "what?" He told me he was taking a cab at 5:00 a.m. to the airport and going home. I was shocked. He was pitching well and seemed to be handling things. But Kevin finally admitted that he was ready to leave after his first three days in Taiwan. It was just too different. But after he thought about it, he decided to give this thing a fair shot, so he would give it a month. That was yesterday. He'd had enough.

I'd heard stories about some guys arriving in Taiwan and getting right back on the plane the next day to return home.

Another time, during a visit from Tami and Logan, we had a short road trip to Taipei. Tami found out there is a section of Taipei called the American Zone. Once you get there, the streets and the buildings—and the traffic—begin to look a lot like America. There are a lot of American stores and places to eat. We decided to go there with teammate Ron Gerstein and his wife, Tisa. We were looking to have lunch, and then we could walk around and go into stores, especially the clothing stores, which got Tami's attention. The only way for us to get there was in a taxi. We all got into a cab together—five of us—and we gave the driver the address to the restaurant. The American Zone wasn't close to our hotel, so I wasn't familiar with how to get there.

We drove for a little while, and I thought we must be getting close. At one point, it seemed like the cab driver may have been lost. I asked him in Chinese if he knew where he was going. He said yes. We were on a road that wasn't quite a main street. The cab driver said he needed to turn left and get to the next main street over. We came to the next street to turn left. It was very narrow, and it had a bunch of scooters and cars parked along both sides. This street was probably about 40 yards long. I was in the front seat, and this narrow path looked way *too* narrow to me. I didn't think we could squeeze through. I was right, but that didn't stop our cabbie.

Against my advice, the cab driver slowly turned left onto this narrow street, and we got no further than 10 feet when he began scraping the cars to the left of us, taking off side-view mirrors of parked cars. We heard metal scraping on the sides of the cars, scratching and leaving dents. All of us stared in disbelief. I thought the cab driver would just stop and back out of this mess. Instead, he continued to drive slowly forward, turning slightly right to avoid the cars. Then he began crunching and knocking over the scooters that were on the right side of the street. I was right there in the front seat, inches away, watching him hitting and knocking over one scooter after another. He kept on going, doing this all the way to the end of the path. It was like a scene from a movie. This guy did a ton of damage. He wasn't even thinking about stopping or doing anything about the damage he'd caused. No notes, no messages of any kind about who did all this.

When we got to the end, he asked me if we should turn right onto the main road. I immediately told him no in Chinese, just stop right here. We were good. He said that we weren't there yet. I politely told him we could walk the rest of the way.

Everybody quickly jumped out of his cab. We couldn't believe what we just witnessed. He must have damaged at least 15 cars on the left, and about 40–50 scooters that were on the right. It was crazy. We ended up getting another cab to go the short distance that was left. We returned to the hotel with a great story to tell.

When I arrived in Taiwan, those scooters looked like death traps. As much as I cringed when I saw people riding them, at the start of my fourth year in Taiwan, I decided that I'd had enough of constant (and sometimes scary) cab rides, and reluctantly joined the scooter crowd.

I didn't really do it by choice. More out of necessity. After all those cab rides, some of the guys started thinking that we should just buy our own scooters and save the money on taxis. At first, I said no…. I was always scared to death riding on the back of one. I was afraid to ride a scooter of my own in this crazy traffic in Taiwan. Just before Opening Day, that same teammate, Ron Gerstein, bought a scooter because he was the only one living in the Twin Towers, and it was a long ride to get to the team apartments to catch our bus for anything. It was more costly for Ron to take a cab back and forth by himself every time. From the apartment complex where I lived, I and a couple other teammates had a short cab ride to the team apartments, and we had three guys to share the cab fares. But right after Ron bought his scooter, so did another teammate, Corey Powell, and then right after that, a third teammate, Brad Straus, bought his.

That left me as the only foreign guy without a scooter.

This meant that whenever we had to go to the team apartments, I had to take a taxi alone. Whenever we went out at night, the guys rode their scooters together, and I had to take a taxi and meet them there, which also meant I didn't have anyone to split the taxi fares with. If we wanted to leave and go somewhere else, they rode off, and I had to find another taxi and follow. Sometimes I had to ride on the back of one of the guys' scooters, which scared me shitless. Riding on the back of one of those things left you feeling helpless.

I think I had a lot of good reasons not to like scooters. While I never did see anything terrible happen with my own eyes, I did see the aftermath. A couple of years earlier, around 2:30 in the morning, I was in my apartment, playing my Sega Genesis video game *Operation Pacific,* when I heard a very loud noise from the main street below my apartment. It was a loud metal bang. My first thought was that somebody was driving drunk and sideswiped a parked car. I didn't immediately jump up to see what had

Three. Travelin' Man 55

Scooters—the most popular mode of transportation—lining a small road in front of Don's apartment in Kaohsiung, Taiwan, 1998.

happened. But eventually I made my way over to the window and looked down to see what was going on. After looking around, I finally saw an intersection with a scooter lying on its side with two guys lying next to it. No one else was around, which was strange, I thought.

After a few minutes, some people started to show up. The two guys on the ground weren't moving. Finally, an ambulance arrived. Two men got out, grabbed the two guys on the ground by the hands and feet, and kind of haphazardly began swinging them from side to side before tossing them onto the stretcher. Like it was some sort of game or something.

I realized both those guys were dead.

The ambulance drove away without a siren or emergency lights. I still have this image of these two guys lying there, the victims of a hit and run. The next day, I walked past the intersection and the scooter was still there, tossed off to the side like a piece of trash. Cars and other scooters were flying by, with no one acknowledging what had happened there just a few hours before.

That's why I never wanted a scooter.

But I caved. After about a week of being the only holdout, I finally broke down. Corey and I went to a scooter shop that fixed and repaired scooters near our apartment complex. The shop was located right on a busy main street. The guy who owned the place did some work inside the small shop, and he had a couple of his workers working right on the sidewalk in front. I approached the owner and asked him to show us some used scooters for sale. This guy was a big baseball fan. He instantly recognized me and was very excited. I saw one that looked all right, so I took it.

The owner didn't speak any English at all, and now I had to tell him in Chinese that I wanted to buy it, and then I had to negotiate with him to get a lower price. He offered it to me for 9,000 NT dollars, about $300 U.S. I bargained him down to 7,750 NT dollars, now about $250 U.S. In Taiwan, it was a law that you had to wear a helmet when you rode on a scooter. So I bought a helmet from him too. After he gave me my paperwork, I had to drive this thing back to my apartment in the crazy traffic. No big deal? I'd never driven a motorcycle and had only been on a motor scooter a few times before, so I wasn't just climbing back on the horse, so to speak.

The scooter was a "150," the biggest a scooter could be in Taiwan. There were no motorcycles allowed on the streets of Taiwan. I was sure that I was going to get killed riding this thing. When I rode the scooter back to my apartment, I had to focus on unwritten rules of the roads. Those actual rules were that ... there weren't any rules. I went with the rule of yield to the bigger guy and to drive where the other scooter riders rode. But now I had the freedom to drive anywhere I wanted and not have to walk or pay for cabs. Now I could ride my scooter to the bank rather than taking the long cab ride back and forth from my apartment that wasn't so close anymore. So it wasn't all bad, I guess.

I used that scooter for the next two years. During the off-season when I went back to Milwaukee, I actually just parked it on the sidewalk by the team apartments. I wasn't sure what to expect when I returned to Taiwan, but miraculously it was still in the same spot! When I left Taiwan for the final time, I sold it right back to the nice little old guy I bought it from. I've never been much of a motorcycle guy, but I do like the photo I have of me and my brother Lance—all 295 pounds of him—riding together on that scooter without our helmets on a crazy street in Taiwan.

Yeah, I got a ticket for that.

Four

Speaking in Tongues

Speaking of traveling ... it had been another long, minor league bus ride starting in our home city of London, Ontario. It was 1992, and I was riding these buses for the first time in about five years. Finally, we pulled into the hotel parking lot in Albany, New York, the first stop on another endless Class AA road trip.

As you do in the bush leagues, we got off the bus and began unpacking the bags from underneath, so we could drag our luggage inside to our cramped motel rooms. It was the perfect moment for some random guy to wander up, look at the bus, give us all the once-over, and say something really ... stupid.

"Uh, are you guys a baseball team?" asked Captain Obvious. Smiling at the absurdity of it all, we said that yes, we were. As he looked back at our bus, he saw the team name and asked, "You guys from London, *Canada*?" I grinned and said, "Yeah, our team is from Canada." He looked around at us one more time and finally said, in a little bit of a "rural" accent, "Well, you guys sure do speak good American."

Duh.

The majority of our roster was made up of American players, obviously. We were part of the Detroit Tigers' farm system; we weren't from the North Pole. We laughed about that one for weeks.

In other places (although not usually in Canada), one of the main things that proves difficult for American players in foreign countries is the language barrier. Over most of the next decade, I saw some very good ball players—guys who had a lot of success in their careers—arrive to play in a different country but not be able to handle the different culture—including the language, the food, the stress of having to be perfect all the time, the playing conditions, and everything that goes with it. I saw those things take down a lot more American players than any opposing team.

Me, I always tried my best to learn as much of the native language as I could. At first, it wasn't all that difficult. At every level of professional baseball, you'll have Latin American Spanish-speaking teammates. If you play enough professional baseball, you're bound to pick up a little of it. For some guys, it comes out as funny-sounding, broken Spanish. But others do try to learn the language. And that can come in handy a lot of times.

I always felt a little bad for the Latin American players who came to our country to play ball as very young men and were forced to try to learn English on the fly. That had to be tough for them. But they also continued to speak fluent Spanish to one another, and listening in can be pretty helpful if you want to try to learn their language, which I always did. It was really important, for instance, for a pitcher and catcher to be able to communicate smoothly. Occasionally in the big leagues, you'll see an interpreter come to the mound to help a non–English-speaking pitcher understand the instructions he's being given. Not in the minors. In the minors, the two of you are on your own. You need to find a way to communicate.

Growing up in Southern California, taking trips to Mexico, and having many Spanish-speaking friends and teammates helped me pick some things up over the years. I always told myself that when I went to another country, I'd do my best to communicate in their language. Even if I had a hard time expressing myself, people usually appreciated the attempt and would at least try to find someone who could help.

That's not an idea shared by all. Something I noticed playing around the world is that sometimes Americans go to other countries and just expect people to understand English. I've seen players get frustrated that people in other countries didn't understand English. Americans have a reputation around the world of being arrogant, and that may have something to do with it.

It's funny, I've encountered people who go to other countries and get frustrated when natives don't understand English … yet when others come to America, those same people expect foreigners to speak English while they're here. Hypocritical? There's a joke I always think of when I consider this dynamic: "What do you call someone who speaks three languages? Trilingual. What do you call someone who speaks two languages? Bilingual. What do you call someone who speaks one language? An American."

I spent two winter ball seasons in Puerto Rico and the Dominican Republic, but the majority of the people I associated with there spoke at least some level of English. It did give me the chance to work on my Spanish. So I was ready in that respect for my first real "foreign" baseball experience when I landed for the first time in Puebla, the fourth-largest city in Mexico.

I got paid well—$7,000 a month—to pitch in Mexico, so that was nice. And I did spend a good amount of my free time in Mexico trying to get competent at speaking Spanish. When I walked around, I was always

Four. Speaking in Tongues

reading street signs and trying to understand them. If there were words I didn't understand, I'd remember to look them up in my Spanish-English dictionary. While I was living and working in Mexico, my Spanish got better over time.

Something else odd I learned about myself. When I have a few drinks, I seem to speak Spanish *better*. I have no idea why, but when normally I'd be struggling to understand, after a few drinks, I could communicate just fine with my Mexican teammates. I was also working to be able to understand the language better, too.

Once during a northern trip, we had an off-day and visited Roy Salinas' home in Eagle Pass, Texas, which was right on the border. As we were walking around town, a Mexican guy said "guero" to us from across the street. I was sort of surprised. Roy quickly said, "Don't worry, he didn't say anything bad. Guero means white person." It wasn't derogatory. Roy added, "As you may have noticed, you guys are basically the only white people around." The guy was probably surprised to see two white guys—me and Chris Bennett—and he just blurted it out loud in surprise.

When we got back to Roy's house, he introduced Chris and me to the people there. They were speaking what was termed "Tex-Mex," using both English and Spanish words in the same sentences. I was able to understand the Spanish parts a lot easier too, but then again, I'd had a few beers, and my Spanish was kicking in. The food was also the Tex-Mex style, which was awesome.

Another time, after a game in Campeche, a teammate and I were a little late leaving the stadium. As we stood by the road waiting for a taxi, the umpires came out of the stadium and got into a van. They pulled up and offered us a ride, and we accepted. First stop was a little cantina on the outskirts of town. It was their little bar. We were the only ones inside. These umpires spoke very little English, so we were using our Spanish with them. Half-English half-Spanish, Tex-Mex style. After a late night out of drinks and conversation, they told us, "We are all family now" and gave us a ride back to our hotel. In the United States, umpires are not allowed to fraternize with the players and can get fired for it.

Even with the improvement in my Spanish, miscommunication over an injury nearly got me released during my first season in Mexico. I was on the mound pitching against the Mexico City Tigres when I felt something pop in my elbow after throwing a hard curveball. I tried to throw another pitch, and it hurt even more. I called our manager, Bernie Calvo, out to the mound and told him what I felt, saying I couldn't pitch any more.

I rested and iced my elbow that night and the next day. The following day was my bullpen day. I tried to throw the ball to see how it would feel, hoping for the best. No dice. It still hurt, and I knew if I tried to throw more, I could damage my elbow seriously. I told pitching coach Max Leon that I couldn't throw the bullpen and that I should skip my next start. I felt that it just needed some rest. Max and Bernie were reluctant, but finally said okay. They were reluctant because they needed me to pitch. Our team was in last place at the time, so when I pitched, it was one of our better chances of winning. Plus, the teams in Mexico expected the American players to perform and win *all* the time. They didn't want a well-paid player sitting on the bench.

With the playoff format, coming in last place in the first half meant it was nearly impossible to make the playoffs at the end of the season, even if you came in first in the second half. And if you're not going to make the playoffs, the owner and the general manager start firing coaches and releasing the higher-paid American players.

So they needed me to pitch to protect their jobs.

My next scheduled start was three days away. Actually, *skipping* my next start would have given me eight days to let my elbow rest and hopefully be ready. This is where the language barrier and miscommunication took place. Their understanding was that when I skipped my start, it didn't mean an additional five days. "Skip" to them meant being pushed back a single day. One extra day wasn't going to help me. That wasn't what skipping a start meant. All they had planned on was one extra day.

I had to tell them I couldn't pitch yet, and now I worried about getting released.

The coaches told me they needed to talk it over with the GM, and they would let me know the next day. The next day came. and they agreed to let me pitch after missing one turn in the rotation. That gave me the five extra days off. I rested and iced it continuously, still not sure if my elbow would be ready.

The 10th day finally arrived. We were facing Minatitlan. I walked out to the bullpen not sure how I would feel. I knew that if I couldn't pitch, they would release me. I threw my first warmup pitch very gingerly. My arm was stiff, but no pain yet. I threw more. It was still sore, but not bad. I warmed up without throwing a pitch full-speed. When I finally threw a curveball, I could feel it. I was nervous going out to pitch the first inning. I got through it, still stiff and sore. I just kept battling through every inning. I was afraid to throw my out pitch, the curveball. I threw very few. But I got through seven innings. Tired and very relieved, I left winning, 4–1, The bullpen held, and I got the victory.

I had more successful moments speaking Spanish than I did problems. After one winter ball playoff win in the Dominican Republic, I was asked to do a post-game interview … in Spanish. I told them I spoke only a little Spanish, and they said that was ok, just do the best you can. The fans

Four. Speaking in Tongues

will like it if you try. Along with the radio guy, there were a couple of people from my team listening in. The radio guy asked me some basic questions, like how I felt, what was working, what winning this game meant for the team. I gave my answers in Spanish, and not one-word answers. I elaborated the best I could. As I was talking at one point, I realized I said a word incorrectly to a question earlier, so I corrected myself. The interviewer said "no problema." When the interview was over, they all said I did a good job. I was proud of that moment. I was fitting in.

I won't say I ever got fluent in Spanish, but for an American with no formal training in the language, I was happy with the level I reached. I never expected to be bilingual.

How about *Tri*-lingual?

After being released by the Pittsburgh Pirates organization in the spring of 1995, I learned about the opportunities to continue my career in Taiwan. I didn't want to go back to Mexico, but going to Asia to play?

Professional baseball didn't begin in Taiwan until 1989, and they only used Taiwanese players that year. Everyone had heard about those Taiwan Little League teams that won the Little League World Series every year. The first year of professional baseball in Taiwan didn't go over that well with the fans. It was decided that, to make the game better they would need to bring in foreign players, mainly from the United States and Japan. They couldn't get Major League players. At first, they were able to get some players with A ball and AA experience for the 1990 season. The fans loved it. They sold out all their games. The Taiwan teams started to get players with AAA experience, and then some players who had some Major League experience.

What I had been promised about opportunities in Taiwan proved to be correct. After those first couple of years, they started to pay the better players over $100,000 a year. I was told that with professional baseball growing like it was there, players could get up to a million dollars a year in Taiwan soon. They could compete with Japan, which was still the best league in Asia. In the meantime, if I could get to Japan through Taiwan, that would help me get more attention from Major League teams ... plus I could make *really* good money while doing it.

As I boarded that first all-day flight to Taiwan, I was nervous. I was going to the other side of the planet, and I didn't speak a word of Chinese. At least in Mexico I knew how to speak some Spanish. This was going to be totally different.

Chinese-Mandarin is the official language of Taiwan, it's what they speak on TV, in the newspapers, everything. When I met my new manager—who was Japanese—we had to communicate through a translator. Before my first game with my new team, he pulled everyone together for a pre-game pep talk. All the players took off their hats whenever the manager spoke, one on one with you or within a group. It's a sign of respect. The manager first spoke to the team in Japanese. When he was done, he paused. The team translator repeated everything in Chinese for the Taiwanese players and coaches. Then she repeated everything again in English. Off to the side, our Korean assistant coach repeated everything in Korean to our Korean teammate. Most of our Latin teammates understood English, but sometimes we had to translate some Spanish for them too.

This all took some time. The manager spoke some more, and the whole translation thing happened all over again. If someone had a question or response, the translator went right back to it. You couldn't be long-winded. This process also took place at team meetings and practices. It took a long time for a simple team meeting.

After games, going out to eat and drink, we'd get into taxis, and most of the guys were able to speak Chinese to the cab drivers. I was impressed with the guys speaking Chinese and that the cab driver understood them. I told my American teammates I wasn't sure if I was going to be able to get this Chinese language stuff.

Slowly I caught on, sincerely trying to learn how to speak decent Chinese. The hardest part is that in the Chinese language, they speak in four different "tones." There's a rising tone, a lowering tone, a flat tone, and a

Chinese newspaper.

lowering to rising tone. So one word can have four different meanings. Just when I thought I understood a word I would hear, it turned out that I didn't hear the tone and I misunderstood. For example, at a restaurant, the word "tang" could mean either soup or sugar. One time I asked a waitress for soup, and she brought me back some sugar. I had used the wrong tone. The word "ma" could mean horse, mom, asking a question, or an exclamation of a scolding.

It was a lot harder to grasp than Spanish.

On the other hand, most of my new Taiwanese teammates *understood* English ... especially music lyrics, even if they didn't speak it. Singing was really big in Taiwan. They always wanted me to sing songs in English. I'm not much of a singer, but I always tried. There was a chain of karaoke bars all over Taiwan called KTV's. We spent a lot of time in those, and we did a lot of singing.

But we didn't just sing along with music being played in a nightclub. We had to sing on our own from time to time. In some very odd places. Think *speaking* a foreign language is hard? Trying *singing* in it.

One year, our team owner thought it would be a good idea to have us go out and about, before and after our workouts, prior to the start of the season, to promote the team. We went to various places to meet people, take pictures, sign autographs, etc. Once he had us go to one of his other businesses. We did all this in full uniform. We lined up inside, and we sang three or four songs to his office workers. We were singing in Chinese, so I just stood in the back, loitering there, mouthing along. Music may be the universal language, but what could I possibly add to this if I had no clue about what I was supposed to be singing? It was the exact opposite of karaoke. Nobody was buying tickets to hear us sing, that's for sure.

Everywhere we went, we signed autographs and took pictures, but we were mostly as a team, singing all of the time.

We did one such "promotion" that would outdo them all.

On this day we had to wake up a little early—like 7:30 a.m.—and board the bus in full uniform. Our coaches wouldn't tell us where we were going. They said it was just another promotion, which by now we were sick of doing, especially the singing part. The next thing I knew, the bus was pulling up to what looked like ... a prison. Sure enough, we were going to do a promotion *in a prison*. I asked no one in particular, "How's this going to help promote our team? Pretty sure these guys can't buy tickets."

The bus pulled up to the big gate, which was several feet high. It opened slowly, and we drove forward before stopping at another huge gate as the one behind us closed. When the next gate opened, we slowly drove in and stopped by a closed door. We stayed in the bus until someone came out and got us, and we followed the guard inside.

I was now inside of a prison, and I was wearing a baseball uniform.

We followed the guard through a bunch of security checkpoints. We eventually reached this big auditorium and found ourselves on a large stage. Down below, there were rows and rows of chairs where the prisoners sat, wearing their white t-shirts, blue gym shorts, and sandals. These prisoners were all tattooed up, sitting there staring. I can't imagine what they were thinking. There must have been at least 400 prisoners sitting in front of us. Sitting in the middle of this crowd was the warden, with some of his officers.

What the heck were we going to do here? The next thing I knew, music started playing in the background, and my teammates began singing to the prisoners. I was hoping that just mouthing along wasn't a crime. You could see this becoming a hostage situation if our singing was bad enough.

I mouthed away ... and we escaped the place without further incident.

Another time, an American teammate named Ron Jones and I were told we were going to Taipei to promote our team and the league. We would be driven to Taipei and told to bring our baseball uniforms. When we arrived, we drove straight to a TV studio. We were scheduled to appear on a Taiwanese TV variety show that was broadcast throughout the entire country.

During this period in Taiwan—before the internet and streaming—every evening each of the different TV networks had their own variety show. It was *the* thing at that time. I sometimes watched these when I was flipping channels in my apartment or hotel room. There were skits, famous Taiwanese singers, interviews with other Taiwanese celebrities, guest actors and athletes, with everyone partaking in silly games and so forth. I was hoping they weren't going to ask Ron and me to sing.

They were taping an episode. Ron and I were sitting behind the set, watching and enjoying the show. There were maybe 15–20 people sitting in the "live studio audience." Later, when I watched the episode, they had added in other taped audience shots, which made it look like there was a full house, with over 100 people there. They also added laugh tracks, making it sound like there were a lot of people busting up.

Eventually it was our turn to appear on the show. At first, we sat together, and the host interviewed both of us in English, asking us questions about our team, how we were doing playing baseball in Taiwan, and a bunch of typical questions. The host translated our answers into Chinese. It went smoothly. I was hoping it would end there. Interviews were no problem. I just didn't want to have to sing.

So much for that wish coming true. Turned out we were there to play a game with the other Taiwanese celebrities. There were five celebs sitting in chairs that had buzzers. Ron and I would take turns putting on headphones so only we could hear popular Taiwanese songs—sung in Chinese.

Then my worst nightmare: They wanted us to sing the songs—in Chinese—*out loud,* and the celebrities would try to figure out what these two non–Chinese-speaking fools were actually singing. No faking it ... and no chance this would be anything but totally embarrassing. The celebrities would only ring their buzzers *if* they could figure out what song we were singing. That was a big if. If they were right, they'd get a point. This was supposed to be funny at our expense, with us mumbling songs in broken Chinese where nobody else could hear the words or the music. Ron, one of the leading power hitters in all of Taiwan baseball, had to go first. (Just imagine watching, say, David Ortiz, standing there with headphones on, trying to sing along with a Taylor Swift song, and you had to guess which one. Yeah, it was like that.)

When Ron began, I saw him with his eyes squinted closed, concentrating on the words to mimic. He was squealing the words and then mumbling them. He couldn't hear himself singing. It sounded totally awful, with a nasally sound too. I must admit, it was pretty funny to watch. The celebrities were making funny faces, trying to figure out what the hell he was trying to sing. They took turns ringing their buzzers, making funny guesses just to make the audience laugh. I had no idea what words he was trying to sing.

At some point, he finished. No surprise, nobody was able to guess the song he was trying to sing. Everybody had a good laugh. Now it was my turn to make a fool out of myself. I put the headphones on, and I waited for my song to come on so I could attempt to sing along. The song began, and I started to sing words that I could barely understand. I was just babbling out incoherent Chinese words. I saw the celebrities with their eyes squinting, tilting their heads, trying to figure out what song I could possibly be trying to sing.

Finally, I thought I would just make up some words that I knew in Chinese to try to be funny. I began singing the words in Chinese for "I am crazy," because that's how I felt standing on this TV stage. Right after I sang the words "Wo shi sun jin been," which meant "I am crazy," all the celebrities rang their buzzers. The celebrity who hit the buzzer first correctly answered the song that I was supposed to be trying to sing. He figured it out ... but I have absolutely no idea how.

After I was done, it was Ron's turn again for round two. I was off the stage, waiting for my turn again, so I asked a Taiwanese person next to me how they possibly knew the song I was singing, because I just made up the words saying that I was crazy. The person told me that when I sang, "Wo shi sun jin been," those words were in this really popular song in Taiwan at that time, that they all understood my Chinese, and rang in all together. Imagine that.

We played three rounds before we were mercifully done. Everybody gave us a good round of applause for being good sports. When the show was a wrap, everybody came up to us—the celebrities, the stars of the variety show, the producers, the director, the studio workers—they all thanked us for coming and told us we'd done a good job. Ron and I left relieved, and it turned out to be a fun thing to do.

That was perhaps the only time we had fun singing that did not involve a good amount of alcohol. When I was with Taiwanese teammates, it was usually at the KTVs, and it involved some *hard* drinking. They always wanted to hear me sing English songs, so I ended up getting my "go to" song that I was becoming comfortable with, once I'd had enough to drink. Everybody who speaks English knows "Come Together" by the Beatles. The song has some great lyrics that don't make a lot of sense, but it was fun to sing. I would get up in front of everybody with the microphone in front of a video of the Beatles, and I would get into it. We had some fun with it since it made my Taiwanese friends so happy.

In Taipei, we had several team meals, with the usual drinking and the unusual food that you eventually get used to, good and bad. This time there was a microphone in the room with a podium, which meant there would be karaoke. The Taiwanese guys were taking turns singing. It was just a matter of time before they would ask me to sing an English song. The mood was more relaxed, and I remember singing "Yesterday" by the Beatles. This wasn't in a private KTV room with my teammates—it was in front of the other customers in the place. Thank goodness for the booze.

In everyday life, I did surprisingly well with language issues. I had my dictionary, and I really tried to study street signs, newspapers, and anything else that could help me get better at understanding and communicating in Chinese. But understanding and speaking some is never quite enough.

One day I noticed my teammate, Tony Metoyer, reading a Chinese language newspaper. I asked him what he was doing. He replied, "What does it look like?" I shot back, "It looks like you're reading the newspaper … but it's in Chinese characters." Tony smiled and told me he didn't read all of the words, just the sports page. He learned to memorize the characters for the CPBL standings and box scores. He could read the players' names to figure out the league leaders in the major statistical categories. He showed me, and after a while I was able to read the sports page, too.

There was also a national newspaper in Taiwan that was written in English. It was a good read. It had world news, Taiwan news … and of course, sports. I read this newspaper whenever I could. I remember reading a local news story in Taichung. It said that in a single night, dog catchers picked up over 400 stray dogs in just one small section of the city. They

Four. Speaking in Tongues

could have caught more, officials said, but they ran out of room and space to put them.

For the most part, I enjoyed interacting with the locals. But sometimes the language thing—because it worked both ways—was funny. During a road trip that featured a couple of day games, we had some time off after a game before it got dark. A group of us had found a trail that led to a little river stream in the mountains. As we were getting ready to head out, a couple of young Taiwanese baseball fans started talking to us, and they decided they'd follow us along the trail. We hiked pretty far and found a spot we'd discovered the year before where the water got deep in one spot, and where there was a high rock above the water. We liked climbing up on top of this rock and relaxing, and then we'd dive back into the water below. It was a lot of fun. This rock was 10–12 feet above the water, and when it was hot out, hitting the water felt really good.

Near this rock, the river curved a bit, so it had a little current flowing. Right there the water wasn't deep, maybe waist-high. One of the Taiwanese baseball fans stayed on the other side of the river, watching us diving into the water. Eventually he decided to step into the water, but the current knocked him down and he fell under the water ... which was only waist-high, mind you. When his head popped up, he panicked, and he screamed loudly, "HELP!!" He went back under and was going down the stream, screaming for help. Corey dove off the rock into the water and swam about 30 feet to him. He basically pulled this guy to his feet in the water where the water was barely to his waist, and then Corey helped him out of the water. The guy didn't know how to swim. He started to cry very hard and loud, sounding like a squealing pig. This had really scared him. Again, he was only in waist-high water. He could have just gotten to his feet and walked back to the shore. After he finally stopped bawling and pulled himself back together, he thanked Corey over and over.

After a while, we decided we'd get cleaned up and eat dinner at the Mongolian barbeque restaurant in the hotel. When everyone got to the lobby, Corey said the weirdest thing had just happened to him. He was getting ready to get in the shower and heard someone knocking on his door. When he answered it, there was this extremely old Taiwanese man with a cane who began speaking Chinese to him. Corey said he didn't understand a word the guy was saying, and suddenly the old man grabbed Corey's arm and started pulling him into the room towards the bed. Corey tried to pull away, but that made the old man pull even harder as he continued babbling in Chinese. Finally, Corey out-tugged the old man and shoved him hard out the door. At that point, Corey said he realized the old man was blind as he began walking away.

Listening to this story, we laughed out loud ... hard. As we began walking toward the restaurant, we saw the young guy Corey had "saved" in the shallow water. With all of us standing there, the guy asked Corey how he liked his massage. Corey was puzzled. "What?" he answered. The guy said, "I bought you a massage as a thank you for saving my life, somebody was supposed to come by your room." It suddenly hit us that the old man was there to give Corey a massage. With Corey having no idea about any massage, he just thought the old blind man was crazy and lost. Corey told the guy he didn't know who the old man was and had thrown him out. The Taiwanese guy said, "No … no…. I bought you a massage!" None of us could stop laughing while listening to this. The Taiwanese guy walked away so disappointed that Corey didn't get his massage.

Communication did not just mean speaking the language. It also meant trying to learn the methods and the ways of a world traveler. I could handle getting paid in pesos in Mexico, but now things were *really* different come payday. Before that first day arrived, Tony Metoyer asked me how much money I was going to keep, and if I was planning on sending any money home. I told him I needed to keep some spending money to live on, but that I was going to send the rest home. I hadn't been told that I needed to let the team know how much money I wanted to keep in New Taiwan dollars, known as NT dollars. Tony told me to tell them to pay me the rest of my money in American traveler's checks.

We'd get our two checks—one in NT dollars and the rest in traveler's checks—and go to the post office. Tony showed me the special label that you filled out and put on the envelope with the traveler's checks. The usual name and address, then when you got to the part asking what's inside, you put "documents." This was express mail in Taiwan, and it arrived in the United States in three or four days, while typical mail could take a month or more. The cost for this express mail was pretty cheap. They had an agreement with the U.S. Post Office that they'd deliver this to my door at home, even on a Sunday. I was nervous about sending unsigned checks around the world. Tony told me not to worry, he never had a problem. No one ever looked inside the envelope. This became my way of sending money home … it was easy, cheap, and fast. Tami would get the mail, sign the checks, and put them in the bank. Never had a problem.

Then there was non-verbal communication. Going into places like the post office or the local banks could be a very different experience in the Far East. For example, I got very uncomfortable waiting in almost any line. More than once while I waited, I'd notice someone I didn't know start to rub my arm. Most of the time it was a kid. They seemed fascinated with the hair on my arms, and they wanted to touch it. Adults did it too, which was a new level of weird. The people of Asia are not hairy at all. They don't typically get hair on their arms, so I guess this fascinated them enough that they were okay just starting to rub the hair on a stranger's arm. It felt good for a moment ... before it got weird. I don't think the people really meant anything by it, so I normally just politely pulled my arm away and smiled.

Other norms in Taiwan weren't so warm and fuzzy. I found that most people in Taiwan aren't good about waiting in lines. A number of times, people just pushed in front of me or tried to push me to the side while I was talking to a bank teller. They had no problem interrupting. It became like a scrum underneath a basketball hoop. At times I literally had to box people out and hold my ground. If I hadn't seen it, I wouldn't have believed it.

When Tami and Logan visited me in Taiwan, the whole language and culture thing became that much more of an issue. One afternoon, a guy selling milk came by my apartment while I was at practice. He didn't speak any English, but he managed to sell Tami on the idea of milk delivery—which we didn't want or need. It turned out the guy *did* speak Spanish, so when I got back, I tracked him down and canceled the milk service. Because I could communicate with this guy in Spanish, I found out that Tami had mistakenly ordered goat's milk.

This was the second time I was able to use Spanish to communicate with someone from the Far East. A couple years earlier, I was in a casino in Santiago in the Dominican Republic. A teammate and I were playing blackjack with some folks from Korea. I noticed they were speaking Spanish to the dealers. Turned out they were working in the Dominican, so they had to learn Spanish. It was sort of weird speaking to a Korean person in neither English nor Korean.

By my fourth season in Taiwan, I'd purchased that scooter to get around, but it required constant maintenance. I'd bought mine from that little old man who had a repair shop not far from my apartment. He was a big baseball fan and always wanted to talk with me when I came by for an oil change or whatever the scooter needed. Remember, he spoke absolutely *zero* English.

Once, when I arrived, he was on the sidewalk working on another scooter. When he looked up and saw me, he became very excited, stopped working on the other scooter, jumped right up, went over to one of his workers, gave him some money, and told him something. He grabbed a couple of folding chairs and set them up on the greasy sidewalk. We sat down, and he started to talk to me as if I spoke fluent Chinese. I did the best I could to speak to him with my limited language skills.

This guy truly loved baseball. He asked me questions about our team and why our manager made some of his decisions and moves. As we sat there talking, his worker came back with a case of Heineken. I guess they figured I'd be there for a while. Several times as he asked me questions, I had to say tee-pe-tone to him, which meant in Chinese "I didn't understand." He would say it again in a different way, which sometimes worked, or we used our hands a lot, or he drew me pictures. We did this while drinking one beer after another. As we drank, my Chinese got better and better. I could understand more of what he was saying. The next thing I knew, several hours had gone by. We drank all of his beer, and his worker brought my scooter to me, ready to go. Now I had to survive the ride back to my apartment.

This happened almost every time I went for an oil change. I was happy to indulge this old guy. He was great to me and very interested in what our team was doing. On one trip to his shop, as we watched a taped baseball game on his little TV, he said something to me in Chinese. I heard the words "shway-jee-ow," which means to sleep. This threw me off, since I was feeling fine, and at first, I thought he was asking me if I was tired. When I asked him that, he said, "mayo" (no). He said shway-jee-ow again, and again I wondered why he was asking me to sleep. My next thought was that maybe I needed to rest before I could ride my scooter home. He said mayo again. He was using his hands trying to make me understand, but I still had no idea. I asked him if he was asking me to spend the night at his home, which was above the shop. He said mayo again. After some more pondering, and him saying shway-jee-ow again and again, all of a sudden, I got the idea that he was asking me to sleep with him and have sex. What else was left?

I wasn't certain that was the case, so I wasn't going to overreact and shout "Mayo" and leave. But I was uncomfortable about this. I didn't know how to ask him if that's what he was asking for. I could not figure any of this out. I was thinking to myself, "I like this guy, but I don't like him *that* much!" I didn't think he was gay, but maybe after a few beers … perhaps he thought I was looking good? He had his wife and son right there, but now I wasn't sure about anything.

I started to feel very awkward. He got out a piece of paper and he drew something that looked like a half-moon. I saw the moon and I thought it meant it was getting close to nighttime. I was looking tired, and he was asking me to sleep with him. I knew he liked me, but how was I going to ask him for my scooter so that I could politely leave? I asked him if I could use his telephone, and I called up Kevin, our team translator. I asked Kevin to speak to my scooter guy and find out what he was asking me. I gave the phone to the old man, he and Kevin spoke for about 30 seconds, and he gave me back the phone. Kevin told me that he was asking me if I wanted to stay and eat dinner with him and his family. His wife was making some dumplings. Kevin said that "shway-jee-ow" is sleep, and "she-ah-jee-ow" means dumpling. One little slight difference in a syllable goes from a guy asking me to sleep with him to asking me to stay and eat dinner with him and his family. I stayed and had some dumplings.

Thankfully, I didn't have too many episodes like that during the five seasons I spent in Taiwan. I worked on being able to communicate in Chinese, and that ended up helping a lot. If you're going to live and work somewhere for that amount of time, you need to try to fit in with the culture.

Over the years, a few guys told me that whenever I thought I was ready to hang 'em up and finally end my baseball career, I should look into playing one more year and go play in Italy. They promised, "You'll love it." I also heard that they didn't pay much, but I still thought I'd look into it.

After five years in Taiwan, I was fortunate enough to find a team in Rimini, Italy, that still had a spot for a foreign player.

Bilingual. Trilingual. What do they call it when you are about to have to learn a *fourth* new language?

By accepting this job, I knew I'd have to learn how to speak at least some Italian. Fortunately for me, a lot of words are similar in Spanish. I remember when I first landed in Taiwan, my brain went to say something and my words sometimes came out in Spanish, not Chinese. Now in Italy the same thing would happen—words would come out in Chinese, not Italian, and the people would just give me a strange look.

When you try to learn a new language, one of the first things you need to learn is how to order food. During my season in Italy, some friends from Milwaukee, Tim and Mary, came to visit me while they were touring Europe. We traveled to Venice when I had a couple of off-days and went out to eat.

The place we ended up at wasn't all that big, but it was crowded. We found a little table, and Tim went to get drinks. It took a little while before he returned with a cold pitcher of beer, excited to tell us the reason it took so long was that he started chatting with two guys at the bar who spoke very little English. In their brief conversation, one of the guys said he was from Argentina and spoke Spanish, and the other guy was Italian. Tim told the guy from Argentina that I spoke some Spanish, and they were on their way over to join us.

When they arrived, I became the middleman, the translator. When Tim and Mary said something to me in English, I translated it to the Argentinian guy in Spanish, who then translated it in Italian to his buddy. They spoke to each other in Italian, then the Argentinian guy would tell me in Spanish what they were saying, and I would tell Tim and Mary what they said in English. We sat there together for a couple of hours doing this. The Italian guy said that when I spoke Spanish, he understood a lot of what I was saying. The guy from Argentina said he was in Italy for a job, and his Italian buddy was a guy he worked with. Tim and Mary were amazed. Once again, after a few beers, I totally understood Spanish. To this day, I still have no idea why.

We decided to go to a Chinese restaurant that we'd seen nearby. The menu was in Chinese and Italian, and that's what the workers spoke as well. The waitress came by to take drink orders. I answered her in Chinese, saying we wanted three large beers, please (woman yao san ge da pijiu ching). She was surprised to hear me speak Chinese to her. Later, when the waiter took our order, I spoke Chinese to him too. As he was walking through a door to the kitchen, I could hear him saying to the people in the kitchen in Chinese that there was an American guy out there speaking in Chinese. He seemed shocked and impressed. When they came back to our table, they spoke Chinese to me, not English or Italian.

Within a couple of hours, I'd translated for a group of people from three different countries—who had never met—in Spanish and Chinese … while we were all in Italy. I do know for sure that all the people I met and interacted with in those foreign countries appreciated the effort.

Learning to speak the language of the foreign country you're living in came in handy when it came time to choose what to eat.

Five

Cheeseburger in Paradise

Making plans to travel to places like Puerto Rico, Mexico, the Dominican Republic, and Taiwan, I was totally focused on baseball and trying to revive my big league career. Getting past the language barrier was a big deal everywhere I traveled. Down the list were things like living arrangements and meals. At least at the start.

They pay for your flights, and you figure the team is going to help set you up with a decent place to live. (Of course, that was not always true.) But with food? You're *totally* on your own.

Growing up in SoCal, my favorite food was Mexican, and I had a pretty tough stomach. I knew from my trips crossing the border that Mexican food in Mexico is not quite the same as it is in the U.S. I loved eating "Americanized" tacos, enchiladas, burritos, and chimichangas. When I reported to Mexico to start my first stint in the Mexican league, I got a taste of the real thing. A real taste. Some of it was great ... and some ... well, not so much.

And yes, I did NOT drink the water.

For instance, in America our tacos have a big crunchy shell loaded with meat, cheese, lettuce, tomatoes, and salsa, but in Mexico a taco is a small corn tortilla that you put a small piece of meat in and roll it up. They're good, but not what I was used to. You order food such as chicken or pork, and it's prepared in a Mexican style. I don't recall ever eating a burrito in Mexico. You definitely don't get the portions that you enjoy in America.

In Mexico, there are a lot of differences between the northern part of the country and the southern part, especially the food. They had different types of foods and how they cooked it—using flour tortillas in the south or corn tortillas in the north.

The differences weren't always good. I was just five days into my first stint in Mexico with the Puebla—the regular season hadn't started yet—when I got a taste of what I'll call "rural" Mexican food. We played an exhibition game in Libres and were invited to stick around for a post-game cookout "fiesta" meal with the locals.

Chris Bennett, Phil Harrison and I were very hungry as we walked about a half-mile from the field, where we played our exhibition game, to where we saw some tents. They had these big barbecues cooking up the post-game meal. We looked to see what kind of food they were cooking. It wasn't the Mexican food I was used to eating back home. This was a country barbecue, and the food was … pigs' ears. They still had long hairs in them. There were also pigs' feet and either pig stomachs or cow stomachs … it was this purple, sack-looking thing.

We were so hungry, but none of us could eat this. They had several little tables set up for people to sit at and eat. Each table had bottles of whiskey along with tubs filled with ice and beer. We decided we'd just drink, hoping the event wouldn't last too long and we could maybe eat when we got back to Puebla. There was also music, and the people of Libres were great hosts. We started drinking pretty well, but we were so hungry that we couldn't stop talking about when and where we could eat.

It didn't look like we'd be leaving Libres anytime soon. Add two hours of driving back … and *then* we'd have to try to find a place to eat that was open late. We realized we wouldn't be able to eat until tomorrow morning at the team breakfast. We thought drinking beer and whiskey would suppress our hunger. It didn't.

You know the saying that if you're hungry enough, you'll eat anything? I gave in, and I tried a big hairy pig ear. I just bit in, crunched my teeth up and down a few times, and swallowed it without it touching my tongue … and I chased it down with a beer or whiskey shot. Did it again with another pig's ear, and then the rubbery, chewy stomach. I just couldn't do the pig's foot. I ate just enough to kill the hunger pain.

Mexican street food.

Five. Cheeseburger in Paradise

Surprisingly, it didn't make me sick.

I wasn't always so lucky. In the Dominican Republic the following winter, I found out that getting sick due to eating foreign foods is as predictable as the sunrise. One day soon after I arrived in the DR, I went out to eat some with teammates. As we were driving back to the hotel, one of the guys told me very casually that it wouldn't take long, but pretty soon I would get diarrhea. Bad. He added that it would last for at least three days. He said everyone gets it. My stomach wasn't used to this food and how they cooked it.

As soon as it hits you, they said, go right to the team trainer for some of these tiny little white pills. "It will help plug you up." I thought, wow, this is something to look forward to. Then I thought nah, my stomach handled the food in Mexico. How different could this be?

He was right, it didn't take long. The shits hit me ... hard! The first night, I was in the bathroom all night. No sooner would I try to lie down to sleep than I'd be up and headed back to the bathroom. It hit me again ... then again ... and again. I literally used up a whole roll of toilet paper. The next day I did get some of those pills from our trainer.

They did help, but it didn't end there. We had a day off, and some teammates invited me to spend the day at the beach in Puerto Plata. I decided I'd go, even though I wasn't totally sure if my stomach could handle the bumpy and winding mountain roads. Things started okay, but every turn and every bump, I began feeling it. I just kept concentrating, and it got harder and harder, but I made it through. We arrived in Puerto Plata, found a nice beach, spread out our towels, and opened up our cooler full of beers. There were people there who looked like Europeans. At first, we assumed they were Europeans because the women were sunbathing topless. The best thing for me was to just lie down, soak up some sun, and not move. No beer, either. Just hang out. After a while, all of them went into the water to cool off.

My stomach was actually doing pretty good. I got up, went down to the water, and started swimming around. They had a frisbee and threw it to me, I dove for it, trying to enjoy myself. But it didn't take long before my stomach turned and began to gurgle again. I made my way back to my towel to lie down and focused on not crapping in my shorts. I desperately needed to use a bathroom. I hoped the pain would go away if I sat still, but it didn't. I got up and started walking toward the van, hoping I could find a bathroom.

There were no bathroom signs anywhere. I tried to focus the pain away, but it got worse. Finally, I saw a motorcycle repair shop. I went to the back where the mechanics were working on motorcycles. In Spanish, I told one of the mechanics that I needed to use a bathroom ... like right now. He walked me to the back of the shop, where there was a toilet with no tank, no toilet seat, and no walls. It was totally open and exposed to everyone. The guy filled up a bucket with water, and told me when I was done, I had to pour the water in the toilet bowl to flush the diarrhea. I sat down to do my business with everyone there able to watch me. I didn't care.

Relieved, I poured the water into the toilet and walked out of the shop and back to the beach. I had to share my story, and everyone got a good laugh. I did feel better and got to enjoy the beach more after that.

When it was time to leave, everyone wanted to eat before we headed back to Santiago. We found an outdoor burger place right on the beach. I decided to pass. "You guys eat, I'll just sit here and wait for you," I smiled. I couldn't eat. My stomach was starting to feel weird again. After they finished eating, we headed back. I wondered if I'd make it through the mountain roads. Fortunately, we made it back to the hotel without incident, and I headed right to my room—or should I say my bathroom. Shortly thereafter, my stomach got used to the food and I was functional again.

When we traveled to away games, the bus would sometimes pull off at the big rest area that had a building that was sort of a food court. There wasn't anything "American" style, but fortunately my teammates would help me out. I ended up ordering something that looked and tasted good, so I ordered it every time we stopped there. No use risking trying anything else.

There were a few things I felt safe to eat just by the sight of them. Like fruit. Once, when we got off the bus, there were two young boys trying to sell some oranges to the ball players. I went up and asked them how much for an orange. They said something like two pesos. I gave them six pesos and they gave me three oranges. I kept one for myself, because an orange at that moment sounded really good, and I gave the other two back to them and told them, "These are for you guys." I don't know if they ate them or just resold them later.

Of course, eating also included drinking, and we were usually able to get the bus driver to stop at one of these little roadside tavern-type places just off the road. Guys would go in and buy beer, usually a bottle of Johnny Walker Black or Blue … and everyone shared. Some of the places we'd stop at didn't even look like they had electricity. They were on an open two-lane highway in the mountain jungle. But they had cold beer. I learned that even in a country stricken with poverty, you can always get a cold beer.

At the end of my time in the DR, we decided to have dinner together one last time at one of our favorite places, Palo Taco. As usual, we were eating outside, and I was having the tacos. When I was done eating, the tacos left a funny taste in the back of my mouth and throat. That wasn't normal. But we had a good time and went back to the hotel for our last night in Santiago.

Five. Cheeseburger in Paradise

I woke up early the next morning, got my bags, went down to the hotel lobby, and checked out of my room. When the rest of the guys showed up, we got onto the van and left for the airport. I noticed that the bad taste from the night before was feeling thicker, and I had a slight headache. When we got to the airport, I told one of my teammates, Jeff Pico, that I wasn't feeling so good. Didn't matter—feeling good or not, I was getting on that airplane. We got on our flight, I told Jeff I was feeling worse and worse.

We hung together until it was time to depart on different flights. I was going to Chicago, then to Milwaukee. As I boarded the plane, I was feeling sicker, wondering if I might throw up. Luckily, I didn't. When I arrived in Milwaukee, Tami and her dad picked me up at the airport. When we got home, I hugged Logan and immediately lay down on the couch. I felt like shit. Tami asked me what I wanted to eat. I said "nothing, I can't eat." It wasn't too much longer before I finally did throw up. I went to bed hoping that when I woke up, I'd feel like myself again.

Instead, for the next three or four days, I was sicker than a dog. My stomach was in constant pain. Tami kept telling me that I should go to the hospital, but I could only lie on the couch in pain. This had to end soon, right? I told her I'd give it another day. If I didn't feel better, then I'd go to the doctor. I began to gradually feel better. But it took a while.

I discovered later, after talking to some people and describing my symptoms, that I'd gotten food poisoning. It made sense. On my last night in the Dominican Republic, I ate those tacos, which I normally loved. But that night, they tasted different, and it was from that point on I began to feel sick. When I weighed myself, I was down to 168 pounds. When I left to go to the DR in November, I weighed 194 pounds. I lost 26 pounds due to how little I ate there and the food poisoning I got from my final meal.

The good: I'd learned a couple of key things in Mexico which served me well in the Dominican and everywhere else I traveled. I called them my "Top two foreign country survival skills." First, always, without exception, keep two rolls of toilet paper with you when you travel, wherever you go. Even in your home city. You could never just assume that the facilities you'd need to use were adequate. For example, in Puebla, we had a nice bus with air conditioning, but it didn't have a bathroom. So when we stopped, you were on your own. You might have to go off somewhere near the side of the road. At the ballparks, they didn't have toilet paper in the bathrooms at any of the places we played.

Second, always have two bottles of water with you *everywhere*. Some guys laughed at this the first time I said it, but at the end, they realized I was serious. And correct.

Many of the ballparks only had backed-up, dirty toilets full of crap and urine that didn't flush. They were for extra emergency use only. Once during a game in the Dominican Republic, my stomach started gurgling. I really tried to hold it in, but it got worse, and I couldn't hold it any longer. I ended up sneaking to the "toilet area." It was actually an open area under the bleachers. Luckily nobody was around. I had to take a crap right on top of all the backup that was already in the hole. It was gross, but you learn to block the "hole" experience out of your mind … like it didn't happen.

Part of the problem with the "just don't eat that stuff and you won't get sick" thing is that some of the food tasted really good! Like I said, growing up, Mexican food was my favorite. Now I was getting to sample the authentic thing. And I'm supposed to say no?

Most of the time, I couldn't. I thought I'd eventually adapt. In Puebla, there was a taco place right next to a spot where our bus would normally park and wait for us. I *really* liked their tacos. Right on the street, you watched the guy carve the meat off and put it into the little tortillas, add salsa, roll it up, and have them ready to eat. The bad thing was we were about to get on a bus without a bathroom. As good as those tacos tasted, they always made my stomach churn. I always had my two rolls of toilet paper with me, so when our bus driver pulled off the road to let everyone stretch and go to the bathroom, I needed that TP. Even if we got to use a public toilet, chances were there wouldn't be TP in there, either.

Remember, some of those bus rides were 12 hours long … or longer.

There's also such a thing as bus etiquette. While I was playing for Campeche, we had a bus *with* a bathroom, but there were certain things you weren't supposed to do in there. Shortly after I arrived, we were on a trip when I felt my stomach start to gurgle. I tried to hold it, but eventually slipped toward the back of the bus so I could use the bathroom. I had that roiling that said I was going to have diarrhea. When I was done, I went back to my seat. One of my Mexican teammates who was sitting across the aisle asked, "Did you just take a shit?" I replied, "Yeah…. I had to." He was upset with me.

I was told that nobody uses that bathroom to take a crap, only to piss. If I needed to take a shit, I was supposed to take a box or a bag in there with me and shit in it, and when I was done, throw it out the window. Since this was my first trip on a bus with a bathroom, they cut me some slack. I noticed that whenever we were on the road, if anyone had any trash, they just opened up the window and tossed it right out, then closed the window. Didn't matter where we were—on a country highway or in the middle of traffic in a big city. Bottles, cans … everything went out the window!

In that regard, things couldn't have been more different in Taiwan from what they were in Mexico. In Taiwan, decorum is *everything*. You'd never toss excrement or any kind of trash out the window of a moving bus, for instance. All the buses had restrooms, although using them for anything other than a urinal was still frowned on, for obvious reasons.

In Taiwan, it wasn't just about getting sick from eating food my system wasn't used to, but I also had to wonder what exactly I was eating, since most of it I didn't even recognize. I had to be very careful how I was eating, with whom and where. It was all very complicated and took some time to learn.

At first, I couldn't pick my own places to eat. The signs were in Chinese, and the buildings were tall and squeezed tightly together. This contributed to my culture shock and education. To start with, I looked different from everyone else—I'm taller, had light brown hair, blue eyes, and white skin ... so I stuck out. Plus, I had no idea where to go. I just had to trust the other American players to guide me in the right direction. They always did.

There are a lot of American fast-food places in the bigger cities in Taiwan, such as McDonald's, Wendy's, and Texas Chicken, for example. At Wendy's, they sold their Wendy's burgers, but the menu also included Asian food. There were other places like TGI Fridays and Tony Roma's that had American food at very high prices.

There was no way around it, I ate a lot of Taiwanese/Chinese food while I was playing in Taiwan.

There were customs to learn that revolved around meals. Even at the ballpark. My first game in Taiwan was in Taipei, where I was introduced to my first meal custom. After batting practice, somebody brought in several plastic bags filled with "bin dongs." These were boxed meals—typically some sort of meat in a sauce with white rice (bai fan) and some type of vegetable. In the Chinese culture, it's typical to have a meal before any gathering or event, even a baseball game. Somebody handed me a bin dong, and I wasn't sure what to do. I was surprised to see the players eating a meal just before taking the field for the game. One of the American guys, Cecil Espy, said, "Eat it, it's actually not bad."

You immediately noticed that the food looked and smelled different. Through the years, we'd have these before every game. After a while, you learned which bin dongs you liked and which you didn't. The only way to eat it was with the cheap wooden chopsticks (kuaizi) they gave you. We also got bin dongs after practices.

Teammates would take me to places for lunch, mostly Chinese places. I followed their lead, since they promised the food would be all right. The guys knew their way around and would order everything in Chinese. I ate several things that I wasn't very sure about. I had no idea what I was eating. My stomach had to get used to a very new diet. Again.

On one of my first long road trips, we were going to play two games in Taipei and one in Hsinchu, a city just outside of Taipei. During batting practice in Hsinchu, my stomach began gurgling. Just like in the Dominican and Mexico, I found out it's not unusual in Taiwan to get a bout of diarrhea. Again, it's due to the different food and how it's cooked.

To this point, I'd been lucky, not having to take a crap in a hole at a Taiwan baseball stadium. Really. At the stadiums, I noticed that the bathrooms didn't have *actual* toilets. They were just a hole in the ground on the floor. You were supposed to position yourself over the porcelain hole, then remove your pants and underwear off one of your legs, holding your underwear up so it didn't touch the floor. Then you had to squat over the hole and relieve yourself. At first glance, I vowed that I'd never *ever* take a crap at that ballpark. I later noticed that *all* the ballparks had these types of toilets ... and a lot of public places too. Keeping that vow was going to be ... difficult.

Now we're in Hsinchu, and I can't hold it. You never know when you'll get hit by the gurgles. This time it was bad. I went to the bathroom while the team was on the field taking batting practice.. I went over to the spot with the hole in the ground toilet. When I opened the door and looked inside, there were spider webs hanging everywhere. Hot and humid, mosquitoes flying around ... and no toilet paper, of course.

I turned around and decided I'd just hold it. I couldn't in those conditions. I headed back onto the field to shag fly balls. My stomach kept

Taiwan squat toilet.

getting worse. Cramps would come and go, and I had to concentrate on not crapping my pants right there. It faded away ... and then a few minutes later it hit hard again, and I literally almost crapped in my pants with diarrhea. Finally, I realized I couldn't do this much longer, let alone for the entire game. Defeated, I gave in, walked to my baseball bag, and took out one of my rolls of toilet paper.

I went into the hole in the ground stall. I took my pants and underwear completely off because I needed a clear path, or else I'd crap all over myself. I pushed the spider webs away from my face and hair before I squatted over the hole and let loose. It didn't take long before my legs began to get tired, and I was trying not to lose my balance. I had spider webs in my hair, I was being attacked by mosquitoes, and I was sweating bullets. Good thing I had my own toilet paper, or else I don't know what I would have done.

It was all part of this entire experience of learning to adapt to situations I could have never imagined before I left the USA.

Again, I could have chosen to steer clear of some foods, but I'm not all that sure which ones. Sometimes I didn't have a choice of what I was going to eat.

There was a custom in the Chinese Professional Baseball League to have team meals. We didn't get a vote; we just did as we were instructed. Shortly after I arrived, we went on a road trip, and after the game, we were told by our manager that we were going to have a team meal. We changed clothes but didn't get on our bus. Instead, we started walking down the street through the traffic. I wondered what people driving by thought, seeing 30 guys walking down the street in a pack.

The people at the restaurant were waiting for us. We sat at big round tables that could seat eight, so we took up four of them. On every table there were three bottles of whisky, and on the ground beside every table were little coolers filled with beer. If they ran out, somebody refilled them. Everybody immediately started drinking the whisky while we waited for the food to come. That was the best part.

I learned the term "gan bei," which means "cheers"... but what it really means is to gulp down your full drink. Whenever you meet someone new, the custom is to go up to them, put both hands on your glass of whisky, and say gan bei ... then both of you down your whole drink.

It was inevitable that there would come a time when, being the new guy, I'd be at a bar with a group of people I didn't know—a half-dozen or more. They were in a line waiting to say hello. To welcome me, they each took a turn saying gan bei. The first guy and I both downed our drink— and a glass full of whisky kicks you right in the face. Now I meet the second person. My glass gets refilled ... same drill. He says gan bei, and we both down a glass of whisky. The third person comes up to me to do the same thing. Of course, each of them only had to drink one glass of whisky, while I had to drink six. I couldn't say no, or I'd make them lose face.

After drinking six glasses of whisky, my immediate goal was not to suddenly fall flat on my face. Only now I had to be ready for some hard-core drinking for the rest of the night. This was my first month in Taiwan … but this sort of thing would happen again and again over the next five years.

As for the first team meal, the guys are doing gan bei. It takes a little while for the food to show up, and by then everyone has a good glow going. In the middle of our big table was a huge lazy Susan, and it got filled with a lot of food. Everyone spins it to put food onto their own plates. The food looked very different to me. I didn't know what most of it was. Some stuff was green and slimy. The smell was completely different from what I was used to. I had to go with the flow.

Whenever they brought out a chicken or a duck, it was the whole thing, on a big platter with its head still on and its stomach cut open so you could cut the meat out from it. The same thing with fish, head on and cut open … but with the fish, the Taiwanese guys wanted to eat the eyes. My American teammate, Tony Metoyer, a veteran of the CPBL who knew the customs, told me I *had* to eat the food. If I didn't, I would insult them. Tony said I couldn't make them lose face. So I began pecking away at it, with no idea about most of what I was eating.

Over the years, I'd be at many more of these team meals and even be invited to someone's home. I learned the method of taking a bite, quickly taking two to three chews without the food touching my tongue and swallowing the chunks down. Just like I did in Mexico with the pig ears and stomachs. Still, over the years I'd say that about 80 percent of the time, the food was okay—not good, but not bad. Around 10 percent of the time it was really good, and I'd eat it again. The other 10 percent of the time … it was just plain awful—smelled and tasted horrible. I never threw up, and I never spit it back out, you just couldn't do that … ever.

That night, after the team meal ended, the guys hurried down a few more drinks and ended up with bright red faces. The team was paying for everything, after all.

At a certain point—usually after some sort of team bonding event—the Taiwanese guys would get used to their American teammates and come to accept us. They started to ask me out to eat with them—which meant you had to, or else you'd make them lose face. And you must eat whatever the food is; you can't spit it out or make faces when eating. This is their food, sometimes it's their favorite dish, so you can't insult them.

While we stayed in Kaohsiung, the hotel gave us lunch tickets to eat at

Five. Cheeseburger in Paradise

their buffet every day. It was a lot of unrecognizable food, but if I saw the chicken legs, I'd get those and whatever else looked edible. The chicken legs were pretty good ... but I'd find out soon enough that they weren't chicken legs at all. They were frog legs. I never had frog legs before. They were actually pretty good ... they really did taste like chicken.

I got better and better at trying new things. Once the Taiwanese guys caught an eel while we were training in Australia. That night, they slow-cooked it in a dorm room quad and made eel soup. They asked me to have some. I didn't want to, but I couldn't say no and make them lose face. Once again, I was going to eat something that I didn't want to eat. When I took a spoonful, it actually tasted good! I even asked for a second bowl. Really.

Another time, a few of my Taiwanese teammates took me to a restaurant I hadn't seen before. We were in a neighborhood off a small side street. We sat down at a large table outside, and we started right up with the drinking. We were having a good time, and then the "food" arrived. The waitresses brought these big plates with big bare bones on them and put them down in front of everybody. When I looked closer at my plate, there was no meat at all on any of the bones.

I was confused. I thought this was a joke the guys were pulling on me, and that the real food was coming. But it was no joke. The guys showed me a hole drilled into these bones. We were each given a straw, and you had to stick the straw into the hole of the bone and suck out the bone marrow inside. It actually tasted good.

Not every trip ended up pleasurable. During another night out, some

Taiwan street food.

of the Taiwanese players dared one of our American players, Corey Powell, to eat a live beating turtle's heart. He took the dare.

They brought out the turtle and removed its heart while it was still beating. Corey ate it.

Of all of the things that I ate in Taiwan…. I wonder if I ever ate a turtle's heart and just didn't know it? I sure hope not.

Eventually I was able to pick and choose my own restaurants, and I learned how to order off a menu in Chinese. I still went out with my American teammates most of the time. I liked learning how to use chopsticks. Some of the restaurants were wide open, with stray dogs wandering all over the place, right under your legs while you were eating. Teammates taught me the different words for food in Chinese. I learned how to order fried rice (chow fan), and I ordered some fried pork to go with it. When it arrived, I had to use the chopsticks.

There were a lot of street vendors with their carts, and people setting up tables and chairs right on the sidewalk, right in front of someone else's business. They had gas grills and cooked the food right on the sidewalk. I ate at these places a lot. Sometimes your plastic chair was on the edge of the curb and there were literally cars flying by you at 35–40 miles per hour only a couple of feet behind you. You felt the wind blow by, and while you were eating you were breathing in car exhaust. There was one street vendor food I hated. When I smelled them cooking tofu on the street, it gagged me, it was terrible.

Most of the time, the "street food" and the experiences that went with it were cool. In Taipei, Corey found another interesting place right off a main road. There was a guy with his food stand on the sidewalk. He had pots and pans and all the things needed to cook with. Off to the side of the stand, just off the sidewalk, he had a bunch of chickens walking around in a chicken wire cage. To order, you pointed to the chicken walking around that you wanted to eat. The cook grabbed that chicken and threw it into a machine that killed the chicken and defeathered it. The cook pulled it out and with a huge, sharp knife, he cut off the head and butchered it into pieces. He took those pieces and seasoned them up a little, then put them into a pan with cooking oil, where he fried it up. He took it out of the frying pan and put it onto a plate for you. You took your food and sat on a portable table on the sidewalk, about 20 feet from the street where cars were driving by, and that's where you ate your dinner. We watched the whole process from a live chicken to a meal on a plate happen within minutes.

In Chiayi, we found a little Korean barbeque restaurant close to our team hotel. We enjoyed the food so much that we went back every time we were in town. One night, we sat at a table that had a round cooking plate. To order, you went to the food bar and got your meats and vegetables, brought them back to your table, and cooked your own food. The cooker

Five. Cheeseburger in Paradise

was big enough for four guys to have a space to cook. It didn't take long. While you ate what you cooked, you put more of your food on the cooking plate. The best part is that you get to cook the food just the way you like it … and it's all you can eat.

On one visit there, we were enjoying our meal when we noticed that one of our American coaches, Mark Budaska, was grabbing his throat, not making any sounds. His eyes were watering. We asked him if he was okay, and he nodded no … he wasn't okay.

Mark was seriously choking. In a restaurant full of people, my teammate Steve Wilson got up and began slapping Mark on his back hard, over and over again. This got everyone's attention, and it turned into a full-blown scene. The slapping wasn't working, so Corey Powell jumped in and began doing the Heimlich maneuver on Mark. Everyone in the place was watching. Suddenly, Corey popped the piece of food out, and Mark began gasping for air. His face was still purple. (Ironically, after Corey was done playing baseball, he became a paramedic.) Mark got his breath back and would be fine. Didn't stop us from teasing him about it, though.

Late in my first season in Taipei, the guys took me to lunch at a Mongolian barbeque restaurant. I loved it! You fill up a bowl (or two) with different meats and vegetables, with water, oils, and sauces all together. You give the bowl to the chef, who throws the food on a hot cooking table, flips it around, stirring it up, tossing it around to cook just right. When it's done, he slides it into another clean bowl. You watch him do all of this in front of you. You go back to your table and eat it fresh and hot. This would be my favorite meal during my entire five years in Taiwan.

Of course, we also needed the occasional late-night pizza. We found a place called the Harley Bar in Kaohsiung. It was a bar that had a real Harley Davidson motorcycle in the front window. It was a decent place to have a few beers, but we usually went there late at night for the pizza.

You couldn't eat out all the time, of course. But when you bought groceries, you needed to be careful—and a little picky, too.

Three blocks from our apartment complex was a Taiwanese grocery store. It was all Chinese food. In the middle of the place was a barrel filled with chicken and/or rooster talons, basically about three to four inches long with the gummy skin. These were used to make a chicken claw soup, where you sucked the skin off and ate it.

On her very first trip to visit me in Taiwan, Tami and I stopped by this store. I distracted her from seeing a big barrel of chicken claws. I knew soon enough, she'd say there wasn't anything there for us to buy. As soon as she finally said it, I replied, "Hey, turn around, let's buy some of this for dinner tonight." When she turned around, she saw the chicken claws in the barrel and she literally screamed out loud, "Oh gross!"

There were American-style grocery stores and convenience stores we would frequent, too. They sold these Chinese noodle bowls, a huge selection of all the flavors and spices you could want. You'd take one and open it up right in the store, put the seasoned pack in with the spice paste, and add some boiling water from one of these big thermoses that they had at all the stores. Pour the hot water in the bowl, put the cover back over it, and in two minutes you had this noodle bowl. These were so good, especially after a late night out ... and of course you had to eat it with chopsticks. At the end of every season, I'd take a bunch of these home with me.

There was also a Hooters in Taipei. They had a grand opening while we were there. Of course, we went there to eat. We met the manager, an American who told us he was there to open the place and to train the locals how to run it before he returned home. They brought in a bunch of American girls as the waitresses, who were really good-looking in their sexy outfits. It was nice to see and talk to some American girls. They were also there to train the Taiwanese girls how to do the job. On the next trip to Taipei, we went back, and the American manager and American waitresses were long gone. The Taiwanese girls looked cute, but they didn't quite fill out their outfits like the American girls did.

One night on a road trip in Taipei, Corey said he'd discovered something cool he wanted to show us. We went with him to a section of Taipei that had a lot of bars. Off on a side street, there was a snake show going on. They had a guy doing all kinds of things with the snake, entertaining people. At the end of the show, the dude cut open the snake and had its blood drip into a cup. He said that this drink would make you very potent, a natural male enhancement. He was asking for someone from the audience to come up and drink it. Sure enough, some guy went up and did. This was weirdly ... entertaining.

Meal time could oftentimes be plenty entertaining. On the last day of road trips to Taipei, we'd each buy a sandwich from Subway to take back to the hotel and save for the long bus ride home. On one "getaway" day, after lunch at an Australian diner nearby, we stopped at a Subway just a few blocks away. As we walked in, we saw this guy who looked like an American out front, drinking a beer. As we waited in line to order, the guy strolled into the store with his open can and took a big drink out of it. I thought it was unusual ... and it turned out to be against the law in Taiwan. The Subway manager went up to him and said in English, "You cannot bring that beer in here." The guy replied, in what sounded like an Australian accent (while slurring his words), "I'm an alcoholic ... it's what I do."

We were listening, and we began laughing out loud at this guy as he turned and walked out of the store. Not something you see every day. Anywhere.

We made a lot of traditional American meals with what we bought, and even ended up having cookouts on the roof of our high-rise apartment building. It gave us a chance to pretend we were home again, eating hot dogs, chips, and the rest. I found places to buy American food in Kaohsiung. There was an American store that imported food from the USA, run by an old man who was drunk every time I was there. He would slur and rant and rave in Chinese. I just nodded my head up and down and said yes to whatever he was going on about. We also found a Costco, believe it or not. They had USDA meats. It was worth the trip across town—even on a scooter—to get the good stuff.

There were some Taiwanese foods—like Mongolian Barbeque—that I absolutely continued to eat when I returned to the States. Some of the food, though, was better left on the island.

Of course, after I got home one season, Tami and I were invited to go out to dinner with some friends. They wanted…. Chinese. I just couldn't.

As you can imagine, going to Italy was a *much* different experience, food-wise. While I had to start over language-wise, at least I knew what kind of pasta I liked. And there was A LOT of pasta.

Even so, things were still different.

During my first few days there, I was taken to a restaurant called Oliver's. I got to know Oliver, the owner, during the season. It became my favorite place in Rimini. There was a variety of food to choose from on Oliver's menu. I usually ordered an individual pizza and a salad. The salad was basically lettuce with vinegar and oil dressing—that was it. You got bread on the table. On a small plate, you put olive oil, and you dunk your bread in it. I learned quickly that in Italy, you don't get your pizza sliced. You have to cut it with a fork or use your butter knife to cut pieces off to eat. The pizzas are not exactly round either—some cheese sort of covers it, and a little bit of meat is put on it. It still tasted good, but it was definitely different from what I was used to in America.

I also was not used to eating what was pretty much a full meal in between games of a doubleheader. Since we played doubleheaders every Saturday in Italy, we had a lot of pasta meals. After the first game was over, both teams got fed, whether playing at home or on the road. The meal was always pasta; you could get it either with a white sauce or red sauce. The drinks came in glass bottles, either regular water or aqua fizzi, which was carbonated water. There was always a long time between games. We had this same pasta meal when we arrived at a new city. We'd eat in the team hotel before going to the ballpark for the Friday night game.

Eating out in Italy was easy once I learned how to order in Italian. We went to Oliver's most of the time, but there was a McDonald's in town too. They basically had the same menu as we did in the United States, with one interesting exception: "McBirra." These McDonald's had brews. You could go into a McDonald's in Italy and order a real beer.

This didn't mean I gave up on my enjoyment of "street foods." They just weren't as available in Italy as they were in Taiwan. I did have a favorite—hot panchitos, a hot wrap with meat and melted cheese. It was cheap, but it tasted so good that I'd buy two of them at stops along the highway after road games when the bus pulled over. American teammate Eric Pini and I laughed at each other because we both loved them so much.

I ate most of my meals in my apartment. The local grocery store was very similar to small grocery stores in America. To get lunch meat, you had to go to the deli department and take a number. I had an Italian teammate who taught me how to ask for deli meat, like ham, and how to order

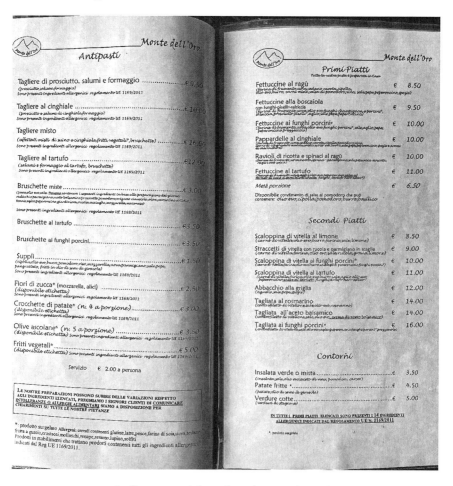

Italian menu (photo by John Henderson).

cheese slices in Italian. I learned to say "sette fette di formaggio Suisa, per favore," which meant "seven slices of Swiss cheese, please." Same thing when I ordered ham. This grocery store had everything I needed. I bought all of the essentials for lunch, snacks, and meat for dinner. I got bread, chips, soda, canned goods, beer, and of course … toilet paper! The grocery store didn't give you grocery bags to put your stuff in, you had to buy them. I wouldn't have understood that, but I figured it out with some help from my teammates. I could reuse these bags whenever I went back.

And Italy was where I discovered the awesomeness of gelato. Once I tried that, I was hooked.

In Taiwan, most meals were accompanied by hard liquor and lots of beer. In Italy, I drank less beer, and I learned that most of my teammates drank wine instead. The wine in Italy was inexpensive and really good. I drank it a lot. On a side trip into Germany, I discovered Guinness, a dark beer from Ireland. You have to learn to pour it just right, so the foam rises upward and so forth. When I took my first drink, I was hooked again! To this day, I love drinking Guinness.

Looking back, I'm glad to have expanded the kinds of foods I could eat, even if I paid a high price a few times while finding out which ones my stomach could—and couldn't—handle.

Six

Family of Man

Travel. Language barriers. Strange foods. Still, without a doubt, the toughest thing a professional athlete has to deal with on a recurring basis is leaving family behind. Now go ahead and multiply that times 10 when you're talking about leaving the country to play.

Tami and I were married in October of 1989 and had our son, Logan, in July of 1992. Fortunately, I was able to travel home and be there when Logan was born. I wouldn't have missed it for the world. It was scary to think that I was someone's dad now.

I missed Logan's first Christmas while I was in Puerto Rico. I would miss several more "firsts" by being out of the country. That part sucked.

All you could do was stay in touch the best you could. We take communication for granted today. Back then, whenever I wanted to call home and talk to Tami, I had to find these special pay phones that could make international calls. The calls were expensive, so we couldn't talk very long. We could catch up on things, and after seeing how she and Logan were doing, I'd always try to get Logan—who was still an infant—to make some kind of sound over the phone, so I could just hear him.

The biggest issue making calls from Taiwan wasn't the money—although the calls weren't cheap—it was the time difference. If I wanted to call at 4:00 in the afternoon in Taiwan, that was 3:00 a.m. in Milwaukee. When I was in Italy, they gave me a cell phone to use since my apartment didn't have a landline. That was cool. It would have been great to have that cell phone in Mexico and Taiwan.

Things were a lot better when family could visit. It wasn't easy for any of us—Tami having to bring our infant son on airplanes, trains, buses, and taxi cabs—and me having to make sure they were taken care of and safe while I was doing baseball stuff. We had to plan well ahead of time for all their travel, meals, and entertainment. It was taxing … but of course, it was more than worth it.

During my first season in Mexico, Tami, Logan, and Tami's mom, Eileen, came to visit. Puebla didn't have an international airport, so they

Six. Family of Man

had to fly to Mexico City. First I had to get from Puebla *to* Mexico City. I had to take a two-hour bus ride to the airport in Mexico City, greet my family, and grab their luggage. Then it was the bus for all of us back to Puebla—making sure we got on the right bus, the *Estrella Roja*.

Once they got to my hotel, the hardest thing was finding places for Tami, Logan, and Eileen to eat and spend time when I wasn't around. Not surprisingly, they were finicky eaters (pig ears was a definite no) in a foreign country. After my bouts with diarrhea, I understood why.

The day after they arrived, we needed a taxi to go to the grocery store. We'd made friends with a cabbie named Carlos in Puebla, so I called him. When he got there, he asked to hold Logan while we were talking. When he took Logan into his arms, he jumped into his cab and sped off. Tami freaked out (of course). After about 50 feet, Carlos stopped, reversed, and came back with a grin on his face. He got a good laugh from everybody (except for Tami) with his fake kidnapping.

A typical day with family in Mexico included walking around the downtown area called the Centro, grabbing something to eat, and looking around at the shops, where Tami liked to check out the clothing stores. When I had to leave for the ballpark, the fam would have Carlos drive them to the stadium for game time. Tami held Logan tight.

Tami was always expecting the worst, but nothing wild or crazy ever happened, thankfully. Getting them back to the airport was every bit as tough as picking them up ... but well worth it. Every trip was.

You can imagine that Tami wasn't all that thrilled with me leaving the country for those eight seasons ... plus two winter ball stints. It was hard for her to be home with Logan without me there, too. I'm sure it was hard on Logan, although he never complained.

During my second winter ball season in the Dominican Republic, I still didn't have much experience being a parent, but I started to notice the actions of those who did. For instance, Tony Peña is well known for his stellar big league catching career. But I saw another side of him off the field. He was a really good dad, too.

Some of the Dominican players lived in Santiago or nearby, including Tony, who had a house there. After most games, he'd just go home. But one night, he was out with the rest of us, along with his wife and two kids. We were eating outside and noticed this little boy walking around. He was very small, nine or maybe even 10 years old ... but he looked more like he was five or six. The little boy was walking around all by himself late at night. Tony brought him over to sit at our table and bought him some food. I noticed that this little boy had six fingers on each hand. During the rest of the season, Tony more or less took this kid into his own family. We'd see the kid at the ballpark, and I heard someone say that Tony and his wife took him to buy clothes. One of the few times that we stayed at a hotel on the road, I saw the boy again with Tony and his family. I wondered what kind of arrangement Tony had with the boy's real parents. Maybe he adopted him. His care and generosity with that kid were amazing.

You find out that being a parent is hard. Maybe the hardest job ever. And sometimes, things can go horribly wrong, even for great parents who do things right.

Back in Mexico the following season, I made friends with a new teammate, Marty Clary. Marty played three seasons in the majors with the Atlanta Braves. He joined our team in Puebla. Marty also made plans to have his family come and stay with him for part of the season. He was a great family man and a terrific dad himself.

Early in the season, Marty found an apartment he was going to take. He told me it had an extra bedroom and that I could stay with him there until his family arrived. I took him up on his offer. That gave me a place to stay and time to find an apartment or hotel for myself.

Marty's apartment was on the third floor, and it was very nice. It had a big living room, a nice kitchen, two bedrooms, and two bathrooms. Every two days, a maid would come to clean, including the dishes. The apartment was in a very nice upper-middle-class neighborhood, about 15 minutes from the stadium by public bus, with a bus stop about three blocks away on the main road. Luckily, myself and another pitcher, Tom McCarthy, who just joined the team (and was my teammate from the season before in Charlotte) got the place directly below Marty. Living below them allowed Tom and me to get to know the Clarys.

When Marty's family arrived, he was thrilled. He had an infant son, Weston, who was younger than Logan. While they were visiting, it was Weston's first birthday. We got invited to come up and celebrate. They had a birthday cake, we sang happy birthday, everyone was having a good time. Marty's son had these little bells on his little shoes, and he had just recently learned to walk. With his little clumsy steps, I remember hearing those little bells ringing all night. Weston was also wearing a hat that said #1 on it. We all had some birthday cake, and after a while we called it a night. Everything was good.

Then it wasn't.

The next morning, I was chatting near our door with the landlord's son, Jose. While we were talking, I could hear Marty and his wife yelling out loud upstairs. Jose suddenly yelled, "the window!" He ran right past me to my window, and I quickly followed him. We looked down and saw Marty's son lying on the cement below, in a cement square court area, which had two 12-foot walls on the sides. The other two sides of the square were the sides of the apartment building. It was like a box.

Six. Family of Man

There were only two ways to get into this court: through the bottom floor apartment that had a sliding glass door, or climb over the wall from the outside. As I tried to figure out what was going on, I saw Marty climbing up on top of one of those walls. He jumped down, rushed up to Weston, and picked him up into his arms. Marty looked back to the wall and realized it was too high to climb back up holding his son. He knocked on the sliding door, but nobody answered. He kicked in the glass of the sliding door so he could run through the apartment and out the front door.

At that moment, I realized Weston fell out the window from the third floor.

By the time I threw on a shirt, put shoes on, and ran down the stairs with Jose to the street out front, we had lost sight of Marty and his son. Then we saw Marty down the street, coming in our direction, still holding his infant. When he got back to us, he was still in a panic, saying he ran down the street because he heard there was a doctor living down there. As Marty was telling us this, I saw Weston's head lying on Marty's shoulder. There was blood coming out of his nose and onto Marty's shirt, and the little boy's eyes were glassy and just staring straight ahead. I was hoping he was still alive. I just prayed for him to live. Marty's wife had called an ambulance.

We were waiting on the street for the ambulance to arrive. I didn't know what to do or say. The ambulance arrived, a Volkswagen van, Marty got in with his son, and it took off. Marty's wife and daughter got in a taxi and followed it.

We didn't know what hospital they went to. I went back to my apartment, stunned and upset. After what seemed like forever, my phone rang. It was a lady calling from the hospital. In broken English, she said, "baby not make it."

At first it was hard for me to understand that those were the words she said. I didn't want to believe it. I was hoping she was saying that the baby was still alive. I asked her the name of the hospital, and moments later got into a taxi, still not knowing what she meant. I remember walking into the emergency room waiting area and seeing Marty and his wife, Ginger, just staring straight ahead. Marty looked up at me, and when our eyes met, he began to cry. "He didn't make it."

Ginger was in shock. Just had a blank face, unable to say anything. I stayed with them for a while, before our team owner, general manager, and another woman arrived to help the family. There wasn't anything more I could do, so I left. When I got back to my apartment, I was so upset that I immediately went to the special phone booth about five blocks away to make an international call back home to talk to Tami. I needed to talk to her. I needed to hear Logan's voice. She asked me if I just got released. I told her no, something worse.

There was a pall over the ballpark that night. It was pure sadness. Needless to say, Marty stayed at his apartment with his wife and daughter. The team went about its business, and we played our game. Afterwards, some of us went to Marty's apartment, not knowing what to expect. Marty invited us in, but Ginger stayed in the bedroom. She didn't want to talk. We wanted to let Marty know we were there for him.

Marty spoke softly and told us he and his family were leaving the next morning. The team made arrangements for the Clarys to bring their son home with them. It was so incredibly sad. Marty was a good teammate and a friend. I couldn't stop thinking about hearing those little bells on Winston's shoes, and how it made me think about Logan and how happy everyone was just the night before. All we could do was say our goodbyes, wish the family all the best, and let them grieve. The next day, Marty and family were gone. The upstairs would be a quiet and empty place.

If you're around long enough, you'll be around players and teams that have to deal with sadness and even tragedy. I had another teammate later that season, Mike Browning, who was the closer on our Campeche team. At one point, he had to return home to visit his mom, who was very sick. Shortly after he returned to the team, he and I walked several blocks to one of those special "international calls" pay phones, and we each called home. Mike found out his mother had passed away. On the way back to our hotel, Mike wasn't saying much. I understood. I told him he could cry if he needed to, not to hold it in because I was there with him. He said he would hold it in until he got back to his hotel room in private, and that he didn't want to cry out in public. I felt really bad for him, and if there was anything I could have done for him, I would have. These are the times it's *really* hard to be in a foreign country.

Then again, sometimes I think it's better to have your teammates around in times like that. In Taiwan, we found out that our Taiwanese shortstop's sister had been killed in a scooter traffic accident. She was riding in traffic when a bus turned right into her and ran over her. She died instantly. I always wondered why there weren't more accidents like that due to the crazy traffic that was everywhere in Taiwanese cities.

Our shortstop was away from the team for over a week. As a team, we dressed in our uniforms and took our team bus to his parents' home to pay our respects to the family. It was hard seeing the enormous sorrow and pain in their faces. I always hope that our being there gave them some support.

Taiwan has some very distinct customs, especially concerning death. I found that out very quickly right after I arrived for the first time. I was learning how to use chopsticks, but like a typical American, I wasn't watching how those around me were doing things. Men don't ask for directions, after all.

Six. Family of Man 95

At a team meal, I was enjoying my dinner when I decided to grab something to drink. I needed to set down my chopsticks before I got up and decided to stick them into the rice on my plate. They were sticking upward. Within seconds as I was taking a drink, one of my Taiwanese teammates hurried over to me all freaked out. He pulled my chopsticks out of my rice and handed them to me, telling me I couldn't do that. He told me that the chopsticks, while sticking up in a "V" shape, were making the sign of death.

This freaks Taiwanese people out. They believe in bad omens, such as: Never give someone a clock as a gift. Don't talk about death, avoid the number 4—because it sounds like death—and don't put your chopsticks in your food that give the sign of death. At funerals, people light incense sticks, stick them in sand in a barrel outside the temple before entering, making a V as they stick up, sort of like what my chopsticks did when I stuck them in my rice. I didn't know I was breaking a social rule in their culture.

Obviously, when you're somewhere for five years, you experience a few tragic situations. We went through one with our team sponsor.

Every team in Taiwan had a major sponsor—a business that would put their name (and resources) on the team. We didn't get to know these folks all that well, but most were very passionate about baseball. I first encountered ours after a tough loss in Taipei. All of a sudden, this guy climbed aboard our bus. I was wondering, " How did a fan get on our bus?" I figured it was some crazy guy going to give us crap. The guy started to speak loudly to the whole team. Nobody did anything, and I noticed that everybody was listening to him. It sounded like he was giving a spirited pep talk. It was our sponsor's president.

He did this a few times over the years. I actually grew to like the guy. He was a really nice man, he cared … and a good sponsor.

Two years later, before the season began in mid–February, I was at my apartment when the TV news began covering a major airplane crash not far away. A China Airlines plane was trying to make a second attempt to land in bad weather in Taipei. The plane hit and crashed into some homes in a neighborhood near the airport. On live TV, I could see homes on fire, and other small fires around the street. Debris was everywhere, suitcases, clothes, parts of the airplane, and dead bodies. Where there was a dead body or a body part, the camera showed it. This was terrible to see, but at the same time I kept watching. Everybody on that plane died, 182 passengers, 15 crew … and seven more people died on the ground.

The next day, as usual the team gathered in the basement of the team apartments to have a meeting before a game or practice. Everybody was talking about the plane crash. When our manager came in to talk to us before we got on the bus, he spoke slowly and looked saddened. When his words were translated into English for us, we were told that our team sponsor—the nice guy who regularly gave pep talks on our bus after games in Taipei—was on the airplane that crashed, along with his wife and two small kids.

Later in the week, we boarded the bus and traveled to the funeral in Taipei. We went to the temple and stood outside. Everyone was given two of those incense sticks that were lit. Everyone got into two long lines and began entering. When we reached the door, there were two huge barrels filled with sand, and before you entered the temple you stuck both of your incense sticks into the sand, making a "V." This instantly took me back to two years earlier, when I had stuck my chopsticks into my rice at a team meal.

They have an even more public custom that plays out every summer, called "Ghost Month." This goes on day after day throughout the entire country of Taiwan. Each year on "the fifteenth day of the seventh lunar month," from the middle of August through the middle of September.

"Hungry ghosts" are beings sent to the underworld to suffer an eternal state of hunger for their misdeeds. During Ghost Month, they're free from their hell. Ghost Month rules to live by: (1) Don't go swimming. A ghost may drown you to get a chance at a rebirth. (2) Don't go out alone at night. (3) Don't whistle, especially after dark. (4) Don't pick up money on the street. (5) Don't kill any rare insects in your home, it could be your ancient ancestors reincarnated. (6) Don't hang clothes outside to dry. (7) Don't lean against walls. And (8) Don't pee on a tree, to name a few.

The Taiwanese burn "Ghost (fake) Money" to honor their ancestors and appease the restless spirits. Some wear amulets. They put food outside their homes and businesses to feed wandering ghosts to satisfy the ghosts' hunger, hoping they'll leave in peace. One person went so far as to put two large speakers outside his home, pointing to the sky. He was several blocks away, and I was 26 floors up. He was screaming into a microphone, and he woke me up from a sound sleep.

Like I said, there were many customs that took a lot of getting used to.

I had my own family to focus on. When they made the long trek to Taiwan, I had to make sure they were safe and okay. We needed food they'd like, and a way to be sure they didn't get lost when they were out on their own. Entertainment was necessary. I also needed Tami to help me with a matter of personal hygiene.

Ever since we met in 1988, Tami—who was a professional hair stylist—had been the only person who cut my hair. Before my family's first trip to the Far East, I'd let my hair get really long. I'd considered getting it cut sooner, but I didn't know where to go—safely. I'd heard that there

Six. Family of Man

were certain places in Taiwan where women offer sex to you as part of your haircut. This was called getting a "Yellow Haircut." I had no way of knowing the difference between places that gave regular haircuts or the ones that offered "yellow" ones.

It was best to wait.

I was so dedicated to this that after they returned home, I let my hair grow out again until I looked like Grizzly Adams. (I let my face hair grow long, too.) One year when I returned to Milwaukee, Logan didn't recognize me. I was sitting at the kitchen table, and I could hear Logan running up to our back door. He was three years old. I heard him yell, "Grandma told me my daddy's here!" He ran in the door, looked right at me, and kept right on going. I heard him stop in the living room and say, "Where's my dad?" I called out his name, and he ran back into the kitchen. He stared at me like, "Who is this guy?"

When they visited me, I wanted Tami and Logan to see everything I'd been describing over the phone. We took walks around the area of our apartment complex. I took them to eat at places I liked. She had to get used to finding things to do whenever I was at practice. For games, I had someone write down on a piece of paper in Chinese saying, "Take me to the baseball stadium." All she had to do was give this to the taxi driver, and they'd get there. That didn't take care of all the worries. I was concerned about them getting lost on their own. When we played on the road, I didn't take the team bus, instead I traveled with Tami and Logan and met the team at the hotel. For me, it was hard enough taking care of myself, but now I had to take care of them too. I was always worrying.

It wasn't super safe on those streets, even in the daytime. In many of these Taiwan cities, you have to step over sewer water that's draining from the nearby buildings. It doesn't smell good. Once as we were walking, Logan—who wasn't quite five years old—started yelling out, "Mom, Dad, it stinks!" I ignored him, but then he said loudly, "It smells like poop!" I finally told him to shut up, because there were people around who did understand English. He laughed. We walked about three more blocks, and as we approached a side street, Logan and I noticed, on the other side of the street, something popping its head up out of a hole by a bench. As we crossed the street, Logan went running over toward the hole to see what it was. It was a rat popping its head up. We had to get Logan away from the hole in a hurry.

During the day, I would play with him as much as I could. One day, there was a little Taiwanese boy—about the same age as Logan—playing with some toys inside the apartment complex on one of the floors. In the world of little kids, there's no language barrier or discrimination, kids are kids. Logan and the other little kid ran toward each other and started chasing each other running around. They ran up and down, laughing and having a great time. At one point, as the Taiwanese boy was chasing Logan, he was yelling something to him in Chinese. Without missing a beat, Logan yelled back to him in English, "No, I'm not," as if he knew what the kid said to him. The kid yelled something back to Logan in Chinese again. They were somehow communicating.

I did end up finding a park about six blocks away where we could play baseball. There were some outdoor toys to play on too. On our first visit to this park Tami, Logan, and I saw a group of older Taiwanese people doing Tai Chi, and some stray dogs lying by the toys. I looked for a space where Logan and I could hit the ball. Logan was eager to go play on the toys, but I told him to wait for me. He didn't. He instantly ran towards the playground equipment. When he ran around a corner, there were two big German Shepherds lying there. Logan didn't see them until he made his turn, and when he saw these two big, dirty, mangy street dogs, it startled him. He let out a scream, and frightened, he took off running in the opposite direction from Tami and me. This also scared the dogs, and when Logan began running away, the dogs jumped right up and began barking and chasing him.

Tami and I were helpless.

We took off running while we watched these dogs chasing Logan down like it was an episode of *Mutual of Omaha's Wild Kingdom*. Everything was going into slow motion, the dogs were right on Logan's ass, and he was still screaming. I was just waiting to see them take him down. At the last moment before the dogs were going to pounce, an old man who was doing Tai Chi ran out and chased the dogs away. When we finally caught up to Logan, we were still shaking. They'd gotten so close that we weren't sure if they'd actually bitten him. Thankfully, they hadn't. He was fine, but I gave him a scolding for not listening to me when I told him to wait. I really thought my son was going to get killed. Thank God for the old man doing Tai Chi in the park saving the day!

We were always looking for fun (and safe) things to do as a family. Sometimes stuff just popped up in a spot you'd never expect.

By accident, we found this place on a busy street we passed almost every day. Inside, you could fish for shrimp in a large built-in swimming pool filled with salty, foggy water, and shrimp you couldn't see. You rented a fishing pole, you paid by the amount of time you were there … and you kept all the shrimp you caught.

The first time, it was me, Tami, Logan, and eight others in our group. We got our poles and began "shrimping." You had to be patient to catch a shrimp, and it did take some work. It didn't take Logan long before he got impatient and bored because he hadn't caught anything yet, and he wanted to leave. I told him we had to stay a little bit longer. Moments later, he was instantly hooked when he caught his first shrimp. Now he didn't want to leave. Every time he caught another shrimp, he went crazy. I'll admit, the rest of us had fun, too. We went back numerous times. With limited space in an overcrowded, big city, this was how you went fishing.

The best part of having my family there was having Logan in the stands to see me pitch and understand what was happening on the field. He never got to see me pitch in the Major Leagues, so having him in the stands meant a lot. Before his first game, I got to bring Logan down onto the field during our pregame. He was wearing his mini-Cubs uniform, which he loved after seeing the movie *Rookie of the Year*. At the ending of batting practice, we had a quick game of catch on the field. Back in the stands, Tami bought Logan these plastic bangers that the fans used to make noise and cheer for their team. Logan banged them together the entire game.

A couple of days later, Tami and Logan were able to see me pitch against Agan. When I was on the mound, I glanced up into the stands and saw Tami and Logan right in the middle of all the crazy fans, Logan having a great time. It meant everything to see them here. I ended up throwing a complete-game shutout, winning 1–0. I was the Player of the Game, and afterward I went behind home plate to get my award and have my picture taken.

Another time, a director from a TV station that televised our games asked me if it would be okay to have Logan sing "Take Me Out to the Ballgame" during the seventh-inning stretch for the telecast of the next day's game. They asked us to bring Logan in before the game so that they could tape it and play the tape in the middle of the seventh inning. After the game that night, we borrowed a CD of the song and taught Logan the words. He picked it right up.

The next day, they put an earpiece on Logan so that he could hear the music and sing with it. He knocked it out in one take! Back at the apartment, we had a VCR and were able to record the broadcast. After the game, we hurried home to watch. Logan's little kid voice keeping pace with the music made it look so cute, and he was looking at his fingers as he was counting "for it's one, two, three, strikes and you're out at the old ballgame." The TV station played it several more times that season—and it's still on YouTube.

There was also time to relax. A local told us about a place called Kenting. It was located on the far south part of the island. It was a little beach town, laid back, easy-going, with no traffic. When we had a couple of days off, we went there as often as we could. We rented rooms that were above a convenience store. There were some cool little places to eat along the beach, and a bunch of little bars. It was great to get away from the crazy

Don, Tami, and Logan August with teammate Brad Strauss (left) at the beach in Kenting, Taiwan, 1998.

traffic and noise that we were always surrounded by. We hung out on a nice beach during the day, and then at night there were restaurants and outdoor bars. We found one cool little place where you had to eat outside on the sidewalk. It was a Thai restaurant owned by this interesting dude from Belgium named Marco. Places like this were a great find.

With Tami and Logan visiting, this would be a nice getaway. We checked into the little room above the convenience store, and we hung out with my teammates and their wives. We ate at Marco's, hung out and relaxed, and spent the day at the beach. Having them there seemed to make all the travel issues more than worth it. For me at least.

I relished every moment with them in Taiwan. But it was harder for them being there than it was for me. During their first trip, after being in Taiwan for nearly three weeks, Tami told me she couldn't stay in Taiwan any longer, it was too hard being there. I understood—it was hard for me too, worrying about them all the time. We agreed they would leave a couple of weeks early.

When they left, the apartment became quiet and lonely. While they were traveling, I was waiting for a call to let me know they made it home safely. I didn't get a call when I was expecting it. When I tried calling home, there was no answer. A short while later, Tami called me—from Anchorage, Alaska.

On their flight from Tokyo to Detroit, Tami saw an explosion on one of the engines of the plane. The plane veered down and was shaking really hard until the pilot regained control. Tami got the attention of a flight attendant, who told her to remain calm and that if there was a problem, the pilot would have diverted the plane to Anchorage. Within two minutes, the pilot came on the intercom and told the passengers that they were being diverted to Anchorage. Tami was afraid they would crash into the Pacific Ocean. When they arrived, everybody had to go through customs, and there were no flights out they could get on. They had to spend the night in Anchorage, then sit at the airport starting early the next day to find a connecting flight back home.

It took them three days to get home.

See, I had the easy part.

The following year, we tried it again, and about four weeks into the visit, she and Logan were spent. Tami wanted to go back to Milwaukee earlier than planned again. This time, we arranged to fly to LA together to visit my family in Mission Viejo during our mid-season break, before I had to return to Taiwan for the second half of the season. I got permission from the club to travel, and it worked out great.

Taiwan could be a very lonely place for foreigners without family. I had a manager for parts of my first two seasons in Taichung named Mr. Wu, who understood that pretty well. He was a legendary figure in Taiwan. He'd been the manager of the Chinese Taipei team in the 1984 Olympic games that I played against. Along with coaching baseball, he owned a Mongolian-style barbeque restaurant in the city of Tainan. Mr. Wu tried to treat the American and Latin players like family whenever he could.

A couple of days before our last practice prior to the league shutting down for Chinese New Year celebrations, Mr. Wu gathered me and five of my foreign teammates together. He told us that during this holiday break, the Taiwanese players were all going home to be with their families, and there wouldn't be any practices for four or five days. Mr. Wu said he would have us come to his hometown of Tainan, about 90 minutes south, where he would be with his family. He would put us all up in a hotel, and we would come to his home and spend time with him and his family. I think he didn't want us to be alone during this holiday in Taiwan. He would have someone take us around during the day to see the festivals, parades, and Chinese New Year celebrations going on in the city. Otherwise, we'd have been sitting in Taichung, alone and bored. So we accepted Mr. Wu's kind offer.

He got us bus tickets, and he had someone pick us up and take us to the small hotel where we stayed. He checked us into our hotel, and we were told we weren't paying for anything. Mr. Wu told us to hang out for a little bit, and later we were going to eat dinner at his restaurant. Mr. Wu also invited the foreign players from the Lions team, based in Tainan, to be with us too. He didn't want them to be alone either. We had plenty of food, plenty of beer, and plenty of company.

Mr. Wu's restaurant was really cool. It was decorated with all kinds of baseball memorabilia. Pictures from the national teams that he coached, signed baseballs and pictures from players and coaches from around the world along with Taiwanese celebrities. I even noticed a picture with him and Fidel Castro when one of his Taiwanese teams played in Cuba. Things couldn't have gone better.

After we returned to the hotel briefly, Mr. Wu brought our players over to his home. We met his wife, son, and two daughters. One of Mr. Wu's daughters was a student at the University of Georgia, and she flew all the way home because in Chinese culture, everybody returns home to be with family to celebrate the Chinese New Year. He had plenty of food and drinks for everyone at his home. It was incredibly nice of Mr. Wu to worry about the foreign players being alone in Taichung and to take care of us.

Seeing the Chinese New Year celebration up close with my own eyes was an amazing experience. We came across a parade, with people wearing all kinds of traditional costumes. We saw a big, long, decorated dragon weaving and moving down the street through the people. There were many people inside the dragon, maneuvering it. All of this was much like what you have seen in movies—awesome to witness, right before my eyes. There were people everywhere having a good time. We spent all day in town watching and partaking in the celebration, checking out the city. I wish Tami and Logan could have been there.

Two American teammates, Corey Powell and Ron Gerstein, were both married, and their wives, Glory and Tisa, would come to stay with them all season. We lived in the same apartment complex and did "family" style stuff often, including barbecues on the roof of the apartment complex. Glory and Tisa were a huge help to me when Tami and Logan were visiting, even though Tisa was about five months pregnant when she arrived. She ended up giving birth in Taiwan later that summer.

I discovered something I didn't like very much about the Taiwanese culture regarding birth. It was very old-fashioned and outdated. When a couple were going to have a baby, it was hoped by everyone that they would have a son first—or better yet, only have sons. Girls were automatically secondary. A Taiwanese player for another team and his wife were expecting their first baby. He was hoping and expecting to have a boy, so proud he couldn't wait. Their baby was born in the early part of the season, but his wife gave birth to a daughter. This guy was so distraught and upset that he didn't want the baby! He had his new baby daughter go live with his wife's parents. I couldn't believe it. I'd always heard about how important sons were in the Asian culture, but this still shocked me.

Six. Family of Man

This carried on well past birth, of course. In adulthood in Taiwan, there was a distinct difference between a man's job and a woman's. Women were the ones who served, so you saw women working in the bars as bartenders. Women who worked at department stores had to wear dresses. The men were the bosses at work and at home. The wife stayed home with the children. It was normal for the man to go out at night with his friends, and it appeared acceptable for the husband to have a girlfriend on the side … okay as long as the man went home to his wife.

I couldn't see this kind of arrangement working anywhere in America.

Being away from my family, I missed the death of my father-in-law, to whom I was very close, and I missed Logan's first day of kindergarten, too. Stealing time with family members became a focus the longer I was away. With my schedule, I wasn't able to get home to see any of my family members as often as I wanted to. At one stretch, I went without seeing my mom and three brothers for two years.

Somewhere along the line, after I'd made a place for myself in Taiwanese baseball, I talked Lance into flying across the Pacific Ocean to visit me for a month. Several times, I'd flown back and forth from Taiwan and Milwaukee and would have a four-hour layover in Los Angeles. My family would pick me up at the airport, and we'd go to a sports bar near LAX, a few miles from where I grew up. This time, I was picking up Lance for the flight back to Taiwan.

We got to the airport and made the long flight across the Pacific. We arrived in Kaohsiung, and Lance had to follow me around. He was in for some real culture shock. In the taxi, Lance listened to me speak Chinese, telling the taxi driver how to get to my apartment. He had his eyes wide open, looking out the window. It was late at night, so he wasn't seeing a lot yet. When the cab pulled up to my apartment, Lance saw the crowded street scene and the thousands of scooters parked everywhere, more flying down the street through the traffic, even at midnight. I couldn't wait to see his face the next day, to see his reactions.

In the morning, I had Lance jump on the back of my scooter, and I told him, "don't freak out. Don't flinch or do anything. If you do, you'll cause me to crash, and we'll die." In the daylight, he could really see everything as we drove down the main busy road to the team apartments. I took him down to the basement and started to introduce him to the players and coaches. I asked our manager if it was okay for Lance to travel on our team bus to everything. He gave me the go-ahead.

So Lance came to practice. He poured sweat in the high humidity. He ate a bin dong. He struggled with chopsticks. The other players and coaches were great to him, I think out of respect for me. Lance became one of the guys. That night, it was time to hit the town. My scooter was now working extra hard, with me and Lance, at 295 pounds, both on board. I introduced him around, and he fit right in, no matter which bar or club we went to.

For the month that Lance was in Taiwan, it rained 23 days. Sometimes a little sprinkle for about 10 minutes, sometimes a full-on downpour. Still, somehow, we got most of our games and practices in. Lance was able to see me pitch and experience the crazy Taiwan fans. He'd been to games at Dodger Stadium and Anaheim Stadium, and he saw a lot of minor league games in Las Vegas at Cashman Field, but this was a whole new experience for him.

The month seemed to fly by. Before he was set to leave, I took him back to my hangouts so that he could say goodbye. During his last visit to one of our regular hangouts, Graffiti's, we were hanging out as usual, relaxing. There was a Taiwanese girl there that we'd never seen before. She spoke English and began talking to us. It didn't take long to figure out that she was nuts. She told us that she had her own French restaurant and gave me her business card. I noticed that she was coming on to me. I was trying to be nice, but she was really weird, and I needed to get away from her, so I got up, grabbed Lance, and sat him in my chair next to her.

Lance didn't want to talk to her either. A little bit later, she said she was going to take Lance to see her restaurant. He didn't seem that sure about this. After they left, my mind started to play with me. I started thinking crazy thoughts. What if she was a Black Widow or something? Someone who goes to bars to pick up men and then takes them home, where she murders them?

I started to really wonder. I told Corey, and he agreed. After a few more minutes, I was very worried. Corey and I had to find Lance and save him. I had her business card in my pocket, but it was written in Chinese. So instead of looking for her place on our scooters, we got in a cab and showed the driver the business card. The driver said he wasn't exactly sure where that address was, but he could get us close.

We drove to a part of the city that wasn't familiar. Corey and I got out on this little dark road. It was around midnight. We looked at the numbers on the business card. The numbers stopped and didn't match where this place was supposed to be. We were starting to believe that her business card was a phony and that she was probably getting ready to kill Lance at any moment, if she hadn't already.

We walked back and forth on that street. Then we decided to go between two buildings where the address was supposed to be. We were walking by people's windows. Suddenly we popped out onto what looked like an alley. We walked up to several front doors to see if addresses matched. We knew we were going to freak someone out, thinking we were trying to break in. We checked several more buildings on this alley road. Finally, one address appeared to match ... but we weren't sure. We peeked inside the window. It looked like someone's home that could have been made into a small restaurant.

I knocked on the door, but nobody answered. I was afraid we were going to wake up some random family. As we were about to walk away, the crazy girl answered the door! It was a miracle we'd found the place. She was wondering why we were there, but she let us in. I was still worried until I saw Lance in a dining room upstairs. He was sitting at this big table all by himself. I walked up to him, glad that he was still alive, and I said "let's go." The strange girl was cooking some food and didn't want us to leave. She offered to make Corey and me something to eat too. My imagination didn't want me to stay, but we said we'd have an appetizer.

While she was cooking, she brought us out a bottle of wine. The food was good. She was weird, but not as crazy as my mind had convinced me to think. Finally, we thanked her and left, relieved.

Lance made it to the airport, got on the plane, and returned safely to Los Angeles. The following year, I had him fly the other direction and visit me in Italy. They say that in baseball, teammates become like family, and that's true. But nothing ever really beats the real thing, especially when baseball takes you across oceans.

Seven

The Replacements

I didn't want to travel overseas and be an ocean away from my family. I wanted a job with a big league organization in the good ol' US of A...or maybe Canada. I was running out of chances. Then something happened that rocked the baseball world and presented me with a golden opportunity. It was one I was absolutely *not* going to take.

You see, I was the perfect candidate.

I had big league experience, with a good measure of success. I was a free agent, and I was still active in the game. My name could maybe help sell some tickets.

I fit the profile of the perfect Major League Baseball "Replacement Player" in the spring of 1995.

But.... I wasn't having any part of that. No freakin' way.

As every fan knows, the 1994 Major League season was marred by a players' strike and subsequent owners' lockout that caused the cancellation of the 1994 World Series. The entire off-season was filled with arguing and bickering between the two sides who were supposed to be "negotiating." With those negotiations at a standstill, the Major League owners made plans to start the 1995 season using replacement players—or in more accurate terms, scabs—filling out big league rosters.

Here's how I got entangled in the mess ... and how it ended up sending me to Taiwan.

I spent the entire 1994 season in Mexico, first with Puebla and the second half with Campeche. I had a very good second half, and my agent, Chuck Berry (insert your own joke here), had set me up to finish the last three weeks of the minor league season with the Double A team of the Cleveland Indians in Akron, Ohio. I was excited. Cleveland seemed to still like me, since I had pitched for their Triple A team the previous season.

Then I got a phone call. It was from Reggie Waller, the scout who had signed me out of college and who was now the assistant general manager of the San Diego Padres.

There were rumors that the general manager of the Padres was going

Seven. The Replacements

to be let go after that season, and Reggie was more than likely the person to replace him. Reggie is also an African American, and at the time Major League Baseball was working to get more minorities in front office jobs. Reggie was more than qualified.

He told me he could sign me right then and that I'd have to start out in Double A Wichita. If things went well, in about 10 days, he'd try to move me to Triple A Las Vegas to get a couple of starts there to finish the season. Then the Padres would sign me to a Triple A contract for the 1995 season. He'd try to get me a Major League spring training non-roster invite, but he wasn't sure he could do that. Either way, I was going to get some exposure in front of the big league coaches.

This was the best possible news. At the very least, I'd have a job in AAA Las Vegas, and an opportunity, if I pitched well, of returning to the majors. When Reggie told me this, I was pumped up and immediately took the deal with the Padres. It was off to Wichita to finish out the rest of this minor league season ... and I had a job already for next year, so I wouldn't have to stress out or travel to Puerto Rico looking for a job over the winter. Most importantly, I wouldn't have to return to the Mexican League. The Padres would be a great opportunity for me with Reggie in my corner.

The team was in the middle of a series against Arkansas when I arrived in the middle of Kansas. I walked into the clubhouse, and some players were already there. They looked at me like, "Who is this old dude, and what's he doing here?" I was just 31 years old, but most of these guys were 21–24 years old, and they all looked very young to me. I made my way to manager Keith Champion's office. He was in there with the pitching coach, Rick Adair. The season before, Rick had been the Major League pitching coach for Cleveland. I introduced myself, but they both knew who I was. Rick remembered me from last year when I was in Charlotte, and the time we met in Cooperstown when I was supposed to pitch in the Hall of Fame Game. They told me that I'd be coming out in the bullpen, pitching in relief. I was fine with that. I figured it would be good for me to get an appearance or two in to get my touch back since I hadn't pitched in a game in over a week back in Mexico. I'd be ready for a start after that ... like Reggie said.

I'd only been in Double A Wichita for a few days when the Major League Players' Association strike happened on August 12. We knew it was coming, but I figured that, as in past strikes, it would only last a few days. Both sides had to see how bad this would be for baseball and come to a deal. I was surprised when it dragged on ... even more surprised to see the rest of the season canceled ... and downright shocked to see no World Series.

After that, it wasn't a surprise to see the ordeal last the entire off-season—there wasn't anything to lose until Opening Day. Surely they'd come to an agreement before spring training that would allow the season to start on time. No one would be stupid enough to blow an entire season and ruin professional baseball.

But that wasn't all the baseball news that shocked me. One morning shortly after I arrived in Wichita, I picked up a local newspaper. As I glanced over the sports page, I saw a headline that rocked my world. "*San Diego Padres Assistant General Manager Reggie Waller let go by the team.*"

I froze. After a few moments, I swallowed hard and read the story. I couldn't believe it. I was just talking to Reggie a few days ago. We had all these plans, I had someone backing me up in the front office, and he was supposed to be the general manager next year. After I got back to my hotel room, I called Reggie. He told me there were things going on there that he didn't like, and instead of just being quiet and saying nothing, he spoke out, and they let him go. We both knew he had a good chance of being the GM next year. We chatted a little more before I said good luck to Reggie and hung up the phone.

What a bummer for him … and for me.

I was still hoping that the Padres would offer me a contract for the following season, but that didn't happen. Not at first. When my short season in Wichita ended, I headed home ready to look for another job … and maybe even think more about winter ball again. Ugh.

As the off-season turned into winter, the owners and the players' union weren't getting anywhere in resolving the strike. The owners came up with a new and epically bad plan to put pressure on the players. They announced they were going to sign "replacement players" to take the place of real Major Leaguers. They'd have these scabs come into Major League spring training, put on Major League uniforms, and play Major League exhibition games … and prepare for Major League Opening Day.

Teams began to call former and recently retired big league and minor leaguers, along with current minor leaguers, to sign as replacement big leaguers. The owners offered $25,000 just to sign and cross the strike lines to play. Obviously, this was going to piss off the current Major Leaguers out on strike. The owners were going to put an inferior product on the field and expect fans to buy tickets to watch. Meanwhile, the real Major League players saw scab replacement players wearing their uniforms with their numbers and the scab replacement players' names on the back.

Of course, my phone began ringing. I was that perfect candidate. I got phone calls from nearly every Major League team—including my hometown Milwaukee Brewers—pretty much every day over the next several days. None of these teams had called me for the past two years. I wondered how they even had my phone number. Now my phone was ringing off the hook.

Seven. The Replacements

They weren't calling to offer me a major or minor league contract for the upcoming season. They were calling me to invite me to be a scab replacement player. Every team offered me the same $25,000 to sign. I'd get big league meal money during spring training, I'd work out with the other replacement players at the Major League spring training facility, and if the strike lasted into the Major League regular season, I would get a Major League minimum salary to play.

Tempting? Sure. But I told every single one of these teams the same thing: "Sorry, no thanks, I can't cross." I could not cross that imaginary—but very real—picket line and betray my former Major League teammates or the Players Association that had been pretty good to me. I knew that any player who crossed the line would be blackballed *forever*. People have long memories, and the union would hold a grudge. I turned down over 20 Major League teams with zero regret.

Just when I thought I wasn't going to get a chance at anything else, my phone rang again. It was the Atlanta Braves calling. I assumed they were going to offer me a replacement deal too. But they had a different approach. They said they *didn't* want to sign me as a replacement player; They wanted to have me as a veteran player on their Triple A team to help support their young roster of players. It was a chance for me to pitch and have an opportunity to get back to the big leagues as an experienced major leaguer if I did well.

It was a relief to know I had a team for next year and I could avoid all this strike stuff (or so I thought). The minor league director made me an offer and told me that if this strike were to end, I would be invited to the real big league spring training as a non-roster invitee. The Braves' minor league director told me to think about their offer and to call him back in a couple of days. I told Tami about the Braves' offer, and we were both excited and decided we'd accept it.

Just as I was preparing to call the Braves' minor league director back to accept their deal, my phone rang once again. On the other end was Pete Vukovich, an assistant to general manager Cam Bonifay of the Pittsburgh Pirates. I'd known Pete for a number of years. He was a former Cy Young Award winner for the Brewers. When I was traded from the Astros to Milwaukee, I was assigned to the Brewers' Triple A Vancouver team, and Pete and I were teammates briefly while he was in Vancouver working his way back from an injury. After he retired, Pete became the TV color analyst for the Brewers' broadcasts while I was pitching for Milwaukee. Vuke called me to offer me a minor league deal as well, just like the Braves had. He said I wasn't being asked to be a replacement player. He said the Pirates wanted to have me as a veteran player with Major League experience on their Triple A team. I told him I already had a deal in place with the Braves and that

I planned on calling them back and accepting it. He asked me how much money they offered me at the Major League and Minor League levels, and I told him. He said he'd match it. I told him I had a Major League spring training invite as a non-roster invitee when the strike was settled, and Pete said he'd match that too. I told him that I was *not* going to be a replacement player with the Braves, and Pete repeated that the Pirates weren't looking to sign me to be a replacement player, either.

I asked Pete if I could call him back, that I needed some time to think this out, and he agreed. I told Tami what Pete offered. So now it was between the Braves and the Pirates. They were both promising that they didn't want me as a scab replacement player. The money was the same. At the Major League level, the Atlanta Braves had a great pitching staff with Greg Maddux, Tom Glavine, John Smoltz (all future Hall of Famers), and Steve Avery. Not much of a chance of me breaking into that rotation, unless someone got hurt and I was pitching great in Triple A. Another plus for the Braves was that their Triple A team was in Richmond, Virginia, a hot, humid pitcher's park where my breaking pitches would be better.

At the Major League level, the Pirates' starting rotation was not nearly as good as the Braves' (nobody else's was at the time). I'd have a better chance to make the Pirates' staff. A negative with the Pirates was that their Triple A team was in Calgary, Alberta, Canada. Obviously it was really cold at the beginning of the season, and it was a hitter's park—the ball carried well there. But the biggest plus, the deciding factor, was that I would have Pete Vukovich, a friend, the assistant general manager, on my side. That made my decision.

I called Pete back and I accepted the Pirates' offer. Now that I had a contract, I could relax the rest of the off-season and didn't need to go to winter ball. Everyone, me included of course, was hoping that the owners and the players union would come to an agreement and end the strike before spring training. I wanted to go to Major League spring training, but if this continued to linger, there wouldn't be a Major League spring training, and I'd go to a minor league spring training while the game itself was stuck in a big mess.

A day or so after I signed my contract with Pittsburgh, I was watching the news on TV at home in Milwaukee. The sports came on, and the sportscaster announced that former Milwaukee Brewers pitcher Don August has just signed a deal with the Pittsburgh Pirates to be a replacement player. I was caught off-guard and stunned. It was wrong, *I wasn't a replacement player*, but now it was announced on TV that I was. I was worried that the Major League Players' Association and the players would be mad as hell at me. Professional athletes don't look kindly on people who cross that line. I didn't want to be blackballed over something that wasn't true.

Seven. The Replacements

I immediately called the TV station and asked to speak to Steve "the Homer" True, the local sportscaster who announced this. I told him he made a big mistake, and he needed to go back on the air and recant it. He said he couldn't because he wouldn't be back on the air until the next day. He said he would recant the story on his radio show. I felt like the damage was done and that perhaps this was going to hurt me over time.

The rest of the winter flew by, and the owners and the players' union still didn't make a deal. I was going to minor league spring training, and the Major League spring training would be for the replacement players. Off to Florida I would go, diving into baseball's big mess.

At first, all of the players were there together working out, the replacement players with the Major League invitees, nobody knew who was who, until one day the replacement players went to the big-league facility, and the invitees stayed at the minor league facility. The replacement players would train to get ready for the exhibition games. Since I was an invitee to Major League spring training, the Pirates paid me big league meal money while I was there in minor league camp.

Things began to get testy at that point. The Players Association put out a statement to all players: "Do Not Cross the Lines!" Most of the "big league" replacement players (scabs) didn't have big league experience. Most of the guys who did, such as myself, said "No" to crossing the line.

A lot of the guys who did cross acted like they were big shots, even though they were scabs. I knew a few of them, and they were all right guys who did it for the bonus money, hoping the strike would be resolved and then they could go home with the money. But there were guys in those positions who got the big heads, thinking they were actual big league players. They would talk crap.

We'd run into them on a few occasions. They wore their Pittsburgh Pirates jackets out to the bars, wanting people to notice them, particularly the girls. It was so "Joe College." They were getting big league meal money, so they felt like they were big leaguers being big spenders at a local bar. Those of us who refused to cross, real current and former major leaguers, saw them as a bunch of wannabe dumb asses. We had to watch and listen to their dumb shit.

I was still clinging to hope that the strike would end, and I'd get the chance to go to the real Major League spring training, where I could impress the coaches and perhaps be a long shot at making the team. I was there working hard every day. All the Major League teams had scab replacement players except the Baltimore Orioles, whose owner said he wasn't going to do that. My good friend from the Brewers, Mark Lee, was with the Orioles then and said it was great not to have that problem.

Despite what I was wishing for, things actually got worse.

Before the replacement games started, Pirates GM Cam Bonifay called a meeting for the non-roster invitees. Most of us were former Major Leaguers: Todd Frohwirth, whom I knew from the Milwaukee area; Mackie Sasser, a roommate and teammate from Puerto Rico; Dale Sveum and George Canale, former teammates with the Milwaukee Brewers; Sam Horn, my teammate in Charlotte; Luis Mercedes; Matt Maysey; Nelson Simmons; Randy St. Claire; and Jay Baller, just to name a few. In Bonifay's meeting, he told us that just like in any other spring training, the Major League team could call up guys from the minor league camp to play in a game that day, so he said that if they needed a player, we should have no problem doing it.

Ah. There it was. The actual reason for signing all of us to "minor league deals" was to have us available when they didn't have enough decent scab players to compete. Even though we weren't specifically signed to *be* replacement players, the front office knew all along they were going to ask us—expect us—to cross the line.

Of course, we had a problem with it. We'd be replacement players, crossing the strike line. I thought to myself, "Vukovich said I wasn't going to be used as a replacement player." Bonifay told us that if we refused to play, we would get punished and probably get released. I was still not going to cross, but now I was put in a position where I could get released because of that. Bonifay added, "We're not saying we will for sure ask you, but if we do, we expect you to do it, and if anybody here has a fucking problem with that, then let me know in the next couple of days! If I don't hear anything from you, then I can expect you will do it."

The meeting ended, and we left feeling like we were being sucked deeper into this mess. That night, I called Vukovich and told him what Bonifay said. Vuke replied, "I guess he can do that." I told him, "You told me I was brought here to not have to do that." All he could say was, "That's the way it is." I hung up with Vuke, and I was pissed off at him. This *wasn't* what my deal was.

We'd all been played over the winter. Simple as that. My guess is that Vuke got misled, too. And I'm sure the offer I got from the Atlanta Braves would have worked out exactly the same way. It's easy to see why teams would want to do this. They didn't like the replacement player crap any more than we did, but they had to make plans to work around it. Having some experienced guys at Triple A would be a safety net for them.... *if* we'd cross.

The next day, I went to Bonifay's office to let him know where I stood. When I walked in, he looked up at me with a big smile on his face as if expecting to like what he would hear. Instead, I told him not to pick me to pitch in a replacement game because I wasn't going to do it. That was

Seven. The Replacements

not part of my deal with his team. The smile quickly left his face. He was now a bit angry, telling me that I'd still be in the minor league camp and if they needed me, they would ... and if I declined, I knew the consequences. I said okay, and I left his office. I hoped this damned strike would end so that I wouldn't have to deal with any more of this garbage.

Several Major League Players Association meetings were scheduled in Florida. These meetings were for all minor league players to attend and get the inside information from the union execs about the negotiations. They wanted to let the minor league players know what the union expected from them. It would be a meeting to get answers. A lot of minor league players were being squeezed in the middle, especially about playing in replacement games.

We heard there was a meeting in Tampa, so a few of us decided to go. The meeting was held in a big banquet room, and there were a lot of players there. My guess is that over 400 were in attendance. Guys wanted answers. The Players Association had an executive there, I don't remember if it was Donald Fehr, Gene Orza, or someone else. There were also a few current Major League players on hand to speak on behalf of the Union. Wally Joyner was one of them. They gave us an update on the current situation and told us in no uncertain terms, "Do not cross the lines."

As a loyal, dues-paying member of this union for a number of years, my loyalty was solid. But I have to admit, this was not our union's finest hour, either. A few of the players in the audience spoke up about the consequences of being released if we were asked to play in a replacement game and refused. The union reps told everybody that since we were all minor

Newspaper column on replacement players by Mark Knudson.

leaguers and not under a Major League contract, they couldn't help us. So basically the message was, "don't cross … but we can't help you when you get released." That was not well received.

Another guy stood up and asked, "what about us former Major League players who have been with the union? What can you do for us? We paid union dues, and you kept some of our licensing money." They again said they couldn't do anything at that time. The player said, "So you don't want us to cross … but when we get released, you still can't do anything?" The exec said yes, that was the case.

I thought to myself that this was a bunch of bullshit! I thought about all the money the union kept from my licensing money, around $32,000, during my last year in the Major Leagues. They kept that money supposedly to give to *me* in case of a work stoppage that would linger a long time. It was to be used for costs to represent us in a strike … but now that appeared to be only if you were currently on a major league contract. They were using my money, but they still couldn't help me when I needed it?

Joyner got up to speak. He also told the guys to not cross the lines, that there would be consequences. He said he understood our positions, but we had to work together, or the strike would never get resolved. Some players from the audience said they were former big leaguers trying to get back to the Majors, just like myself, and that we needed some help. Wally's reply wasn't very good. He basically said guys like us should just quit trying to make it back … that if we weren't in the major leagues right now, our careers were pretty much over anyway. He didn't say it exactly like that, but that was the message. It was a piss-poor answer.

There were a lot more questions and no good answers. The message was consistent: Don't cross. All the minor league players left the meeting still unsure what to do. We were caught in the middle, and there was nobody to help us … yet both sides were warning us of consequences. That seemed fair. Not.

Spring training moved along, and we were approaching the end with no deal between the owners and players. If the strike wasn't resolved, then the owners were going to use replacement players. Minor league seasons would start on time either way. I was expecting to make the AAA team, especially if I had Pete Vukovich on my side. As a bonus, so far Bonifay hadn't asked anyone to come up and play as replacements in a spring training games, which was a relief.

The fans were upset with all this strike business, but they were coming out to those replacement spring training games, and the players who did cross and play were still acting like big shots.

I was scheduled to pitch against the White Sox's Triple A team. I was looking forward to it because Michael Jordan was in spring training with

Seven. The Replacements

the White Sox, preparing for his second professional baseball season. The previous year, 1994, he played the entire season in the minor leagues during the period when he quit basketball and decided to pursue a professional baseball career.

When our bus arrived at the White Sox complex in Sarasota, there were a lot of news trucks all over. Something big was happening. I thought maybe the baseball strike was settled. Nope, the strike was not settled ... but Jordan had announced that he was returning to the NBA. That turned the sports world upside-down. I was really disappointed that I didn't get to pitch against him. I read later that Jordan said one of the reasons he gave up on his baseball dream was due to the baseball strike. He said he felt he was being dragged into the middle of it ... being asked to be a replacement player. Imagine that. We all felt his pain.

Finally on April 2, the owners and the players' union settled, and the work stoppage was over. It was decided that the real Major League spring training would be extended by three weeks. This would allow the Major Leaguers to show up at their spring training sites and get ready for the regular season, pushing back Opening Day to late April. It would save the season. The minor league spring training was to end within the week, and the minor league baseball season would start on time.

While I was very happy things were settled, the timing sucked for me. During this new Major League spring training, the Pirates wouldn't bring up their non-roster invitees. I was one of those non-roster invitees that wasn't going to get a chance now. Only two non-roster players got a chance with the Pittsburgh Pirates—Todd Frohwirth and Mackey Sasser.

I finished out the minor league camp, and now I had to worry about making the Triple A Calgary team. I wasn't worried at first, but when I came to the minor league complex one morning, some minor league guys were gone ... released. They were called into the office and let go that morning. The reason made a lot of us very angry. There were five or six replacement scab players in the locker room in their place. It came out that some of the replacement players had made deals with the owners, that if they agreed to be replacement players, when the strike was settled, they'd be guaranteed jobs on the Triple A team for the regular season.

This meant that some better minor league players who didn't cross lost *their* jobs to these guys for the entire season, not just on a temporary basis. That part didn't get a lot of media attention at the time, but it was one of the shittier things to come out of the whole, ugly ordeal.

It was decided that when the Major League season started, every team would start out with a 27-man roster, rather than the usual 25 for the first couple of weeks. It was also decided to begin the Triple A teams with 27-man rosters too, and these would be reduced to 25-man rosters a couple of weeks into the season. This meant that most of us were starting the season in tryout mode.

To finish the last three days of minor league camp was going to be uncomfortable with the replacement players mixed with the guys who didn't cross, especially us former Major League union members. Before we had our first official workout as the Triple A Calgary club, manager Bobby Meacham called a meeting. He said, "everybody in this locker room will begin the season on the team." I was relieved to know that I'd made the team and wouldn't be released before the season started. I found out a couple of the guys who didn't cross had made deals to play in the Mexican League on a team the Pirates had a working agreement with. I was sad they had to go, but I was glad I wasn't going back to Mexico.

Meacham wanted to have a single gathering where everybody had a chance to speak and get the whole replacement player issue off their chest. We would each get to say what needed to be said, and that would be it. No more issues afterward. There was some serious tension in the air. One of the players who had refused to cross began by saying that a few of the guys who got released didn't deserve to. They'd been cut to make room for the replacements only because of the team's replacement deals. No one thought that was fair.

Then one of the players who did cross, Boi Rodriguez, whom I'd been teammates with in Puerto Rico, responded. He said he crossed because he wanted another chance to play in the United States, and he didn't want to go back to the Mexican League. He said, "For you guys who never played in the Mexican League, you don't want to go down there and play, it's hard. I know some of you guys here are mad at me, and I understand. But that was my reason for my decision."

I knew Boi and I liked him, along with a few of the other replacement players. I was still upset about what they did. I didn't want to go back to the Mexican League either. It would have been easy to take $25K. But I didn't. I just couldn't let my former Major League teammates down, or the players' union (which would pay me a nice pension beginning at age 45), and I didn't want to ruin my name.

I know Meacham and everyone else wanted the whole episode to be put in the rearview mirror, but it was never going to be that easy. For years to come, the union and Major League players held grudges against those replacement players. Years later, some guys who had been replacement players would have an opportunity to get called up, but they hit a big roadblock: On some occasions, the MLB players would tell their GMs that they wouldn't play with a former replacement player. The replacement player literally had to get back on the airplane and return to the minors. Those who did make it to the Major Leagues were shunned by teammates.

Seven. The Replacements 117

That was part of the cost of crossing the line.

At our meeting, more guys spoke out about how mad they were over the replacement players, while most of the replacement players said they did it for the money. One of my former Brewers teammates, Dale Sveum—a future big league manager—was one of the most vocal. Dale said, "Yeah, I'm still pissed off," again restating how guys who deserved better had been released. He went on for a while, venting and getting everything off his chest. Everyone had the opportunity to speak, although not everyone did. When the meeting came to an end, Meacham said, "Okay, that's it, I don't want to ever hear anything else about this again!" He should have been so lucky.

A couple of days later, we broke camp and flew to Tucson, Arizona, where we'd open the Pacific Coast League season. Everyone knew there were more cuts to come when the rosters had to be reduced to 25. We had a veteran minor league team with guys who had played a lot of years and had big league experience. I was told I would begin the season in the starting rotation. I knew I had to pitch really good to stay on the team after the roster trickle-down began.

It was fun starting the season back in Tucson, where I'd played nine years before. My first start there lasted just four innings, but I did okay. I was taken out for a pinch-hitter. Meacham told me he needed to get someone an at-bat, and it got another pitcher an inning. Then it was off to Scottsdale.

During the bus ride, one of our pitchers, Will Flynt, was telling us that he had played in Taiwan in their professional baseball league, and what it was like playing there. It sounded pretty ... different. He said in Taiwan they were paying some players up to $100,000 a year, which none of us could believe. As we got to know Will, he seemed like a guy telling big stories that seemed far-fetched. He said that if any of us went there to play, to be careful. There were some teams you'd really want to play for, and one team you'd want to stay away from. That was the team he played on ... the name escaped me at the time. He also told us that in Taiwan, if somebody accidentally hit someone with their car, they wouldn't go back to help, but rather go back to run the person over again to kill them ... because it was cheaper to kill someone and pay off the family than to keep the person alive and pay for their bills and everything else for the rest of their lives. Farfetched, right? It sounded crazy to me ... even after I'd already sucked up a lot of crazy in Mexico.

As fate would have it, before I got to make my second start against the Giants in Scottdale, I got a call I wasn't expecting. Reggie Waller was on the phone. We'd last spoken when I was in Wichita, after he'd been let go as the San Diego Padres' assistant general manager. Reggie told me he could get me a job pitching in ... wait for it ... Taiwan.

There was an owner of a team there who wanted me, he said. It was surprising to hear that somebody in Taiwan would specifically want me. I told Reggie that I was in Triple A with the Pirates and planned to stay there. He said he understood that, and that he wasn't saying he expected me to be released, but … if something happened, I could give him a call. I said fine and hung up. My plan was 100 percent to stay in the United States and make it back to the Major Leagues. I wasn't *planning* on going around the world to Asia to play.

In my next start against the Triple A Giants, I felt like I pitched well again. Yet again, after I pitched the fourth inning, I was taken out for a pinch-hitter. It was a duplicate of my first game: four innings with two runs, and again I took the loss. I was starting to feel nervous because I needed to have some good games with the roster cuts coming.

When we got back to Calgary, Meacham and pitching coach Wayne Garland told me I wasn't going to start on my next turn, I was going to the bullpen. They'd let me know when I might start again. This was a bad omen. Sitting in the bullpen, freezing, hoping and waiting to get a chance to pitch. After the first few home games, I hadn't gotten into one.

Right about this time, Major League spring training was coming to an end. Roster changes were coming. I wasn't starting anymore, and I hadn't gotten into a game in relief yet. All this made me really nervous, especially since we had replacement players with guaranteed deals.

I was walking on pins and needles for the next two days. Finally, after a day game, I was called into the manager's office. I knew what this meant. I walked in, and Meacham was sitting at his desk, with Garland and the Pirates' minor league pitching coordinator. Bobby didn't waste any time, he just flat-out told me that the Pirates were releasing me. Wayne told me he wished I could stay, that I wasn't pitching badly. There were guys coming down tomorrow and room had to be made.

I kept thinking about the deal I thought I had with Pete Vukovich … the one where I was being signed to be a veteran player on this Triple A team, and I had someone covering my back. I thought about how I could have signed with the Atlanta Braves, but Pete lured me away from that job.

That night after the game, a few of the guys wanted to take me out for beers. While we were at the bar, the Pirates' minor league pitching coordinator came in. He was actually a pretty funny guy, so I decided to talk to him.

I flat-out asked him why I got released. He told me that nobody in the Pirates' minor league system is considered a big league prospect unless he throws 95 miles per hour. Velocity mattered more than being able to pitch. I reminded him that on the Calgary team, we only had one guy on the staff who threw that hard, and he was getting beat up every time he pitched. I

Seven. The Replacements

asked, "Is he the only pitching prospect on our team?" He shrugged and said, "Yeah."

I had to follow up. "So.... Greg Maddux wouldn't be considered a pitching prospect, or have a chance in this organization?"

He didn't have an answer for that.

I flew out the next day, and I was back in Milwaukee. Pitching in just two games hadn't been a fair opportunity. Now I had to find a job with another team, and I didn't have an agent since I'd cut ties with Chuck Berry. Professional baseball in America was a mess. Major League teams still had expanded rosters, so in a couple of weeks, more players would be sent down. Then the Triple A teams would be trimmed down to 25-man rosters too. I'd learned the hard way over the past three years that guys without baseball jobs in April don't get called about minor league openings until mid- or late May. With the current mess and the backlog of player movement that was still to come, it might be June or July before anything opened up. I was looking at a lost year.

I told Tami about Reggie Waller calling me about Taiwan. I thought maybe I'd give that a try … go to Taiwan, maybe make some real money like Will Flynt had said. I could go see another part of the world and see what baseball was like in Asia.

Plus, there was no way I wanted to go back to Mexico.

In a strange way, it turned out that it was the 1994 work stoppage in MLB—and my refusal to become a replacement player—that sent me on my journey to the Far East. Little did I know what awaited me … for the next five years of my life.

A few months later, on my 32nd birthday, I was talking to Tami from Taiwan. She told me I'd gotten a birthday present from the Major League Baseball Players Association. I got my check from the union, the money they'd held onto in case of a strike. It was for about $12,000 … out of the $32,000 of mine that they'd kept in the "Strike Fund." The fund was established so they could pay active players during the work stoppage so that they wouldn't crumble and give in to the owners.

The union I'd stood up for never paid any players like me any money during the strike that I know of. I never saw one cent of the $32K before they sent me a portion of it. The money went to the lawyers and to the expenses of resolving the strike. This kind of pissed me off. The union couldn't help me by giving *me* any installments like they said they would, and they couldn't find a way to help us former Major Leaguers who were put in the middle of the replacement mess. it felt like the longer the strike lasted, the more money the lawyers made.

More of the bad side of the business of baseball.

Eight

Ramblin' Gamblin' Man

Business is business in all walks of life, but money was never *the* reason I wanted to play in the big leagues, so paying an agent to help me find a job was something I had no problem doing. Problem is, when you aren't in the show or on the fast track to get there, you don't get a lot of attention from agents, either. When things aren't going all that smoothly for you on the business side, you can end up in some not-so-safe situations.

Even before I headed out of the country to play for the first time, I'd been in a few scrapes. I'd escaped them all. So I had that going for me, which was nice.

You don't see a lot of violent or even potentially violent stuff happen around baseball in America … unless you consider the occasional bench-clearing brawl as some sort of criminal act. I was in a few of those during my time in the bigs. Memorable but never potentially fatal. The best one is still on YouTube—when I was with the Brewers, we had an all-timer with the Seattle Mariners in the Kingdome. Lasted for like 20 minutes.

There were no guns involved.

I did have a teammate with the Brewers, Julio Machado, whom I saw carrying a gun. We were getting on an elevator at a hotel in Milwaukee at the start of the 1991 season when we noticed that Julio was packing more than his baseball gear.

I didn't think much about it until the news broke the following off season that Julio had been arrested and charged with murdering a Venezuelan woman. The news account read this way:

> *Machado faces two charges of "intentional murder" and one charge of illegal possession of a handgun in connection with the December 8, 1991 shooting death of Edicta Vasquez after a late-night traffic accident in the western Venezuelan city of Barquisimeto.*
>
> *Machado, 23, was transferred from a police holding cell to a prison and was not available for comment. Machado was playing for the Zulia Eagles of the Venezuelan winter league at the time of the incident and admitted to firing a shot. But he claims he shot in self-defense and did not intend to kill anyone.*

Julio was convicted and sentenced to 12 years in prison. Sad story.

I came to learn that carrying a loaded weapon was more common in Latin American countries than it was in the U.S. back then. Of course, today "open carry" is allowed in a lot of states, and I'd guess that more than a few pro athletes are doing so these days. Even standout athletes get fearful of their surroundings and feel like they need added protection.

I did see things that caught my attention during my playing days *outside* the USA.

I had that winter ball stint in the Dominican Republic when I was fortunate enough to be teammates with the great MLB catcher, Tony Peña. He was an awesome teammate. Once, after a road game, we returned to Santiago on the team bus. As we were pulling into the parking lot of our stadium, Tony came up to me and said he and his brother, Arturo, plus infielder Felix Fermin, were going out on the town and invited me along. It was kind of late at night, but since Tony was asking, I said, "Sure." We piled into Tony's truck, and out of the parking lot we went. They said there were a few good places we could go check out, but they had one place in mind.

We drove down the main street a little way and turned down a side road. We drove a little longer on that road until we made a left turn onto a dark dirt road. I was getting curious. I saw something run across the road. I asked, "What was that?" Someone said that it was a wild pig. Now I'm thinking, "Where are we going where there are wild pigs running across the roads?" As we went up a little further, I saw a building up to the left with some cars in the little parking lot. As we approached the parking lot, it was blocked with a crossing rail.

We stopped, and I saw a guy running toward the truck with a shotgun in his hands. I'm thinking, "What is this?" Tony rolled his window down and said something to the guy in Spanish, and the guy pulled the guard rail up and let us in. Tony parked the truck … but before we got out, I saw Tony, Arturo, and Felix putting guns in their waistbands and socks, and Arturo was putting a knife into his pocket. I asked, "What the hell kind of place are you guys taking me to?"

"Don't worry," Felix said. "We just have to be careful."

I instantly thought of the right response: "Then where is *my* gun?"

Arturo said, "You don't need one."

Not comforting at all.

I thought, "What do I do if a gun fight breaks out in this place? What then?" Once everyone—except me—was done packing their heat, we strolled into the place like we owned it. Everything looked normal. We made our way up to the bar to get drinks. I couldn't stop thinking that this place *looked* like a nice bar … but I remained on alert for the possible gun fight to break out any second. Nothing bad happened, and we enjoyed our night out. Go figure.

I don't remember any of my other teammates carrying loaded guns around, but we still needed to be careful in certain situations, especially as Americans in a foreign country. You always had to be on guard. We could be targets, or we could just be in the wrong place at the wrong time.

Even a good old-fashioned street party could get out of hand. My first Cinco de Mayo in Mexico was a day to remember. Puebla was my home city, and that's where the famous battle of Puebla, Cinco de Mayo, occurred with the French in 1862. So the people of Puebla *really* take to the celebration. It started out a happy, festive day ... just as you'd expect. But when the sun went down, the atmosphere got even more ... umm ... festive, and we noticed there seemed to be fewer kids and families around. Then some people began throwing things, people started to stand on parked cars, pushing in groups, and little fires were set in the streets and on the sidewalks.

Things started to get bigger, and the scene became more aggressive. This all happened in a short time. With my family there visiting, I was in protection mode. Tami, Logan, Eileen, and I made our way in front of our hotel to watch this take place right before our eyes. As it continued to escalate, someone from the hotel came out and told us to come inside because they were going to shut and lock all the doors. We went up to our room and to the window facing the street. This was starting to turn into a riot.

We kept watching until the telephone rang. The front desk told me that we needed to close the shutters because we'd become targets for the crazy people on the street to throw things at. They might even attack and storm the hotel. I closed the window but kept it slightly cracked open so I could watch. Tami and Eileen took turns watching too. Suddenly I saw these big trucks loaded with riot police storm the road. I don't know how they didn't hit someone. The riot police jumped out quickly with their riot gear on, with clubs and shields, and formed a line. They yelled something out to the people and then charged into the crowd, knocking down anybody who was in the way. The crowd backed off a little, and a second truck arrived. They marched toward the crowd, breaking it up while things were thrown at them. The police were shoving people hard; it got wild and pretty intense. Things like this were happening everywhere in the Centro, and it went on for a long time.

Eventually the crowd broke up and cleared out. The police were able to leave. The next morning, I walked out in front of the hotel, and it looked as if nothing ever happened. Maybe some remnants, but the area was back to normal.

While the Cinco de Mayo celebration was planned, and the police were at the ready, you never know exactly how something like a sporting

Eight. Ramblin' Gamblin' Man

event, followed by passionate sports fans, will turn out and what the reaction will be on the streets.

For instance, the people of Mexico follow their local soccer teams intensely. We were on the road in Torreon, where the Torreon soccer team was playing a big game that day. All the people in Torreon were wearing the team's colors, had face paint on, and drove their cars with the windows painted up with support up and down the main street right in front of our hotel. There were a lot of cars driving in circles around the streets. At some point, the soccer game ended, and the Torreon team won. Now everyone wanted to celebrate. More people came out onto the streets, and it quickly became very crowded.

When there are a lot of people on the streets with alcohol, it gets pretty crazy. After our day game, I decided to walk by myself from the team hotel to get something to eat. When I returned, I was maybe a mile away, and I was having a hard time walking through the crowd. When I got to within about four blocks of the hotel, stuff got *real*.

People were beginning to throw things, like bricks and rocks and whatever else they could get their hands on. It reminded me of the Cinco de Mayo scene from the season before. There were little fires being set in the street and on the sidewalks. People were getting aggressive and shoving, and of course there were fights breaking out. A lot of this was happening right in front of our hotel. It wasn't safe for me to try to get to the hotel, so I stayed about two blocks away, where I felt safe. I just sat there, witnessing the craziness.

Soon enough, several trucks with police wearing riot gear arrived. It took several minutes before they regained control of the street. When I saw an opening to get to the hotel, I ran to the front door and saw some teammates inside. Made it through that, too.

It didn't always take a holiday or special event for things to turn dangerous in Mexico. A place like Mexico City—the second-largest city in the world—had enough going on even without something unusual lighting a fuse. Everyone knows to be careful there. It's a big place with a lot to do, but every day can be dangerous. You could be mugged and robbed on the street. We heard stories of people or families being robbed right on the street. They said thieves came up to them and made them strip naked on the street, and they had everything taken from them at gunpoint, leaving them standing there with no clothes. One day a teammate came into the locker room collecting money because friends of his had come to Mexico City to watch him play and were robbed on the street, just like that.

Mexico City is a big place, and a lot of things go on there, good and bad. It seemed like every time I was there, something different happened. One night, our bus was driving through the city. It was late, and it seemed unusually dark. There was traffic—a backup on a main street, which was a little unusual for this time of day. As we crept closer, we could see the flashing lights of police cars. The two lanes broke down into one, while the other was closed off. As our bus slowly moved by the spot, I saw a young dead woman lying on the street with a huge puddle of blood around her. It was really terrible. I wondered why she wasn't covered up. There were a lot of people walking around her, plus the traffic with people in the cars able to see everything. It seemed like nobody was doing anything while she just lay there dead. Try getting that image out of your head.

Another time I was walking on a street in Mexico City, just looking around, not paying much attention, when I suddenly noticed five guys running toward me with automatic rifles and wearing bulletproof vests. I froze as they made eye contact with me. Then they ran right past me into the front door of a bank I was standing in front of. I looked down the street and saw an armored car coming. Turned out they were coming to get the money out of the bank and hurry it into the armored car before anyone with bad intentions showed up. That's not something you see every day in front of the First National Bank of Wauwatosa, Wisconsin.

Sometimes guns aren't necessarily what makes a situation difficult at best ... and dangerous at worst. I don't honestly know if anyone had guns when two teammates and I wandered upon what appeared to be an anti-American rally in Puebla.

Protests in America are nothing new. But I guess it still surprised me to see it up close and personal. We were about three-quarters of the way back to our hotel when we saw that up ahead of us, the street was blocked off. Some sort of political rally was going on, and we were going to walk through it. But as we got closer, we heard the voice on a loudspeaker saying something about Americanos ... and not in a nice way. We stopped in our tracks and looked at each other. We had heard Americanos but didn't know what was being said. Then we heard Americanos again. That's when we decided to turn around, walk back a block, and go the long way around this rally to get back to our hotel safely. We weren't the targets, but we sure could have ended up in the wrong place at the wrong time.

I saw even more political protests in Taiwan. They weren't targeted at us either, but they weren't as easy to avoid.

During my second year in Taiwan, tensions with mainland China were escalating (much as they have been more recently). The presidential elections were a big thing in the news ... and in the streets. Everywhere you went, you saw campaigning. There were big gatherings everywhere all the time. Candidates would be outside with huge speakers turned up to 11. You could literally hear them blocks and blocks away. One presidential candidate was pushing for Taiwan's independence, and that was making China extremely upset.

Eight. Ramblin' Gamblin' Man

For the prior two decades, China had been sticking to the policy from President Richard Nixon's historic 1973 meeting in China: One country with two systems. There was the People's Republic of China (PRC)—the mainland—and there was the ROC—the Republic of China—or Taiwan as we call it. Hence the name of our league, the Chinese Professional Baseball League.

There were rumors that China might invade Taiwan militarily. When we were at our practice field working out during this time, about every 10 minutes we'd see a Taiwanese fighter jet screaming by, patrolling the coast, one after another all day long, every day. These jets went by so fast that when you looked up, they were already gone. The jets were ahead of the sound. This made a lot of people nervous, including me and my American teammates. I believed at the time that there was a decent chance I would have to put down my glove and pick up a rifle sometime very soon. We could end up in the middle of a war.

This news was so disturbing that a good number of the American professional basketball players playing in the Taiwan pro league left and went home. Every day that passed, more and more tension was building with China.

As the presidential election got closer and closer, the tensions increased. I was still hearing about the possible threat of invasion. I asked one of my Taiwanese teammates about an invasion or war, and he said, "Don't worry. China always says that, but they never do it." I said, "There's a first time for everything."

At practice, we continued to see and hear the warplanes patrolling. Towards the end of our training, the team went to Kaohsiung to play some exhibition games. I wasn't feeling any less nervous about the whole invasion thing when one day I went out to eat lunch by myself. After lunch, I was walking back toward our hotel. I was on a major street that was very busy at this time, with heavy traffic and people walking around everywhere, just like New York City.

Suddenly a loud siren went off, like a loud tornado siren. People immediately began emptying the streets, going into the nearest buildings. I'm thinking this is it! The Chinese army is here, and they aren't taking any prisoners. Someone on the street actually grabbed me and pulled me into the door of what looked like a dress shop. The door closed, and it was full of people who'd just come in off the street. Everybody just stood there for what seemed like forever, even though it was probably 20–30 minutes. I didn't know what was going on, but the more I thought about it, the more I believed that the Chinese invasion had begun.

It turned out it was an air raid *practice* in case the Chinese *did* invade. Obviously, the people of Taiwan were taking this stuff very seriously. It was weird to see these completely busy streets turn into a ghost town in seconds.

As the people went back outside, the streets went back to the usual chaos. We continued to hear about a Chinese buildup of soldiers just on the other side of the Taiwan Strait. The Chinese military was conducting what they called "war exercises" in the international waters just off the coast of Taiwan with their Navy and Air Force. They were practicing shooting live rockets that were very close to the Taiwan waters. It was an intimidation tactic, and it was working. I was intimidated.

According to international law, countries were allowed to come close by to observe other countries' war exercises. The United States, a great ally of Taiwan with lots of common interests, sent the entire *USS Nimitz* fleet to observe. This upset the Chinese even more, claiming the U.S. was "escalating the tensions." We continued to hear more and more about foreigners leaving (fleeing?) Taiwan. I heard that if there was an invasion, the U.S. military would get all Americans out. We were supposed to check in with the AIT (the American Institute in Taiwan), a pseudo embassy, to inform them where we were staying in case something did happen. Was that supposed to make me feel better? Remember what happened at the American embassy in Iran?

Finally, the elections came and ended, and once they were over, tensions slowly died down. There was no more campaigning or speeches on the streets, no more election tension with China, it all just faded away. But in my mind, we had come *this close* to going to war.

The rest of my time in Taiwan, the threats were more ... subtle, but I took them just as seriously. You were in a very different place, with a different culture. It was easy to accidentally upset people even if you didn't mean to. Sometimes that meant you could not just be yourself while you were out in public.

One night, a few teammates and I were out on the town, and one of them, Daryl Smith, came running back inside the bar all excited, saying there were a bunch of Taiwanese guys outside that were going to beat up him and another teammate, Elcilio DeLeon.

"What are you talking about?" I asked. Daryl said he and Elcilio went outside to get a cab, and when they were at the curb, a scooter with a couple of guys came by them real close and Elcilio yelled at them. A couple of minutes later, a bunch of these Taiwanese guys returned with weapons in their hands.

When the rest of us went out the door to look, there were around ten of them holding boards, rocks, sticks, rods, and other things in their hands, and they were staring at us angrily. "What's the problem?", we asked. They replied, "This is Taiwan!" We already knew that, but okay....

It felt like if we walked out to find a cab, we would get attacked. A lady bartender came out and said something to them in Chinese, and they yelled back. She went back in to call us two cabs, and then we waited—while these guys continued standing there staring at us.

When the taxis arrived, we walked out through the crowd to get to the cabs. This group of locals just stood there and stared. I thought this was when they'd attack, but they didn't. We got in the cabs and drove off.

We took moments like that seriously because we'd heard stories that when a foreign person gets into an altercation with a Taiwanese person, the Taiwanese person leaves and returns with a whole bunch of friends, and they proceed to beat the crap out of the foreigner. As we were pulling away in our cabs, I looked back and saw two bunches of Taiwanese guys with weapons arriving outside the bar from two different directions. It looked like there were at least 20 more of them. We probably got out of there in the nick of time. I think the guys out front were just waiting for their reinforcements to show up, then they'd have had us badly outnumbered and could have crushed us. It was surprising that there were so many locals around at four in the morning who could be called to show up like that over a quick verbal altercation. In the years to come, we did hear about other foreign baseball players who did get ganged up on and beaten up.

You could call those loose gangs "un-organized" crime. They were just groups of friends who had each other's backs obviously, even if they did get offended far too easily. Most of us wouldn't let something like being yelled at for coming close to hitting someone on a scooter grounds for a full-scale brawl.

Other threats were not quite so open. But they could be even more dangerous.

It was my second season in Taiwan when we first heard rumors about players being involved with organized crime and gambling on CPBL games. Word was that bookmakers and gangsters were getting involved in trying to fix the outcome of games. They were allegedly getting key players to throw games or not to win by more than a certain number of runs.

At the time, our team was losing a lot, so teammate Tony Metoyor decided we were going to watch closely to see if this was happening on our team. As we began watching carefully, it looked like it might be the case. I remember after we blew a game late one night, Tony got really pissed, and in our dugout, he angrily screamed out, "I hope nobody is gambling!" Nobody said anything, everyone just remained quiet.

We weren't the only ones wondering. With the team playing badly, our coach and GM were putting outrageous curfews on the team when we were on the road. It was now set at 8:30 p.m. I think these curfews were put in place not only because we were playing poorly, but with the rumors of gambling, it was also to deter the guys from running into the gangsters and getting connected with gambling.

There were lots of rumors. I wasn't sure, or maybe I was just hoping that they weren't true. The first time I got really suspicious was when I was pitching late in a game. I threw a good pitch, the hitter just chopped at it, and it was one of those swinging bunts that rolled slowly down the third base line. It was starting to roll foul before our third baseman grabbed it while it was just barely fair at the very last second. It was exactly the wrong thing to do. The hitter was easily safe without a throw.

Our third baseman was one of our foreign players, Hector De La Cruz. He acted like he'd made a blunder. Everyone knew the ball was going foul. I walked over to him and asked why he picked it up. I looked into his eyes, and I saw his expression. I knew something wasn't right. I even asked Tony what he thought, and he said it seemed odd to him, too.

A week or so later, Hector started wearing this big, expensive watch that he just bought, bringing on more suspicion.

Tony and I continued to watch and look for signs of game fixing. We were playing a four-game series against the Elephants in Taichung. On the second day, we began to hear talk about something that supposedly happened to some of the Elephants players the night before. Turned out that four Elephants players had been kidnapped by gangsters and taken up to a player's hotel room. The gangsters had lost $125,000 on a recent Elephants game, and they thought those Elephants players had been bought off by a rival gang. One player got pistol-whipped, and another had a pistol stuck in his mouth.

There was a lot of security around the Elephants' dugout. One of their players had a huge bandage wrapped around his head. It was all hush-hush.

In the days to come, the story leaked out. It was like something out of a movie ... but it was really happening. These players had their lives threatened. The gang members were demanding that their losses be paid back. These were serious threats. There was a story from a couple of years before about an American player who had supposedly jumped off a high building in Taiwan and killed himself. It was ruled a suicide—supposedly he was depressed and ended his life. The inside story was that he had crossed some gangsters, and they threw him off the building. None of us knew for sure what really happened, but what we heard through the grapevine made me wonder.

By mid-September, Hector was not playing well, and the team released him, along with another Dominican outfielder, Sergio Cairo. Before joining our team, Hector had played for the Elephants. Maybe that was just a coincidence, maybe not. Sergio wasn't playing badly, so I was surprised that he got released too. Word got out later that the team not only released Hector for playing poorly, but they were aware of his possible gambling involvement. Since Sergio was his roommate, they assumed he must have been involved too, although we never suspected Sergio of being involved.

Careful who you hang out with.

I knew it was just a matter of time before they approached me. I also knew I had to make it crystal clear from the very start that I was never going to get involved. These people were smart. They did their homework on you and knew how to get close.

We were in Taipei playing a week of games. After one of the games, our team "grunt" (otherwise known as a clubhouse attendant) Stoney, who was a good kid—asked me to come hang out with him and some of his friends at a KTV. I had a hard time saying no to Stoney. He was a big guy, kind of chubby. He'd given himself an English name. Stoney worked for the team and would do all of the dirty work. He took pride in it. "I'm a worker," he'd say proudly. I'd end up spending a lot of time hanging out with Stoney too. Sometimes he was baffled by the things I did and said.

Stoney always had a straight, serious face, so he was a lot of fun to mess with. It was like he didn't understand my American humor, and he'd look confused, which would just crack me up. He could make me laugh even when he wasn't trying to. He would come up to me and say in his broken English, "What is wrong with you?" Which probably made me laugh harder. Once, when I was out in public with Stoney, I screamed out his name loudly. He was mortified. "What is wrong with you? People are going to think you're crazy!"

On this night, we wandered into the KTV and started doing our usual thing. There were people there I didn't recognize. Usually when I'm there, I see people I know … or at least recognize. After we were there for half an hour, a Taiwanese lady came over to me and asked me what my name was, speaking very good English.

That should have tipped me off.

I told her my name, and she asked me what I was doing in Taiwan. I told her I was playing baseball. She asked me what position I played. I told her I was a pitcher. At that moment, it appeared that she didn't know who I was and was just being friendly (I was wrong about that). Eventually she asked me if I knew what the "untruth game" was. I instantly knew exactly what she meant and why she was asking me. I acted like I didn't know.

The "untruth game" was code. It was being part of fixing a baseball game with the gangsters and/or gamblers. She explained—laid it all out. Then she asked me what I thought. I sat there quietly, wondering how to change this subject and then get out of there. She pointed across the room at a young girl and asked me if I thought she was pretty. Being nice, I said yes. She told me I could have her. I didn't say anything. I started wondering about everyone in the room that I didn't know. Slowly I figured out that these guys were gangsters who were there to "recruit" me.

The lady pointed to another young girl and said that I could have her too. I realized this lady knew who I was all along. She told me I could make a lot of money playing in the untruth game, and she asked me what I thought. She needed to tell the guy sitting across the room. I began to stare at the ground, thinking, "I'm not going to do this, but how am I going to get out of here?" The lady said to me that I looked ... sad.

I paused before I replied. "I can't do it ... even if I wanted to.... I wouldn't even know how to do it." I told her to tell "her friends" the gangsters that I said no thanks. She told me again that I should do it, that I could make a lot of money. They'd give me $10,000 right now if I'd just think about it. I told her no thanks again. After an awkward pause, she told me—in a very different tone—that if I *didn't* do it, I still wouldn't win another game for the rest of the season.

What the hell did that mean?

Now I was really nervous, and I began thinking about the American who got thrown off the building, and about the Elephants players being threatened and pistol-whipped. She walked over to one of the men sitting on a couch with other people around him. Apparently he was the Boss. When she spoke to him, he looked right at me, and I looked back at him, right in the eyes. I'm thinking, I'm in deep shit now. One gangster stood up and said something in Chinese in a loud voice. Within five seconds, the music stopped, the party stopped, and all of the people stood up and started leaving.

This was supposed to be a celebration party for me in joining the gangsters to fix baseball games. I was told that I had to leave, that they were mad. As everyone headed for the door toward the elevators, I tried to hang behind and not go with them. I wanted to leave later when I felt it was safer, but some people shooed me toward the elevator. An elevator door opened, and I got led in. We were on the 10th floor. I was up front with my back to everyone else. The elevator started to go down, which was a relief, because if we were going up, that would have meant we were going to the roof, where I would have been tossed off.

Even though we were going down, I was now literally waiting and expecting someone to come from behind and wrap a wire or something around my neck and strangle me. When the elevator made it to the lobby floor and nothing had happened, I couldn't believe my luck. I jumped off quickly. When everyone was off the elevator, the passengers all went one way, I went the other.

Then I exhaled.

Eight. Ramblin' Gamblin' Man

My heart was pounding in relief. I was expecting them to do something to me because I saw their faces. When I looked around, I saw Stoney, and I went right up to him. "What the fuck was that!" He stammered something back, but I cut him off. "Don't you *ever* do something like that again, or else I will kick your fucking ass!" He said he was very sorry ... but that he was told he had to get me there ... or else.

I felt like I literally dodged a bullet. I thought I was dead. I'd lost my last five games, even though I was throwing the ball pretty well. The gangsters felt I was vulnerable and that I'd just go along because I was losing anyway. But I wouldn't do it. I couldn't do it; I had my integrity.

I'd learn that some guys were getting $15,000 to $40,000 *a game.*

I wasn't going to ruin my name and everything I'd already done as a Major Leaguer. I never wanted my son to be embarrassed about anything I did. I wanted him to be proud of me for what I had accomplished in baseball, and not be remembered as a gambling cheat.

No amount of money was worth that risk.

I obviously don't regret the decision. I came out of it just fine. In fact, I got things going better after that.

I had another teammate, Jackie, who took me out a lot and always paid for everything. At dinner just a few weeks later, Jackie said to me, out of the blue, "You want to know why I always pay whenever we go out?" I replied, "Yeah, I was wondering about that." He said that he bet big money on me through a bookie—nothing to do with gangsters—and that he always bet on our team to win when I pitched. He said he bet on me ten times and won eight of them. He'd won around $40,000 that way. I was never sure if he said he won a total of $40,000, or if it was $40,000 per bet. He said he never wanted to tell me because he didn't want to make me nervous. He felt like he could tell me now because the season was just about over. I was glad he didn't tell me earlier.

The end of the season arrived. Our team struggled to the finish line. We finished buried in last place with a 28–69–3 record. But after my gangster meeting—where I was told that if I didn't participate in the untruth games, I wouldn't win again—I won my last five games of the season, along with a single no-decision. In those final six games, I was 5–0, with five complete games. I pitched 51 innings and gave up just 17 earned runs with 35 strikeouts. I punched out 13 batters in one game against the Lions, and I had a 3.00 ERA.

I wondered what the gangsters thought of that.

On the season, I finished with a 14–13 record, meaning I won half of the team's games ... and I had a save too. I had 13 complete games and 30 starts (setting league records at that time) and three shutouts. It was my final season in the Chinese Professional Baseball League. That off-season, after I couldn't reach a contract agreement with my team, I signed a contract with the brand-new Taiwan Major League. The TV network that had the rights to broadcast CPBL games lost that contract and decided to start their own league so they would have games to broadcast.

That off-season, the CPBL branded the 30 players—including me—who left the CPBL for the TML as "traitors." I didn't feel like a traitor. I had given my old team plenty of opportunity to re-sign me, and they didn't act. So I took a better offer. Finally, the business of baseball was on MY side.

During that off-season the rumors about the gambling got stronger. Investigations were done, and a lot of players got arrested for their involvement. It became official that Taiwan had a problem with gambling in professional baseball. The team that was investigated the deepest was the Eagles. They were nicknamed the "Black Eagles" because so many of their players were caught up in it. If a player was proven to be involved with game fixing, that player was banned for life in Taiwan. Some were arrested and served jail time. The Eagles lost so many players that they had to borrow players from the other CPBL teams to field a team for the next season.

The Taiwanese fans took this game-fixing news hard. They loved baseball and really supported their teams. They were very upset that they weren't watching legit games. Taiwan went into the 1997 professional baseball season under a dark cloud.

About a week before the new league season was to start, we found out that one of our best pitchers, Kuo Chin-hsing, was found guilty of participating in gambling the previous season. He was considered the best pitcher in Taiwan—a true baseball hero. He was banned for life, and while he didn't have to go to jail, he did have to pay a big fine. This was a big loss because he was supposed to be a big part of my new Fala team in the TML.

The new league wanted to start out right and avoid the mess that gambling had made of the CPBL. That league was going to suffer at the box office, big-time. A couple of days before the season was going to start, the TML brass had all four of the new teams meet in Tainan. Players and coaches were there, and the players were in uniform. The owner of the league spoke to the large group about his excitement for this new professional baseball league and the inaugural season. It didn't take him long to address the gambling situation. He warned everyone to stay away from the gangsters and the gambling. At the very end, everybody had to stand up and make a pledge that we wouldn't engage in game-fixing. Then, one team at a time went up front where there was a large poster declaring that you would not get involved in gambling. You had to sign your name on it. Every player and coach did.

This didn't make the new league immune. It was just a matter of time before the gangsters would try to get to many of us—again.

Eight. Ramblin' Gamblin' Man

I probably should have known better than to accept an invite from Stoney to go out with him and a new "friend" of his after a game. Some of my old friends from my former team, the Bulls, were also in town, so we agreed to go out on the town. Strength in numbers, I guess. We were having fun when Stoney's "friend" showed up. After a while, Stoney and his friend wanted to take me to a KTV. I agreed, but I was suspicious about Stoney's friend. There'd already been rumors that gangsters were getting involved in the TML games. I told Stoney I'd go with them … but only if my friends could go along, too. I figured if this guy was a gangster, I had my guys as protection. Stoney's friend agreed.

I told my friends that we were going to another place, and Stoney's friend would pay for everything. But I reminded them that I thought this guy could be a gangster trying to get us involved in game-fixing. Be careful, I said, and let everyone know if anyone gets propositioned.

In hindsight, I should have just said good night to Stoney and his friend much earlier. Fool me once, right? We went out to a KTV and were having fun, nothing was happening. Maybe I'd been wrong, and everything was innocent. When it was time to leave, we were walking down the road to get a taxi back to our hotel. Stoney and his friend were walking away in the other direction. Nothing bad had happened, right?

Suddenly Stoney yelled out to me to wait, he wanted to tell me something. He ran over to me; it was just me and him. I asked him what he wanted. He started to tell me that he'd made a big mistake and lost some money gambling and asked if I could help him. He was my friend, but I had to say no, I can't help you with that. I asked who his friend was, he told me it was a guy who worked for a gangster. They wanted to know if I would work with them. I told Stoney, "You know me better than that. You can tell that guy they can bet on me to win, and that's fine, but don't bet on me to lose. I will pitch to win, and I will not take any money from them, period."

Stoney looked down at the ground. "I know, all of the gangsters know that you won't do it, but they wanted me to ask you anyway." This was the second time my friend had put me in this bad spot with the gangsters. He looked at me, said he was sorry, and asked me if I was mad at him. I told him I was just disappointed. I said good night and walked back over to the other guys, who were waiting to get cabs. I told them that I was right, that the other guy was a gangster looking to get me.

I was really worried about Stoney now.

I don't know what that other guy told his gangster boss about me, since he and I didn't speak much, and he never asked me to throw a game. Maybe he wanted to see my resolve. Two days later when it was my turn pitch, I pitched 10 innings again. I came out of the game after the 10th tied 2–2. If he bet on me that day, I guess it was a push.

Later, I thought about those close encounters with gangsters and wondered how close I'd come to getting tossed off the top of a building. I'm glad I wasn't desperate enough for money to take any from them. That was a sure way to end up getting pistol-whipped … or worse.

Nine

People Are Strange

Growing up, we all get to know some, umm … memorable characters. Hopefully none of them are too dangerous or ask you to do things—like fixing baseball games—that could get you killed or jailed. Maybe we stop short of calling them crazy … then again, some of them are.

Crazy. Maybe "strange" is a better term. And "strange" isn't always a bad thing.

Strange can mean fun, adventurous, and all that … or it can mean … yes, a little bit dangerous. Over the years, I've known my fair share of both … and a whole lot of in-betweens.

My college roommate, Ed Puikunas, was an in-between.

Ed was your stereotypical left-handed pitcher. Nutty, fun-loving, and willing to do pretty much anything. And I mean anything. Besides being teammates and roomies at Chapman College, we went to Alaska to play summer ball together. Ed was nuts, but he was still very good at baseball.

We lived with the same host family in Alaska, so we did pretty much everything together. After a night out, we were driving back to our host family's house. On the way, Ed told me he had found something he needed to show me, and that I'd love it. He was really excited. Knowing Ed, this could literally be anything … that wasn't close to normal.

We drove through this wooded area on a single-lane, winding road. It was about 2:00 a.m., but in Alaska during the summer, it's still kind of like dusk. We were driving along when suddenly, Ed told me to turn and yelled out, pointing, "There it is!" Ed had discovered this place on one of his jogs.

The Alaska Psychiatric Institute. The region's mental hospital. Really.

Ed was so excited he jumped out of the car while it was still moving and told me to park. He could barely wait to start running up to the secluded building. Now I like a good adventure probably more than the next guy, but even I didn't think this was such a good idea. Before I knew it, Ed was peeking inside the windows! The way he was acting, someone was likely to mistake him for an escaped patient. He was bouncing around, looking inside and yelling for me to come over. Eventually I went over just to shut him up. I couldn't keep him quiet. He wanted me to look inside to see what was going on. I humored him and looked inside, then finally got him to leave before we were discovered and locked up ourselves.

I still consider that a narrow escape.

Ed and I were drafted and signed the same year. I went to the Astros; Ed was drafted by the Oakland A's. Since both organizations held their fall instructional league seasons in the greater Phoenix area, we were back together again in September of that year in the desert. One night, he was supposed to come and pick me up at my motel. I sat there waiting, watching TV. Then I heard this loud thump on my door. I was on the third floor of this motel, and when I looked outside, Ed was throwing a baseball at my door—which had glass windows on each side—from the parking lot below. He didn't want to climb three flights of stairs to tell me he'd arrived.

On several occasions, we got a six-pack and drove up to one of the bluffs that are all over Phoenix. We didn't want to do anything except avoid the snakes, bats, and scorpions ... relax, talk, and enjoy the scenery. That off-season, Ed was traded to the Giants for All-Star turned renowned big league manager Dusty Baker.

Years later, when I was playing in Taiwan, Ed was living in Micronesia. He and his wife and kids were living on one of the islands amongst the natives, living primitively. Ed was nuts, but he had a good heart. He mentioned that some of these people didn't have electricity; some had never seen soap before. He would treat them by giving them some. He said he would sit with the men while they chewed on roots, which made their mouths numb.

He invited me over, and I wanted to go see my old friend, it sounded like an adventure. A pretty safe one by Ed standards. Unfortunately, I was never able to make that trip.

Ed was, of course, not the only "character" I ever played with. (Some of them would say the same about me, but that depends on who's telling the stories, I guess.)

Another college character was Dangerous Doug Newark, and he was as crazy as they come. Coach Deese once said that Doug had more lives than a cat. I did sneak Doug into the Olympic Village during the 1984 Olympic games. That's all I'll say about that. Doug helped guide me early on with my sense of adventures. Three weeks into my first season in Mexico, Chris Bennett, Phil Harrison, and I were all pitching pretty well. It was evident that we weren't on a good team, and we were last in our division. While Chris and I continued to do well, Phil was up and down. He would have a decent game, then another tough outing, and he wasn't happy. Then he lost another game ... and now he was getting mad and irritated with everything.

Nine. People Are Strange

He wasn't laughing anymore; he wasn't having fun. Remember, we were all about the healing power of laughter. But Phil started to complain about everything. We were playing in another country, and things were going to be done differently. We learned very early that you have to laugh a lot or else everything will get to you.

At the beginning of the season, the three of us were having fun, making jokes, and laughing at the different things we were going through; we weren't getting mad. Now, Phil wasn't laughing anymore, and everything was getting to him. Phil complained all the time, even at the ballpark in front of the team. It got to a point where one of the Mexican players finally spoke out in English and said to Phil, "Where you are!" It was perfect broken English, making the point that this was their home and you are not in America, so deal with it.

Phil didn't make it. One of the last straws for him came on his day to pitch. We were in Puebla and sharing a hotel room. It was early in the morning, and we were sound asleep when suddenly construction noise started coming from our hotel, and it was very loud. Phil, who was a high-strung guy in the first place and already in an unhappy mood, woke up literally screaming and cussing that it was his day to pitch, and he needed his rest. When Chris and I were awakened, we just laughed and said, "of course." After the noise went on a little longer, Phil got up, opened the window, and screamed at the workers outside. He put on some clothes,

This clubhouse attendant was Mr. Do Everything.

went yelling down the hallway to the front desk in the lobby, and began yelling at the front desk people in English. They probably didn't understand him. He came back very frustrated and unhappy.

Needless to say, that night Phil pitched badly and lost again. He was mentally beaten down. Shortly after that night, Phil was called into the general manager's office, and he was released. I think if the team didn't release him, he would have quit and left (again) anyway. It was sad for me and Chris to see our buddy gone, since we had such a good time at the beginning together. There are guys who just can't handle playing in a different country.

Over the next few years, I would see good ball players who had similar problems. They'd had success earlier in their careers, but they arrive to play in a different country unable to handle the different culture, the language, playing conditions, the food … the stress of having to be perfect all of the time. These factors took down a lot of American players.

I met some very interesting folks *in* Mexico, too. During my first season in Puebla, I was adapting pretty well. But you're never prepared for everything. Imagine playing for a professional baseball team and one day having the general manager ask *you* to borrow some money? Really.

One day during the first half of the season, our GM asked to speak to me in private. I'd pitched well in my last start, so I wasn't worried about getting released … but you never know. They may have needed to save a few pesos. Instead, he asked me if I could loan him $2,500! I was shocked.

He said his daughter needed surgery, and he had to pay the hospital some money right now. He said he would pay me back in five days, on payday.

This was more than a little awkward. No one would expect a professional team's GM to ask to borrow money. I really didn't want to do this, but I saw he was desperate for his daughter, and I figured he'd do what he said and pay me back within a week, so I gave him the money.

How could I know that two days later, I'd get a phone call from my agent, Chuck Berry, with some great news: Chuck had gotten me a Triple A deal with the Cleveland Indians. I'd leave the following day. It was back to America. What a great feeling, getting another chance. I packed everything up, and I was ready to leave the next day. The Indians would fly me from Mexico to Milwaukee, and the following day I'd meet the Charlotte team on the road in Norfolk, Virginia. It was all good.

I was excited to call Tami to tell her about my new deal and said I was coming home for a day. She was obviously happy about the news. But I also had to tell her I had loaned the GM—a guy I hardly knew and was now leaving—that $2,500. What would any wife say? "*You did WHAT?*" I explained myself and said I'd get the money back. In reality, all I could do was cross my fingers.

Nine. People Are Strange

That night, I went to the park a little early to meet the GM to tell him about my deal with Cleveland ... and that I needed to collect the money he owed me. I'd be leaving tomorrow. He was really surprised. He wasn't expecting me to land a Triple A deal. I asked him not to tell the team, that I wanted to do it after the game, and he agreed. I asked him again about the money he owed me, now that I was unexpectedly leaving. He explained he didn't have the time to get it, that he could pay me on the next payday like we'd agreed. He'd send it express mail, including my paycheck and the money he borrowed. I couldn't do much but say okay, we'll go with that. "The check is in the mail" as they say.

Tami was understandably mad that I left Mexico without getting my money back. I promised her it would come on the next payday. I hoped.

While I was in Charlotte, payday came and went. The team sent me my final paycheck ... but nothing from the general manager.

Now I had to call Mexico and ask him why he hadn't sent it. He said he wasn't able to get it yet but would send it the next payday. Well, the next payday came and went, and the money still hadn't arrived. Tami told me to keep calling. It's not easy to call Mexico from Charlotte. I was having trouble getting him, his secretary would answer the phone and say he wasn't there ... so I'd leave him another message, doing all of this in Spanish over my hotel room phone. When I did finally reach him, he told me he was having money problems and he was just unable to get my money at this time ... and continued to promise he would pay me back. Tami was becoming more and more upset with me for loaning him the money. Not hard to understand why.

When I got home in mid–September, I still hadn't gotten paid back. I had to keep calling and calling. I didn't think I was ever going to get it.

Finally, in late October my money from Mexico showed up.

Needless to say, Tami "discouraged" me from being a lender ever again.

Most times, the crazy meant entertaining. One day in Puebla, teammate John Jensen got a haircut. It was your normal, typical haircut. Nothing out of the ordinary. A couple of the guys and I were eating lunch in a Mexico City diner, when the freshly trimmed Jensen wandered by, and we invited him to have a seat.

John said he had just gotten his hair cut at a barber shop around the corner. The haircut was fine, nothing wrong with it. We just started to mess with him and told him it was horrible.

We pointed to the back of his head and said, "Look! The barber messed up here *bad*." John was gullible and believed us. When he sat down at our table, we kept saying how bad it looked.

Now we got him pissed. We told him he had to go back to that barber shop, tell the barber his haircut looked like crap, and insist on getting his money back.

When we finished eating, we had John take us to the barber shop. We had John all fired up. He said he was going to let the barber have it. When we got there, John got nervous. He stood outside of the barbershop, staring in the window at the barber. The barber eventually looked up and saw John out front, looking in. This was becoming a funny scene. John wouldn't go inside, but he began making gestures and faces at the barber and yelled at him from outside. The rest of us were laughing so hard we couldn't hold it in. The barber flipped his hand at John, turned around, and went about his business. John made more gestures and walked away. Walking back to the hotel, we made fun of John for being afraid to go inside, tell him off, and get his money back, and we kept telling him how bad his haircut looked. We even told him that he had to go to another barber and get another haircut to fix it up. It was so funny getting him all worked up when his haircut was just fine.

Eventually, we confessed. John wasn't happy.

Usually, if you wanted to pull one over on someone, you needed more than a lie about a bad haircut. Props were very helpful. One day, an American teammate and I were in a mall on the USA side of the border in Laredo, Texas. We found a shop where you could buy gag gifts, and he wanted to buy some stink bombs. They came in a box with very thin glass vials. When you broke open one of these vials, within seconds it produced the most God-awful rotten-egg-dead-animal smell. We both bought some. In the days, weeks and years to come, I would use these stink bombs very selectively ... and effectively.

One of the best places to use them was a bar that had music and a dance floor. When the bar was full and the dance floor was crowded, we'd make our move. You could bop out on the dance floor with a vial in hand, drop it to the floor, and in a dance maneuver step on the vial, breaking it open ... then instantly dance right back off. Within seconds, people were making sour faces and looking at those around them as if they had just crapped their pants. That cleared the floor. Quickly.

We'd watch this go down from a distance, laughing so hard we had tears coming down our cheeks. We also dropped these in the locker room, getting some great reactions from teammates. We would drop these things in any crowded area and watch the reactions. The healing power of laughter, remember?

I still had some stink bombs left over the following spring in 1995, when I was with the Pirates' Triple A team. I was always ready to use them. During a bus trip to Scottsdale, a teammate named Luis Mercedes got up

Nine. People Are Strange

and announced that he was going into the bathroom on the bus to take a crap. He said this to get a big reaction out of the guys, which he got. Everyone yelled at him not to, of course, knowing if he did, he would stink up the bus.

In my own twisted way, I knew this would be the perfect time to pull out one of those stink bombs I just happened to have with me in my travel bag. I was sitting at the back of the bus next to teammate Matt Maysey, and I showed him the stink bomb. I told him what I was going to do … because you need someone to enjoy the prank with.

We knew Luis wasn't going to take a dump on the bus. When he came out of the bathroom, he had a big smile on his face and he acted like he did, just to tease the guys. As he walked by, I dropped one of my precious vials on the floor and broke it open with my foot. Within seconds, while Luis was still walking back to his seat, the stink overwhelmed the bus, the smell making its way all the way up to the front. Everyone started yelling at Luis, and they were really mad at him. He yelled back, defending himself. Everyone was laying into him, and Luis was getting mad. He said he didn't crap in the bathroom, and everyone was calling him a liar. It got heated.

All the while, Matt and I were hiding our heads because we were both laughing so hard that it hurt. It was hilarious. I literally had tears coming out of my eyes. Like most successful pranks, we never did have to confess what we did. Luis just had to take all that grief.

The joke was on me shortly thereafter. Hello? Karma? Is that you?

At the end of minor league spring training that season, I was among the group that got assigned to start the season with Triple A Calgary. The team had to make travel arrangements before we left Florida, including choosing our roommates. One of the guys on the team I didn't know very well asked me if I would be his roommate, and I said sure. We had to tell our trainer, who was also the travel coordinator, whom we would room with.

When I told the trainer, he paused. He looked up at me, chuckled, and asked me if I was sure. I was puzzled by his reaction, but I said yes, I'm sure.

We won't use my former teammate's real name here, because I don't want to make light of anyone's health issues. We'll just call him "Joe Smith."

"Joe" is a good guy, but he had a real issue.

After breaking camp and leaving Florida, we began the season on a 14-day, 12-game road trip in Arizona. Joe was a good guy, but it was during this trip that I got to know about his "problem."

When Joe went out at night, he drank a lot, like quite a few of the guys. Nothing all that unusual there. Most nights, I'd hang out with my younger teammates for a while, then go back to the hotel room. Joe was usually still out. By the time he got back to the hotel room, I was normally asleep.

During one of the first nights on the road trip, he woke me up, but not on purpose. It was dark in the room, and I woke up and saw him peeing on the floor in the corner of the hotel room. I yelled at him, "What are you doing?" He didn't reply and crawled back in bed.

I didn't realize that Joe was walking in his sleep when he peed on the floor. When I kept talking to him, he finally woke up and had no idea what he had done. I thought to myself, Oh well, no big deal, he must have had too much to drink and was too drunk to know what he was doing. I dismissed it as a one-time thing.

It wasn't.

The next night he did it again.

When I went out at night, I sometimes ran into other guys on the team, and Joe would be there too. He didn't seem to get carried away with his drinking. Perhaps alcohol intake wasn't the problem. Then the sleepwalking/pissing happened again. And again. I'd wake up and see him peeing on the dresser, on the curtains, on the door. I had to yell at him all the time … but he was asleep.

It got worse. One night I woke up, and when I opened my eyes, I saw Joe's penis about 10 inches away. He was about to pee on my face! I quickly shoved him away and yelled. He woke up all confused and disoriented, not knowing what he was doing. After that, it was tough for me to sleep at night, wondering and worrying that he might come over and pee on me. He didn't do this every night, but he did do it several times on the long road trip. This would not be the end of it.

We flew from Arizona to Calgary. The team paid for our hotel rooms for the first three days, and then we'd be on our own. If you had a roommate, the team paid for six days. I still had Joe as my roommate. He had asked me if I'd room with him. I gritted my teeth and said okay. I figured I could do it for six more days. Then I'd find my own apartment.

The first night, Joe woke me up peeing on the floor again. The next night, he woke me up when I heard him walk out the door. This was new. He was wearing only his underwear, now sleepwalking down the hallway. Could I pretend to still be asleep? Nope. Violation of roommate etiquette. I was really tired, but I jumped up, ran out the door, and headed down the hallway to find him. I saw him trying to open up a door to another hotel room. He was jiggling the door handle. Then he pulled his dick out to start to pee on the door. I had to sprint down the hallway in my underwear to grab him before the people in that room opened their door and found some strange person peeing on it. While I was running, I was praying that a door wouldn't open and that nobody else would come walking down the hallway to see these two guys standing there in our underwear.

I pulled Joe back the several doors to our room and got him inside. In the process, he woke up, wondering what was going on. Imagine waking up in your underwear with your roommate dragging you back to your room.

I don't know what happened to Joe after I got released by the Pirates. He was a good player, but that sleepwalking/pissing problem was a tough thing to overcome. I wondered who took my place as his road roommate and how they handled it?

I met people—not all players mind you—in Taiwan that were memorable mostly for the right reasons. Mostly.

One of the first guys was a Taiwanese friend of Tony Metoyer's named Jordan, who was the manager of a night spot called the Pig and Whistle. Jordan was his English name; he gave it to himself because he loved Michael Jordan. Jordan would always take care of us. If there was a line to get into his club, we walked right on in. We never paid a cover charge, and a lot of times we didn't pay for our drinks. If we did, we didn't pay much.

We didn't only go to see Jordan at the bar he was managing, we went to other spots with him as well. I went to Jordan's bar a lot by myself, usually until way past closing time. People there would want to take both of us to a KTV, which meant staying out and singing karaoke until the sun rose the next morning.

A couple of times, we didn't just go home and get some badly needed sleep. Jordan took me to a playground that had basketball hoops with a bunch of guys playing early-morning pickup games. He wanted us to play. Jordan was such an easy-going guy. "It'll be fun" seemed to be his motto.

It wasn't a lot of fun when Jordan accidently hit and killed a guy on a scooter while he was driving home from my apartment after drinking. Mind you, the scooter driver was drunk and ran a red light before crashing into Jordan's car. Instead of paying off the family, Jordan spent a year in prison for that.

It was mid–July the following year when Jordan was released. He'd served his time. It didn't take him long to get a job as a manager of a bar in Kaohsiung. He surprised me and came to a game. He gave me the directions, and I went there after the game. I brought a few of the guys along. Jordan had an allowance to spend on the customers, so we usually wouldn't pay for anything. I told him I felt weird about this, but he said, "don't worry, I have to spend it, or else the boss takes it away."

After a short stint there, he became the manager of a big night club in Kaohsiung called Jurassic Night Club. You couldn't miss it. The building was on a very busy road and had a huge dinosaur sticking out of the front. I always had a good time with Jordan, he treated me so good. I asked him how it was in prison. He said he got by fine since he spoke English so well. He had a good job inside, and because of his English, he did favors for some of the gangsters, which made others not bother him. I can't imagine what that was like.

Strange can also mean … well, mean. Greedy. A bit twisted.

That would describe the owner of the first team I played on in Taiwan—the Jungo Bears—a man named Chin Yi Ping, whom we all called "The Boss." The Boss was a cutthroat businessman, not afraid to flaunt his wealth but a penny-pincher at the same time. Since I pitched very well that first season, I didn't have much interaction with him—until the end of the season. Under our contracts in Taiwan, we got paid until the end of December. On some teams, and with certain players, if a guy had a contract already for the following season, he would get paid through November and get his December pay when he returned in January. Not really a bad idea. When you returned, there was money already there for you to live on.

But this was also a trick by some owners to ensure that the player would return for the next season—and if he didn't, the owner kept his December pay. On the Bears, Boss said the foreign players had to stay in Taiwan indefinitely to get our full pay. What he hoped to do was either: (a) get you under a bad contract for the following season; or (b) get you so frustrated that you left before the end of the year and forfeited the remainder of your pay.

Like I said, cutthroat.

It wasn't like he needed to save the money. I think it was mostly an ego thing.

I'd been away from home for over five and a half months. The season was over, and I was ready to leave. My contract said the team could keep me around after the season to play exhibition games. In the past, there had been exhibition games against teams from Japan, but we had none scheduled, so there was no reason to keep us. Boss didn't say how long we had to stay to collect what we were owed.

He did this so we'd get mad and just leave, breaking our contracts. It was crap like this that caused people in the CPBL—including other owners—to dislike him.

When the season ended, we didn't practice or do anything, so there was literally nothing to do. I decided to stay so I could collect all my money. Tami was pissed, constantly asking me how much longer I'd be gone. I didn't know. I hadn't seen Tami or Logan since early May. Four of my teammates were in the same situation. Days revolved around waking up, doing nothing, eating lunch, hanging with the guys, eating dinner,

Nine. People Are Strange

doing more of nothing, and eventually going to sleep, and doing that all over again the next day. During the first week, my roommate got to leave because his visa expired. Same with Tony. Another guy gave in and left, forfeiting his money. He said he missed his family and wanted to go home, which was a win for the Boss.

There wasn't anything to do but to go out and drink. During our second week of captivity, Boss invited me and two teammates to eat at a restaurant he owned. He was playing nice. He said we could come back anytime and eat for free.

I think he realized we were strong and planned to wait him out. He told us if we'd negotiate a new contract and sign, he'd let us go home. I called the interpreter, Jeffrey Wilson, to ask him to come to Taichung to negotiate.

They negotiated in Chinese, and I wasn't able to understand what they were saying. Every so often they'd pause, and Jeffrey would catch me up. This went on a long time, and before it ended, Jeffrey told me what the deal was.

It was terrible.

I used my limited Chinese to tell them both, "No. That's a bad deal for me." Jeffrey told me to give him a call when I wanted to negotiate again. Meanwhile, both my remaining teammates negotiated with Boss and got lousy offers too. A day later after we all refused, we went to his restaurant to eat. The manager told us that after tonight, Boss said we couldn't eat there for free anymore. Of course not.

It was now mid–November. I called Tami and told her that I had to get out of Taiwan. I told her I'd accept the offer, as long as he would give me all of my money through December 31 … and that I had no intention of returning to play for him next season. She agreed. I called Boss and told him I was accepting his deal. I'd sign the contract as long as he gave me everything he owed me, and he agreed. I went to his office that afternoon. He paid me right there, and I signed the contract. I ended up spending an extra month in Taiwan after the season ended.

This time, Karma was on my side.

Shortly after I left Taiwan, the owners of the CPBL voted Chin Yi Ping out of the league. As much as he messed with his players, he ruffled the feathers of the other owners even more. They had enough and kicked him out. With Chin Yi Ping gone, I had a safety net. If I couldn't get a job in the U.S., I could always return to Taiwan to play for a different owner.

I did have a guaranteed $90,000 contract sitting there for me even if I didn't like it very much.

I did return, of course, and got to experience different levels of crazy from different parts of the world.

While we were in Brisbane, Australia, training before the 1996 season, the local team hosting us asked if we could take one of their catchers back to Taiwan with us on sort of a tryout basis. The team agreed. He did a lot of bullpen catching for us, but I never did see him hit or anything else. I doubt he was good enough to play at our level in Taiwan. Still, it was ... entertaining before he returned down under.

His name was Ben, and after we got back to Taiwan, we started to see that this kid was one weird dude.

Teammates started asking me about the Australian kid. One asked me if I could understand his English. They knew he was speaking English, but they couldn't understand him. "I learned how to speak English ... but when I'm speaking to him, I don't understand. I think maybe I forgot how to speak English," I chuckled. I couldn't understand him, either. Ben spoke too fast and had an accent. In Australia, they use a lot of English words that Americans don't know. We hardly knew what he was saying either.

One day at lunch, I went to Montana's bar in Kaohsiung. Several teammates were already there with a few of our Taiwanese teammates. Ben was there, too. He had a huge plate of food in front of him. The guys were laughing about how he ordered this huge, expensive meal for lunch. He had a huge steak with a baked potato, vegetables, the works. It would cost him about $50 U.S. We didn't think he could eat it all.

Ben had this happy, dumb look on his face as he devoured everything. A few moments later, he was finishing the last bite! I was impressed. He said he was still hungry and ordered another steak meal. He ate that whole plate too.

The whole time Ben was with us, he said one stupid, weird thing after another. One of his stories was about the time he took an X-ACTO knife and slowly cut open his own scrotum ... from one side to the other! He said he wanted to see what his balls looked like. He described what he saw and how they looked. We asked him what he did after that. He said he went to his dad, and they duct-taped his scrotum shut.

Okay. Check please.

Ben's stay with us, while entertaining, was short.

When I joined the new rival Taiwan Major League (TML), I met a left-handed pitcher from Canada who became my favorite roommate ever. Steve Wilson played in the Major Leagues with the Rangers, Cubs, and Dodgers. He was from Vancouver, where he married his wife, who was born in the Philippines. They had two kids. He and I roomed together for the next two years.

Being left-handed and Canadian, it was pretty much assured that Steve would be up for having fun anywhere, anytime. If I asked him, "Hey, let's go out and do something," he'd immediately reply, "Sure, let's go." Steve would talk to anyone and made friends everywhere he went. I was amazed. I remember walking into a little Taiwanese bar where there were no foreigners. That didn't matter—he walked right up to some people and started a conversation. If they spoke a little English, that was great, and if they didn't, he still found a way for everyone to have fun.

We started to call Steve "The Chameleon." We noticed he'd sort of adopt the culture of wherever he was. When he first came to Taiwan, he was wearing clothes that the people of the Philippines wore, like a barong. After being in Taiwan, he started smoking cigarettes, and he would squat and smoke like our Taiwanese teammates did. He went to local Taiwanese bars by himself.

Steve never left Taiwan. He divorced his first wife and became involved with a Taiwanese girl named Judy. She had a four-year-old daughter. They got an apartment together not far away, and he stayed there all year 'round. When the season ended, we were all ready to go home and live like Americans again. Steve never left the rat race.

Once Steve and Judy invited me to go with them to Tainan, Judy's hometown. That night, they wanted to take me out to this "different" bar. We went up some narrow stairs, and they decided to tell me we were going into a transvestite bar. Everyone who worked there was a transvestite. Steve said, "Don't worry, it's just something different."

We went in, sat down, and started to play Taiwanese drinking games. Some of the workers joined in. One of the workers was playing around and teasing me … he asked me to kiss … her.

I tried to be polite and say no thanks. But the working … girls … could see I was uncomfortable, and after a while they thought it was funny to keep teasing me like this.

Finally, I jumped up and turned the tables on them. I told one of the … girls to "Show me your dick." Everyone started to laugh. The worker tried to turn the teasing back to me, but I said, "No no no. Show me your dick." The worker pulled up his dress, tucked his penis back between his legs, and did a little wiggle, making everyone laugh.

We were getting ready to leave, and Judy left to get a cab while Steve and I finished our beers. With us alone, the employees came back and began teasing us like they wanted to kiss … and more. Steve and I started to walk slowly toward the bar, but quickly turned and ran to the exit and down the stairs. We could hear them chasing after us, and when we got to the bottom of the stairs, we headed to the alley, where Judy was waiting for us in the cab. As we jumped in, the transvestites ran out the back door towards our cab. Our cab took off, and when we looked back, the "girls" were laughing.

Steve retired after that season, and he and Judy opened up a little bar in Tainan. They lived in a little apartment above the bar. The Chameleon now lived and worked full-time in Taiwan.

He was fitting right in like always.

We'd visit when we could. One night, we had a large group going out together. We couldn't all fit in one car. I took my scooter; one couple went together on another scooter; and Steve, Judy and my brother Lance, who was visiting from California, rode in Steve's car.

I was following Steve, and as we got close, Steve turned onto a little frontage road. He let his eyes wander off the road while he was looking for the place, and I watched him crash his car right into a parked car. It made a very loud noise and caused that parked car to crash into the car parked in front of it, chain reaction-style. I couldn't believe what I saw. It was like slow motion.

I parked my scooter and ran over to see if they were okay. Surprisingly, no one was hurt, and nobody heard the crash, because nobody came out to check anything. Steve was a little dazed, but he was more bummed out. He'd damaged the front end of his car, and he had a cracked windshield where Judy's head hit. She was bleeding from her forehead. Lance climbed out of the back seat and said only his knee hurt. Since nobody came out, everyone got into the car and drove the three blocks to the bar we were going to.

There were probably some pretty pissed-off car owners when they discovered they'd been hit.

Last I knew, Steve and Judy were no longer together, but he was still living the simple life in Tainan. No doubt he's been fitting right in all these years.

One of my favorite Taiwanese teammates was a guy named Da Pan. He was a young player on the team. He was tall and played first base, and he seemed to get better every year. He spoke good English, and I liked to talk to him … and sometimes mess with him. One day we got onto the subject of reincarnation. Taiwanese people are Buddhists, and reincarnation is a part of their beliefs. We would have long talks about this, and I was truly interested. I asked him what he would like to be reincarnated as, and he told me he wanted to be a "green dragon." I asked him why … because dragons are not real. He answered by saying that if I knew what green dragons were, then I would know. I still don't.

Maybe "strange" meant someone had a very different way of doing things.

I remember being on the road early in my first season in the new TML. I had strained my inner thigh groin muscle. While I was getting some treatment from the trainer, Coach Doi San came by and asked me what was wrong in broken English and Japanese, in front of our trainer, who only spoke Chinese. I told him. He informed me that for the rest of the road trip, he would take care of me at the hotel. He came to my hotel

Nine. People Are Strange

room, brought his big bag of needles, and he gave me acupuncture. This was the same Coach Doi San who dove naked into the Kaohsiung harbor from a ferry our team was on the very first day we got together for a team meal at the start of this season. I had no idea if he even knew what he was doing, but I allowed him to stick needles into my groin area anyway. I was thinking, who just carries around a bag of acupuncture needles for the heck of it?

He did know what he was doing. He took these long, thin, sharp needles that he put into a thin tube with the back end sticking out. He would smack the back end of the tube, and the needle would fly right into the spot he wanted it to go. When the needle went in, he tapped the top of it to make sure it was in the right spot. He then moved his finger and thumb down my inner thigh to find the place to put the next needle. He did this again and again until he had the needles in place. There were six to eight needles. They were very sharp, but they never hurt. I think Doi San had a great technique because I barely felt anything when the needles went in. When he removed the needles, all I could see was a pinhead-sized drop of blood, if that. When he was done the first time, I could already feel a difference; my groin wasn't healed, but it did feel better. He did this for the next couple of days. Then it was time for me to pitch again. For precautionary measures, I had my groin wrapped by the trainer, but I felt good and confident. Doi San was a master with his acupuncture needles. It helped, and while it was strange at first, I'm now a believer.

I grew to appreciate the uniqueness of Taiwan. The experience of being an American in a foreign country was the most memorable part. Americans in a foreign country are immediately thrown together, regardless of which team you are on. I spent many nights out with American players from opposing teams. Coaches too. One guy in particular—Tim Ireland—a long-time scout, coach and manager, made his presence known in Taiwan ... and not always for the right reasons.

Strange days indeed.

I'd known of Tim from the Milwaukee Brewers organization, even though we'd never met before. One year, he was managing the Gida team in the TML. When you talked to him, it didn't take long to figure out that he was a bit nuts and didn't have much of a filter. When we talked to the foreign players with Gida, we asked them about their oddball manager. They didn't mince words: "He's crazy. He says off the wall things, and when he goes out and drinks, he gets crazier still. He talks crap to people around him and almost gets in fights all the time."

But they also said that he knew his baseball and was a very good coach.

Whenever we played against Gida, our American hitting coach, Mark

Budaska, was somehow obligated to hang out with Ireland after games. Mark told us stories. Mark said he was uncomfortable a lot and usually found himself waiting for a brawl to break out. The way Tim talked to people always had him on the edge. Mark wasn't sure if he would make it out of the places they visited. Whenever I talked to Tim, I could see that he was certainly … different.

Ireland was all about winning, that's for sure. He knew what buttons to push. For example, he was well aware that Taiwanese players never fight or get emotional. It's always the foreign players who get mad. We're the ones who throw our gloves against the dugout wall after a bad inning and cuss to get the frustration out. The Taiwanese guys never do this. They look at us and laugh. We get mad at them because we think they don't care. But that's just their way. The only brawl I saw in Taiwan was when Corey Powell got hit by the pitch by another foreign player, and he charged the mound. All the players came out, but none of the Taiwanese guys got involved. We learned that the Taiwanese pitchers would never throw at a batter on purpose.

We were in the middle of the game against Gida when I heard a commotion by our third base dugout. I looked over and I saw about five of my Taiwanese teammates on top of Ireland, beating him up. Once everybody realized what was going on, the Gida team began running across the field from their first base dugout. The rest of our team came out too. The Gida team felt obligated to protect their manager, and our Taiwanese guys were hot about something.

It caught me totally off-guard, seeing my Taiwanese teammates in a fight.

After everyone was separated and things calmed down, players returned to their dugouts. I asked one of the Taiwanese guys what happened. He said that Ireland, who was coaching third base, was talking trash to our outfielder, Lu Ming Su, after the end of every inning as Su was running back to our dugout from left field. When Su got tired of it, he approached Ireland, and they began swinging. When our Taiwanese players saw Su, who was a baseball hero in Taiwan, involved in a fight, they ran to his defense, which was the Taiwanese way. Gang up and beat up the foreigner.

Later, the foreign players on Gida told me that Ireland started all this on purpose to fire his team up. Ireland knew that if he messed with Lu Ming Su, the Taiwanese guys would get involved, which was exactly what he wanted. He got his fight and a spark for his flat team.

Ireland's methods didn't go over well in Taiwan. He only managed for that one season.

But he would return.

Nine. People Are Strange

Late in my final season in Taiwan, we were sitting in a restaurant after a game when we saw Ireland walk in. He was now in Taiwan as a scout for a team in the States. He was there for a big Asian amateur tournament being played in Taipei. He saw us and walked up to the wall that separated our table from the waiting area and the bar. As we were saying hello, there was a Taiwanese customer standing next to him, wearing this hat that looked like one of those old Soviet Union military fur caps. Ireland thought this was funny, so while he was talking to us, he pulled the guy's hat off his head, put it on, and started making funny sounds like he was speaking Russian. It was yet another weird and uncomfortable moment with Tim.

The local was surprised by all this. Tim finally gave him his hat back, but a couple of minutes later, he tapped the guy on the shoulder and told him he wanted to buy his hat. The guy declined, and Tim burst out laughing in the guy's face, saying, "Come on, I wanna to buy your hat!" Tim grabbed the guy's hat again and put it on, turned toward us, burst out laughing, then turned back to the guy, asking him how much money he wanted for the hat. The poor guy didn't know what to do, and we didn't know what to think either. It was all very awkward—again. The guy ended up walking away.

We got to talking about a guy who had pitched for Tim last season, and how he was signed by a team in the States. This was, of course, a very sore subject for me. For the past six seasons, I'd been trying to get back to the big leagues through Mexico, then through the whole replacement players and strike mess, and now through Taiwan. I thought my success in Taiwan would at least get me a shot in Japan, which could have led me back to America.

But it took Tim Ireland of all people to finally, after all that, hit me with my new reality.

He told me the reason nobody in MLB signed me after the great season I had the year before was because I was now too old.

What do you say to that?

I was 35 years old. He told me I was *this close* to getting released early that season when I got injured. He said they reluctantly stuck with me—it was my manager, Yamani, who wanted to keep me and give me a chance—so they kept me. All I did was go off in the second half of the season and end up being the league MVP.

See how strange things can get?

Ten

Scenes from the Italian Restaurant

There are a lot of people you meet in and around baseball who aren't crazy or all that quirky, but are memorable for a different reason. Like for making an off-hand suggestion that turned out to be a big plus in your life.

I had a teammate in Taiwan named Daryl Smith. He was from Baltimore. Daryl had been around. He played mostly in the minor leagues, but he briefly made it to the majors, pitching in two games for the Kansas City Royals in 1990, and he had experience playing in other countries. He once played in Italy, and he told me that whenever I decided to quit playing professional baseball, to pause and look in the other direction. Don't hang 'em up yet, Daryl said ... go to Italy and play one more year. He said I would love it. I filed that away in the back of mind.

After my fifth season in Taiwan, I ruled out going back. I had some great times there and some outstanding moments on the field, but it didn't end well. I was done playing in Asia. I still wanted another shot at the big leagues, but there were no bites. I knew what Tim Ireland told me, that my age—I would be 37 during the upcoming season—was a deal-breaker now.

Part of me was ready to hang up my spikes and take a crack at selling insurance. But part of me wasn't.

I thought back to what Daryl said a few years earlier. I called up some friends and former teammates who'd played in Italy. I liked what I heard and started making calls on my own. After being told by a few teams that they already had their allotment of American players, I got lucky. Rimini, the defending league champs, needed a pitcher.

Selling insurance would have to wait.

When I made the decision to go to Italy, Tami wasn't really on board, but I convinced her. We agreed on not going back to Taiwan again, but after we talked about it, Italy sounded exciting to both of us. And it certainly wouldn't be difficult to convince family members to come and visit.

The salary wasn't great—not close to what I made in Taiwan, but still, who could say no to this? Playing in the Italian Baseball League left you a ton of free time. We played a single game on Friday and doubleheaders on Saturday. That was it. We had practice on Tuesday, Wednesday and Thursday later in the evening—because the Italian players still worked real jobs to pay their bills. That left plenty of time for sightseeing. And man, what sights there were to see.

The baseball was roughly Double A caliber. Not as good as Taiwan. As American professionals, we were expected to dominate the league, and for the most part, we did. It's like what's expected from Italian professional soccer players when they come to play in the MLS here.

I was paid the foreign player limit of $3,000 a month. I got them to give me another $3,500 bonus paid under the table. The foreign player cap was in place to keep it fair for teams to compete, so my bonus was a secret from the league. I also got the team to pay for flights for both Tami and Logan to visit, and I was getting my own apartment, whereas the other American guys had to share an apartment. I would get my own car to drive, too. I had a sweet deal.

My flight arrived in Bologna on a Saturday afternoon. There were no customs lines to go through, which I thought was weird. There was a guy from the front office there to pick me up. He spoke no English (or Spanish, or Chinese). We got into his car and took off for Rimini, about an hour away. I mean took off. We got onto the highway, and he started going fast. Like *really* fast. I glanced over at the speedometer, which was in kilometers. When I calculated our speed, I realized we were going 105mph. On the European highways, there are no speed limits. We were going 105mph, and other cars were blowing right by us.

I got to know my new teammates, including my American coaches (no translator was needed, for a change), and saw some familiar faces. I had to figure out my way around Rimini, where to eat, where to shop, and all the rest. This was a seaside resort town, a beautiful place that filled up with tourists every summer. It's in northeast Italy, just south of Venice, right on the Adriatic Sea. Rimini was a big vacation spot for Europeans, mainly from Holland and Germany. Rimini had a normal population of about 40,000 people, but during the height of vacation time, the city swelled to over 400,000 people. There was hotel after hotel lining the beach for miles. I arrived in April, when it was very calm. But when June rolled around, this place got crazy fun.

I enjoyed hanging out with my teammates, but it was great that I was able to arrange visits, like when my friends from back home, Tim and Mary Lineham, came to visit in late April. They were in the midst of an around-the-world vacation. Lance came in June, and Tami and Logan in July.

When Tim and Mary came to Rimini, we spent a few days seeing the sights. They even got to watch me pitch a game. They asked me to come to Venice with them during my off-days. We went sightseeing and had a great time. I found out how easy it was to get around the country. A round-trip train ticket to Venice cost me $12. It was fun exploring and seeing a lot of famous sites, such as the Ponte della Paslia, the famous bridge that dates back to 1360. The Procuratie Vecchi was built in 1520. We walked around and saw the famous gondolas.

On my first road trip to Parma, I ran into a former teammate named Joel Lono. He was a teammate of mine in the summer of 1983 in the Alaska Baseball League in Anchorage. He was a totally cool guy from Hawaii. It's amazing how you run into former teammates when you least expected it. It'd been 17 years since I last saw Joel! That's one of the benefits when you play long enough. After our last game, Joel gave me a bag full of beers for the bus ride back to Rimini.

You make a lot of new friends, too, of course. I really hit off with my new pitching coach, Jim Dickson, an American everyone called "Jimbo." Jimbo was in his 60s, and he had pitched in the majors with the Houston Colt .45s, the Kansas City A's, and the Cincinnati Reds. Jimbo talked with a bit of a country twang, even though he was from Oregon. He'd been coaching in the Italian Baseball League for over a decade, living a simple life in Italy. He actually lived *at* the ballpark. Not near it, or around it. *In* it. When you walked out his front door, there were the stands behind the first base line, and down and to the right was our dugout and bullpen. To the left was the concession stand.

Jimbo had these big bars on his windows. He showed me where gypsies had tried to break into his place. I thought he was kidding. But it turned out there were a lot of gypsies in Italy. They were looked down on by the Italian people. Many said they were thieves and caused a lot of problems. They did look and dress differently. Jimbo had thick bars covering his side window. One of the bars was bent, and Jimbo freaked out, believing the gypsies had tried to break into his apartment. All you had to do was say the word "gypsy" around Jimbo, and you'd instantly get him all worked up. Gypsies became a running joke.

Jimbo was a history buff, and he liked to travel to see the historic sites of Europe, just like I did. We did that as much as we could during our down time. We visited the towns of Anzio and Nettuno when we played there, the sites of major Allied invasions during World War II. They were the largest American invasions until a year later, when the invasion of Normandy took place. We both liked seeing these historical sites, especially pertaining to World War I and World War II. We checked out some war museums that had artifacts and information about the Anzio invasion. We discovered that baseball was introduced to Italy by the U.S. soldiers who were in Italy after the invasion. Some soldiers had their mitts, and they played baseball there. It grew from there. Italy formed its own professional baseball league in 1946.

When we visited the beaches, there were still some pill boxes in place. Time had gotten the best of them, but we were able to slip inside. I imagined German soldiers inside these things decades earlier, facing this shore where Allied warships sent thousands of American soldiers stomping across this very beach.

We also visited the American military cemetery in Anzio. That was sobering. As we were driving there, I noticed how drab the streets looked, the buildings were tan-colored with no style to them, the street kind of barren and dusty. Then I saw the tall wall of the cemetery, which had more of a whitish color. When we got to the front gate, we could finally see inside, and it was a beautiful place. Green grass as far as you could see, perfectly cut and manicured. The crosses and the Stars of David were perfectly aligned, making perfect rows. Jimbo and I walked through, reading name after name, rank, what state they were from, and the date of their death. It was amazing that all of these guys crossed the same ocean I did, ending up in the wrong place at the wrong time. Metal flying through the air would hit and kill some, whereas others who were standing just a few feet away were lucky. These were the soldiers who died during the invasion and the weeks that followed while the Americans were pinned down by the German Army. I felt sadness for the young men who never got the chance to live a full life.

In the middle of the cemetery was a visitors center. Inside it had artifacts, and these huge, high walls, painted to show a map of Anzio and Nettuno with information about the invasion sites. All about the companies that invaded and where they came ashore. This whole place just took your breath away. Jimbo and I walked around, and when I looked back at the visitors center, I saw the American flag flying high overhead. I felt proud to be an American.

Lance arrived in early June, and he got right into my weekly routine. He met the guys on the team, and I started to show him the things to do in Rimini. He came to our practices during the week. As he had done the year before, he brought his cribbage board. I was glad because it gave me a chance to get even after he beat me last year in Taiwan.

At the end of his first week, Lance saw me pitch against San Marino at our home stadium. The first thing he did was to get to know Dante, the guy who ran the concession stand and sold the beer. Lance would become Dante's best customer. He ordered a large beer every inning of the game. Dante was a gruff old guy who never smiled—he just grunted at you. But

Dante was impressed with how easily Lance was able to put those beers away. That first night, while Lance was downing beers, I pitched a complete game and got my sixth win of the season.

Unlike the U.S., baseball is not a major sport in Italy. It's no secret that soccer rules the sports world in all of Europe. People are aware of baseball, but it isn't as popular as basketball or even volleyball. Baseball is competing for fan attention with the other minor sports. We all knew when to step back and let the soccer fans have their time.

Everybody in Italy knows when the big soccer matches are, and they know everything about their national team. They followed their local Italian Soccer League teams with passion. I didn't have to see it on the news to know if the Italian national team won or lost, I could tell by the mood of the Italian people the next day. It impacted their very personalities. We see this sometimes with college or NFL teams, but it's not even close to the passion of Italian soccer fans.

One night we were practicing at the same time as a big match was going on with the national team. Everyone was wondering if the match was over yet. It didn't take long to figure it out when we saw fireworks being shot up into the night sky and began hearing cars honking their horns.

Even so, international baseball competition did bring out the passion of some Italian fans. The Italian League took time off for the Baseball European Cup. This is the same format as the European Cup for soccer—league champions from last season from all of the European countries participate, along with last year's champion. For this year's Cup, there were two groups: Group A was Spain, Germany, the Czech Republic, and last year's Euro Cup champion, Parma, Italy. In Group B were San Marino, Ukraine, the Netherlands, and our team, Rimini. We were in it because Rimini was last year's Italian League champion. This year's Euro Cup was being played in San Marino, so it was a short trip.

This would be my first "international" competition since the 1984 Olympics. Okay, it wasn't *quite* the same thing—certainly not the same caliber of competition—but any time you're competing for your country (in this case my temporary country), emotions run high.

In our first game, we beat up the team from the Ukraine. The next night, we played against San Marino. At the time, they were second-to-last in the Italian League standings. But for this tourney, they brought in an American pitcher. This guy threw very hard, and he was shutting us down. Still, we found a way to come from behind at the end to get the victory. The third game was against the Netherlands, who also had won their first two games. Jason Simontacchi was our starting pitcher, and he threw a shutout as we beat them, 3–0. That was a big one. We also won our semi-final

Ten. Scenes from the Italian Restaurant

(From left) Eric Pini, Brian Thomas, Don, and Jason Simontacchi in Modena, Italy, July 2000.

game against the second-place team in the other group, which put us in the European Cup championship game.

We faced the Netherlands again, who beat Parma, 10–7, in their semi-final game. I got the start in this championship game. In the first inning, I gave up a three-run homer. I threw this left-handed hitter a changeup down, but he went down on one knee and hit the ball over the left-center field fence. There was one thing I really didn't like about this tournament the moment I heard about it: The hitters used aluminum bats. I hadn't faced hitters using those since college. My instincts were right. The guy definitely put a solid swing on the pitch, but there's no doubt that the homer was an "aluminum bat" home run.

Regardless, we were losing, 3–0. I had to battle through every inning, but I put up zeroes. But so was the Dutch pitcher. With one out in the seventh inning, I gave up another home run, and manager Mike Romano took me out, trailing 4–0. We eventually scratched out a run, but the Dutch also scored against one of our relievers, and they ended up beating us, 5–1, to win the European Cup.

The thing that bothered me the most was watching the Dutch team celebrate. They went on and on, acting like a bunch of dumb asses, doing stupid shit. It was very hard to stomach.

When we got back to our normal routine, Lance and I started to spend time with Jimbo. We'd go visit him, and it wouldn't take long for the subject of gypsies to come up to get Jimbo instantly worked-up. He was so freaked out by the gypsies.

We decided to go on a little road trip on our upcoming off-days. We didn't make any set plans on where. Jimbo—who had traveled throughout Europe before—suggested that we just play it by ear. We left on a Sunday morning and needed to be back for Tuesday night's practice. We started out driving northward through Italy and just went wherever the moment took us. I was driving, and we made Venice our first stop. It was cool for Lance to see this unique place. Lance and I walked from one end of Venice to the other.

The time flew by, and we were back on the road, nearing the border of Austria. We were only about five miles away from the border of Slovenia. I wanted to go into Slovenia just to see what it looked like and to say I'd been there, but Jimbo was too nervous about it. The war in Bosnia was over, but it was still fresh to some, meaning they might not be too kind to Americans. So we skipped that side-trip.

We started driving across the Alps. It was everything I imagined it would be. We drove through a lot of tunnels going through the mountains, and as we were driving out in the middle of nowhere, we saw very old castles on mountain ledges. It was amazing to see these huge places

Pitching coach Jimbo Dickson lived in an apartment attached to the right field bleachers in Rimini.

with absolutely nobody around. We got through the mountains and were in Austria. At one point, we could see a large lake off in the distance. It was the town of Velden. We found a bank to exchange our lira for shillings. We went into a little grocery store to buy bread, lunch meat, and beer.

In Austria, everyone was speaking German, and none of us spoke German. I had English, Spanish, and Chinese covered, and Jimbo had Italian covered … sort of. We left the grocery store, drove by the lake, and found a park bench with a table. We made sandwiches, had some beer, and enjoyed the warm sunshine. It was a nice rest. We walked around Velden for a little bit and decided to find a hotel and spend the night. Jimbo was tired. As we were checking into this small hotel, we had trouble with the language. In the tiny lobby was an older Austrian woman who was playing the piano. In broken English, Italian, and German, Jimbo convinced her to let him join in. He wasn't playing that well, but she smiled as he played and told him he was good.

This was what being a tourist felt like, I guess. Being in these countries had always been work for me. I had limited time off to sight-see. I felt grateful that I got this free time in Italy, *and* I was getting paid to be here.

We got up early the next morning and began driving northwest. Jimbo suggested we go northward and go to Salzburg. We could drive by some World War I battle sites along the way. We noticed that there was a little town coming up called Spittal. We decided with a name like that, we had to pull off and check it out. We had no idea what was there or what to expect. That was part of the adventure. We got to Salzburg—close to the border with Germany—and drove around. We were trying to decide what to do. It was hot, so we didn't feel like walking. Jimbo kept saying he wanted to go to Berchtesgaden in Germany, close to Salzburg. He wanted to see the Eagle's Nest, Adolf Hitler's retreat.

As we kept driving, I got very thirsty. We got to talking about how great it would be to find a beer garden in Germany and get a large, cold German lager. That thought kept me going, because I needed to get out of the car.

When we got to Berchtesgaden, we didn't know where to go. Outside the post office, we saw a man and asked him if he spoke English. He didn't. But I pulled out my pocket translator, typed in "beer garden," pushed the German button, and showed it to him. The translator must have been perfect because the man pointed over our shoulders. There was a beer garden only two blocks away. We sat outside and ordered the largest, coldest beer they had. It hit the spot.

After a couple cold ones, we went to see the Eagle's Nest. Sadly, when we arrived, we found out the place was closed that day. Jimbo was so disappointed. We ended up walking around Berchtesgaden, a cool little town.

As we continued driving, we saw a sign for Innsbruck, Austria, the site of the 1972 Winter Olympics. We wanted to see the stadium where the Opening Ceremonies took place. We pulled into the parking lot, and I saw the Olympic rings outside. Now I'd been to two Olympic venues, including the games I played in.

The next morning, we decided to go to Munich, Germany, and check out that city—which hosted the Summer Olympics in 1972 (memorable for all the wrong reasons). But the big thing was going to see the Nazi concentration camp in Dachau, which was just outside of Munich. When we entered Munich from the highway, we got a little twisted around. We finally figured out that we had to drive around the outside of the city on the freeway to get to the other side, we couldn't just drive straight across Munich. We eventually made it to Dachau.

The concentration camp was *really* sobering. We saw the rows and rows where the barracks used to be. There was only one left that they used to show the tourists the conditions that the people had to live in. We saw the building where the ovens were located. There was a tourist center building that had many pictures of the people and the camp. It was amazing to look at a picture and see how awful it was for these people, and then look right outside and see the exact place where that happened.

Inside the tourist center, there was a little theater that showed a documentary of this concentration camp, with a lot of video of the actual people and what took place here. It was horrible, but the point was to show people what really happened, so that something like this could never happen again. We finally left the concentration camp and drove back toward Munich before heading south towards Italy. A little way outside of Munich, Jimbo said there was a little town not too far away called Garmisch-Partenkirchen. He'd been there before, and we could find something to eat.

We pulled into Garmisch, parked, and began looking for somewhere to eat. As we walked down the sidewalk, we approached a building with two guys outside on the sidewalk, sitting at a high, round table. As we walked by, we smelled food from inside and heard these two guys speaking English. We'd gotten lucky. I'd been in quite a few bars and "pubs" now in Europe, but it was still cool to hear other people refer to me and my friends as "Yanks."

We stopped in our tracks and asked if food was sold inside. One of the men, the owner of the pub, offered to take us inside and take our orders. Inside were televisions showing sports, mostly soccer. The place was kind of small, but the owner was a cool guy named Chris. He said he was from Wales, that this was his Irish pub in Germany. He asked us what we wanted to drink, and I asked what kinds of beers he had. He asked me

Ten. Scenes from the Italian Restaurant

if I liked Guinness. Believe it or not, I had to tell him I'd never had one before. This guy should have been on a Guinness commercial. He said it was the best because it came right from Dublin, Ireland. How could we all not order one?

Chris poured my Guinness in front of me, showing me how to pour it just right, the foam rising upward and so forth. When I took my first drink, I was hooked. To this day, I still love Guinness. Chris stayed in the bar and continued to chat with us while we ate. We kept talking and consuming more and more Guinness. He had a bunch of CDs, and we picked out the music. Luckily, he had a CD of my favorite band, The Doors. When I was in high school, I turned Lance onto The Doors, and they had become his favorite rock band too.

Chris told us all about the history of this area. Since I'm a history buff, I enjoyed this a lot. He went back hundreds of years. Time flew by. We were preparing to leave, but Chris told us that we shouldn't go, asking if we'd noticed the big mountains around Garmisch. He said it would be raining within the next 15 minutes because the clouds built up from these mountains, and he could tell that it was about to rain. Sure enough, right on cue it began raining very hard.

So we ordered some more Guinness.

More time passed, and it was now dark. We'd had enough to drink that it wasn't a good idea to drive. Chris had a friend with a condo/hotel place that we could stay at for the night. Jimbo was spent and wanted to go, but Lance and I wanted to stick around. Chris got a taxi for Jimbo. Lance and I had a good time hanging at the bar, meeting some of Chris' friends and some of the locals.

By the end of the night, when it was time to go, Chris gave us the directions to the condo, and he gave us directions on how to get back out onto the highway the next morning. He told us to leave on the main road and said we'd come across a U.S./NATO military base. Turn left, and we'd be on the right track home. We told Chris that if he ever came to the United States, to look us up.

The next morning, we were up and on the road for the long drive back to Rimini. The drive would normally take close to eight hours, but this was Europe, so I drove close to 100 mph, which cut off some travel time. We drove all day and got back to Rimini. We dropped Jimbo off at his apartment at the stadium but were sure to mess with him by mentioning that his apartment had probably been broken into by the gypsies while we were away. We got the reaction that we hoped for.

I kept reminding myself I was there to play baseball, but it was sooooo cool to be able to play tourist on the side.

Lance and I kept right on sightseeing every chance we got. We knew we'd probably never get this opportunity again. During a road trip, the Leaning Tower of Pisa was only a couple of hours away by train. Lance and I decided that we'd wake up early on Saturday morning and take the train from Grosseto to Pisa. I pitched on Friday nights, so I had weekends free, basically. When we arrived in Pisa, we knew to walk down a main road from the train station and eventually we'd see the tower. This was an ancient road with old buildings on both sides. It took a while, but finally we found it. It was just like the pictures I'd seen in books, but now I was seeing it with my own eyes, and it gave me a surreal feeling. We took pictures and walked up and touched it. Basic tourist stuff. I'd gotten really good at it.

The next morning, we were still tired but got up early and took the train for Rome. The three-game series in Grosseto was over, so we had two full days to be tourists. By the time Lance and I got to our hotel, it was still morning and we were both still really tired. We felt the effects of getting up so early the day before to go to Pisa. We had two days to see Rome and do as much as we could before we'd have to return to Rimini. We had to make the time count. But we didn't.

When we got to the hotel room, we decided to take a nap before going out to see Rome. We slept a little too long. I felt like I weighed a thousand pounds and couldn't move. Somehow, some way, we finally found the energy to get up and get moving to see Rome. We could've slept the day away.

Once we got onto our feet, Lance and I followed the map I'd gotten from a teammate. We did all of this on foot. In Rome, the next tourist thing to see is always a walk away. We walked around and saw the Fountain of Trevi, the Pantheon, the Roman Forum, the Spanish Steps, Ponte Sant'angelo and the Castle Sant'angelo, the Piazza del Popolo, the Altar of the Fatherland, the Colosseum, St. Peter's Square, St. Peter's Basilica, the Sistine Chapel, and the Vatican. When Lance and I got to the Colosseum, a couple of guys dressed like Roman soldiers offered to take a picture of us with our own camera. When they were done, they wanted us to pay them a lot of money. When we didn't want to pay that amount, they began to get nasty. Good thing there were no lions around.

We went inside the Colosseum, and it was amazing to see where the gladiators fought and the other things that took place, right there before our eyes. Lucky for us, right across the street from the Colosseum was a little bar where we got a couple of cold beers to rejuvenate ourselves and get back to checking out these sites.

It took us two full days to see them all. On our first day, we went to the Vatican, but we got there too late, it was closed, and we had to return the next day. The next day, we were able to look up at the ceiling of the Sistine

The Leaning Tower of Pisa, July 2000.

Chapel to see Michelangelo's work, particularly "The Creation of Adam." These sites were awesome to see. I always remembered seeing these places in books, but when you're there and see them with your own eyes, it is amazing. At the Colosseum, I kept thinking about how old this place was and that it was still standing. People came here a couple of thousand years ago to see the gladiators, the lion fights, and the mock naval battles.

Finally, it was back to Rimini and back to practice. After one practice, a bunch of the guys—Italians and Americans—were hanging around when somebody broke out a soccer ball, We started kicking the ball around. None of us Americans played much "futbol" growing up. I was not good at all, but we were just having fun. The Italian guys were trying to show off their skills. It somehow became the Italians against the Americans in a playful game that turned into a competitive match. Suddenly we had goals made of baseball gloves. When the Italian guys scored a goal against us, they acted the fool, being funny. One of the Italian guys went up to the guy who scored a goal, had him put his foot on his lap, and pretended to shine his shoes.

They scored four straight goals on us, maybe five, and every time they scored, they did some antics, which made everyone laugh. When we finally scored a goal and we did something stupid, it got a laugh from the Italian guys. Suddenly, we scored one goal after another. The Italians began to get serious because we were starting to beat them. They couldn't score anymore, and we kept scoring on them. We were now kicking their asses, and our antics weren't making them laugh any more. We completely dominated them, and it got to the point where they got mad and embarrassed. I remember telling our guys to tone it down, so we ended up stopping the game. A bunch of Americans who didn't even know how to play just beat them at their own game.

Our next home series against Parma would be Lance's last games to see; he would head home next week. Friday night was my day to pitch, and Lance was there watching. When he was making his way to the concession stand to get his first beer, Dante saw him coming, and the smile on Dante's face was priceless. His best customer was back. Lance returned every inning, and Dante had a beer waiting, Dante took special care of Lance.

The month with Lance went by very fast, just like the summer before in Taiwan. I really enjoyed having him with me in Italy, and we had another great time together. Just like in Taiwan, we played hundreds of games of cribbage, and while Lance beat me in Taiwan, in Italy I beat him. It was close, but I won. We called it a draw.

Lance left for home the same day Tami, Logan, and Eileen were arriving. It was July 3, my birthday, and while I on the train to Bologna to pick them up, I thought about the fun Lance and I had. During the last week, while we played cribbage and hung out, Lance casually drew some pictures, one of them a Vietnam War scene. It was very detailed and very graphic. I still have that drawing.

It was quite a chore getting Tami, Logan, and Tami's mom, Eileen,

Ten. Scenes from the Italian Restaurant

from the airport in Bologna to my apartment in Rimini. Trains, buses, and my automobile. Several big, heavy suitcases and all the other stuff they brought across the pond. By the time we got to the apartment, I was wiped out. I decided that people that do this sort of thing for a living don't get paid enough.

When we finally got everything upstairs, Tami began complaining about how she didn't like the apartment, it was a lot smaller than what I had told her, and there was too much dust. She wanted me to take their bags back outside and said they were going to stay in a hotel. I bit my lip. I'd just busted my tail getting all those bags up here. I stayed as calm as I could and politely informed her that no, we were not going anywhere else. I mentioned that my American teammates were rooming together in a much smaller place than this, and that the team was giving me special treatment. Once we got settled in, Tami decided that with a little sprucing up, it could be a nice place.

Their first day was an off-day for me, and after we rested, we drove around to show them where everything was. Tami wanted to go to the grocery store, and I had to show her how things were done. When we returned, we had a full refrigerator. I took Logan across the street to play some baseball on an open space of grass. The next day, we went to the beach. It was hard to find a parking place because the beach was packed with other tourists. That afternoon before I had to go to practice, I took them to Oliver's

Don and Logan August in front of the Roman Colosseum, July 2000.

restaurant. Every day I'd show them around Rimini—the Piazza, the mall outside of Rimini, to San Marino, and to McDonald's. Eileen especially liked the idea of getting a beer at McDonald's. We went to the beach practically every day.

It was about a mile and a half to the beach. Mostly we drove, but a few times we walked there. We ate most of our meals at my apartment, which meant we made a lot of trips to the grocery store. We ate out sometimes, mostly at Oliver's. On the days of the flea market, we made our way to the old piazza. Tami loved seeing the stuff there, especially the clothes. I showed them the gelato shop, which they of course loved. We went there often.

The week ahead featured a home series against Nettuno. Thursday was Logan's birthday, and we found a bakery and bought him a birthday cake. We celebrated his eighth birthday. We found a spot at the beach that we liked and returned there every chance we had, at least five days a week. It was July, meaning the beaches in Rimini were completely full. We rented our four lounge chairs, and we soaked up the sun, played and swam in the Adriatic Sea, and took walks down the beach. By midday every day, it was so hot we'd rush to get our daily slurpees. They were so good and hit the spot every time. My tan was getting really good—but not as nice as Tami's of course.

Now that Logan had turned eight years old, we noticed him reacting to the topless sunbathers. Logan would tease his grandmother—he'd say, "Grandma, what color is that girl's bathing suit?" When Eileen turned around to look, it would be a topless girl standing there. Logan got the reaction out of his grandma that he wanted: "Oh, Logan!" When we put our lounge chairs on the beach, everyone was squeezed very close, side by side, about a two-foot space between you and the chair. It was just enough space to walk. You had strangers lying right next to you.

One day, lying right next to us were three people, a girl about 21 years old—who was sunbathing topless—her mother, and her boyfriend. They'd been there for a little while before they got up to go for a walk. I was on the end next to them, so they had to squeeze past me. First the boyfriend walked by. As the young topless girl was moving past me, Logan made a loud whistle at her, the kind you'd imagine hearing from construction workers when a pretty girl walked by. Logan followed that by saying— loudly—"Smokin'!" The girl stopped and made a sour face at *me* as she kept walking. Her mom made a face at me too. It was like they were saying, "What's up with this crazy kid?" When I looked at the boyfriend, he had a sour face too. Like this was all my fault. After they walked away, I turned to Logan. "What was that about?" Logan didn't miss a beat. "I liked her bathing suit!" Tami and Eileen were both mortified. But it made for a good laugh later.

Ten. Scenes from the Italian Restaurant

Don, Tami, and Logan August sitting on the famous Spanish Steps in Rome, July 2000.

One Sunday morning, we took the train to Rome. Since I'd gone there earlier with Lance, I kinda knew my way around. Our hotel room was right around the corner from the Spanish Steps, and we were eager to see the sites. Tami wanted to go to the main shopping area, so while Tami and her mom did that, I took Logan to see the Colosseum, the Forum, and a couple of other places where we took pictures. After being tourists for the day, we ended up finding a good place to eat dinner, a cool little café where we ate and watched the people wander around. The next day, we went to see the Vatican, St. Peter's Square, and the Sistine Chapel. I'd already seen these places with Lance, but they were still awesome the second time. Being a tourist is hard work. After another full day of seeing the sights, we were spent. The next morning, we were back on the train to Rimini.

The following week, we went to Florence, and there was a line at the train station for help finding you a hotel. Does it get more touristy than that? When we left our hotel, we went to the Piazza della Signoria. This piazza has a lot of restaurants, nearby works of art with a lot of statues on display, and it was centrally located. One of the places nearby was the Ponte Vecchio. Tami wanted to go to this bridge because she heard they had a lot of places that sold jewelry. I wanted to see this famous bridge for its history.

Until the year 1218, this was the only bridge that crossed the Arno

Don, Tami, and Logan August in a horse-drawn carriage in Florence, Italy, July 2000.

River. It had collapsed a few times but was rebuilt; the current bridge has been there since 1345. It was the only bridge that wasn't destroyed by the retreating German Army in World War II. Later we went to the Florence Cathedral to see the Duomo. It's a magnificent building with a dome that was constructed and completed in 1469, and it's about 370 feet high.

We decided to take a horse carriage ride around Florence. As we were flagging down one of the horse carriages, two competing drivers got into a big argument right there on the street over who would give us the ride. One guy charged the other and began throwing punches, and the other guy got scared and ran away. I suppose we ended up riding in the victor's carriage. He got real charming real quick. Had a big smile as he began to treat us to his horse carriage ride. He spoke some English and told us about everything we were seeing and the history of Florence. After a long day, we returned to the Piazza della Signoria for a nice dinner at a restaurant, sitting outside in the piazza.

While in Florence, we saw Michelangelo's statue of David in a museum called the Galleria dell' Accademia. There was a lot of other great artwork there, but the main attraction for me was the David. I took a lot of pictures because of its history and importance. For Logan at eight years old, it wasn't all that. I thought maybe he'd appreciate the moment later in life.

In the early evening, we were by the Duomo and saw an artist drawing people. After he was done, we asked if he would do a drawing of Tami, Logan, and me. We took turns sitting in front of him, and it took over an hour for him to finish. The drawing turned out very good, all three of us in it together, and it looked just like us. We had it framed, and it still hangs on our wall at home today.

During the evenings when we were "touristing," we'd find a restaurant—and *all* of them were excellent—and just sit outside, enjoy the surroundings, and watch life go by. It was so relaxing.

After a month that produced a lifetime of memories, my family returned to Wisconsin. They had a bit of an adventure with their airplane connections in London, but nothing like when Tami and Logan were diverted to Alaska. Once they were home, it was back to being very quiet in my apartment. I missed them immediately. But I had a season—and a career—to finish.

Eleven

The End

The finish line may have come in Italy, but the beginning of the end happened much closer to home. It was *at* home, actually.

Only a scant few Major League pitchers know when they've played their final game or thrown their final pitch in the big leagues. You always expect there will be a "next game." That's sort of what baseball is all about, right? Lose today? Go get 'em tomorrow. There is always tomorrow.

Except when there isn't.

I didn't realize I'd won my final Major League game on August 16, 1991, over the Baltimore Orioles. Nor did I know that on September 25, I'd get my final major league decision in an extra-innings loss to the New York Yankees at County Stadium in Milwaukee. I also didn't know at the time that I was making my final big league appearance on October 1 of that year, when I pitched an inning of relief against the Cleveland Indians.

To me, I'd just finished up a mediocre 9–8 season. My ERA (5.47) was too high, and I had work to do to make 1992 better than 1991. Tomorrow was just an off-season away.

But things don't always turn out the way you planned. After completing a lackluster 83–79 season, good for fourth place in the packed American League East (yes, the Brewers were in the AL East and not the National League Central), the Brewers front office decided to clean house. It began with the dismissal of long-time general manager Harry Dalton and manager Tom Trebelhorn. "The Purge" also included mainstays like Greg Brock, Chuck Crim, and Gary Sheffield, who was traded to San Diego the following spring, having complained his way out of town.

I would have loved to stay, but new GM Sal Bando called me and told me they were taking me off the 40-man roster. I could opt to become a free agent or accept an assignment to Triple A. I took that to mean I needed to find a new team, so I went about doing so. Not the best decision in retrospect.

Spring Training with the San Francisco Giants in Scottsdale in March of 1992 was a rude awakening. So was ending up in Double A with the Detroit Tigers a few weeks later.

Eleven. The End

After spending the previous four seasons in the big leagues, I was now in the minors, making just $1,000 a month. But I thought it was a good chance for me because the Tigers' starting pitchers were struggling at the major league level.

The Tigers' Double A team was based in London, Ontario, Canada. In late May, I made my way there to start what took me about seven years to figure out: I was now in "Phase Three" of my pro baseball career. "Phase One" is making your way up the ladder to the majors through the minor leagues. For me, that happened in the Houston Astros' organization before I was traded to the Brewers. "Phase Two" is bouncing back and forth between the majors and minors. I did a little bit of that with Milwaukee and Triple A Denver. "Phase Three" is when a player is back in the minors, but never returns to the majors. You don't realize you're in Phase Three until your career is pretty much finished. You always think you're still in Phase Two, working your way back up. But when you're let go for the final time, or when you retire without making it back, you realize where you've been all along.

Perhaps, then, the next eight seasons were "Phase Four" for me and my playing career?

In between bus rides and nights hanging out with younger guys, I pitched pretty well for the Tigers, up until the end. In my final appearance in Double A London—just days before I was going home to be with Tami for the birth of our son, Logan—I pitched a complete-game shutout in Binghamton, New York. After the All-Star break, I went up to Triple A to pitch for the famous Toledo Mud Hens. I was happy and relieved at the same time.

My first start with Toledo went well. I got into a game in relief and did okay. Through my first 10 innings, I gave up three earned runs and my ERA was 2.70. I didn't do well after that. After a couple of rough outings in August, I got released by the Tigers. It was the second time I was released in the same season. But I never, ever stopped believing in tomorrow.

Honestly, I felt like a failure. I called my agent and told him I'd been released. The 1992 season was over, so I focused on finding a team for next season. I needed to get to winter ball to be seen, and I needed my agent's help with that. I started having trouble getting through to him. Finally got him one day, and I could tell he wasn't enthusiastic about our conversation. He had some other clients he was dealing with. If I was a star, he'd be getting right back to me.

People will quit talking to you when you're on the way down. They won't return calls, and I thought that was very disrespectful. I called again and left another message. This time, I called to fire him. I wish I could have talked to him about it, but again he didn't answer. I had to leave that on a message, too.

I got a new agent, Chuck Berry, who got me a job that winter in Puerto Rico and then a job for the 1993 season in Mexico. The team in Puebla wasn't good, but I was a mainstay in the rotation. But there were bumps along the way. Foreign imports are always supposed to run perfectly, right?

I survived a bout with a sore elbow that almost got me released mid-season. One day, just like that, I got a phone call from Chuck. He'd made a Triple A deal with the Cleveland Indians. I was going back to America, getting another chance.

I was joining a juggernaut, managed by Charlie Manuel, one of baseball's all-time best characters. I started four days later in Toledo—the same team that had released me the season before. Obviously, I wanted to pitch well, show them they'd made a mistake. Unfortunately, it didn't go well—went just four innings and gave up seven runs. No way to make a first impression. Still, they told me I would start again in five days in Columbus, Ohio.

When you're in Phase Two—which I firmly believed I was—you keep your ear to the ground about personnel moves. I was hearing rumblings that my start against Columbus could be make or break for me. It was even in the newspaper. After one game, I was already on the hot seat. I just left a job in Mexico for this? No pressure, huh?

Whether it was fair or not, I had to pitch really well to keep my job. Game day arrived, and tender elbow and all, I was able to clutch up, and I shut down the Clippers for six innings before giving up a single run on a misplayed fly ball in the seventh. We won the game, and I kept my roster spot.

Charlie told me I was being moved to the bullpen, and he didn't know if/when I'd start again. I wasn't thrilled, but beggars can't be choosers, right? I was just hoping to get the ball on a semi-regular basis. I did well in two of my first three outings—the exception being a bumpy two-inning stint against the Cleveland Indians in an exhibition game. Then, out of the blue, they told me that they needed a roster spot and were putting me on the DL, even though I wasn't hurt. My elbow had healed by then.

Three weeks of practice followed before I came off the injured list. I got to start again and went six innings, giving up a single run and getting another win. It felt so good to get another chance. I started again five days later against Syracuse and had another quality start there.

Now I was sure I was still in Phase Two.

Things were going well. After more relief work, I got another start and bested one of my former Brewers teammates, Mike Birkbeck. After six innings, we were tied, 3–3. Richmond took Mike out for the top of the seventh, and we scored some runs. In the bottom of the seventh, Charlie took me out. So Mike and I both pitched six innings and gave up three runs. Mike got a no-decision, while I got the win. Things were good.

Eleven. The End

Out of the blue came another stint on the Phantom DL for the exact same (non-injury) reason.

This was something I had to live with now that I wasn't a hot prospect or vested member of anyone's organization. I just wanted to get enough appearances in to solidify a future with the Indians. This was my path back to the show. But there was no happy ending to this chapter of my career either. I came off the DL, and my first relief outing was awful. But I bounced back. In my last four relief appearances to finish the season, I pitched six innings, gave up just one run, walked three, and had five strikeouts. I felt like I did a good job to end the regular season. I finished with a 3–1 record and threw 44-plus innings in my five starts and nine relief appearances. Overall, excluding two games, I felt like I'd done a good job.

Nonetheless, the Indians told me they didn't have any future plans for me. Pitching coach Dyar Miller told me that he didn't think I'd make it back to the majors. I respected his opinion, but I didn't want to believe that. I appreciated Cleveland's up-front and honest approach, but I respectfully disagreed with their evaluation. I believed that if I'd gotten regular work and not been put on the Phantom DL twice, things could have gone a lot better. I still believed I was in Phase Two, even if they didn't.

That belief sent me to the Dominican Republic to play winter ball in front of a bevy of MLB scouts. If I could pitch well in the Dominican winter league, which featured a lot of established big league standouts, I'd show I was worthy of at least another Triple A contract.

By the end of the winter league regular season, I'd pitched myself into the starting rotation. My first start went great. After six scoreless innings, they took me out with a 6–0 lead. I'd done my job and picked up my first win in the DR. I finished the regular season with seven outings—including the one start—15 1/3 innings and a 1.18 ERA.

I got my first playoff start against Licey in Santo Domingo. I pitched into the sixth inning, and with two outs and the tying run on base, they took me out with a 4–3 lead. The bullpen held the lead, and we won.

The next start—arguably my most important since I left the Brewers—didn't go as well. Before my first pitch, I looked into the stands and saw Cleveland Indians general manager John Hart. For whatever reason, I didn't have my best stuff ... but I got by for a while. In the third inning, I gave up two runs and got pulled. Two and two-thirds innings. We never came back, and I took the loss. I think I could have battled through it, but the manager made the move. Hart didn't see anything good out of me. I was disappointed we lost the game, but I was more disappointed that I blew an opportunity with someone important watching me. That game was my only subpar outing of the winter.

At this point, other free agents on our team were getting deals for the coming season, but nothing came of my strong finish to the Dominican Winter league season. By mid–February 1994, with Spring Training about to start, I still didn't have a team. I had good numbers—11 games, five starts, 2–2 record, 36 ⅓ innings, 20 strikeouts, and a great ERA of 1.98. Chuck kept calling. No offers, not even for a Triple A, minor league spring training.

Was betting on myself and refusing to accept the Brewers sending me to Triple A two years ago still haunting me?

I told Chuck I'd be willing to go back to Mexico. My mind—and my pitching arm—were still firmly in Phase Two.

Sure, I was a little bitter about going back. But after having my "poor me" moment on the plane, I felt good about knowing my way around Puebla and the Mexican League. This time around, Puebla wasn't very competitive. I ended up starting 10 games during the first half of the season, threw five complete games, including a shutout, and had an ERA of 3.36. The team, mired in last place and looking to shed payroll, released me after the first half of the season, and I went back to Wisconsin. After I was home for a week, my telephone rang. The Campeche team wanted to know if I was interested in playing for them. It was back to Mexico. Things went better with a much better squad in Campeche. I started 12 more games, had an 8–2 record, threw five shutouts, and posted an ERA of just 1.34. Combining both halves, I had 22 starts, an 11–9 record, 13 complete games, six shutouts, 76 strikeouts, and a 2.22 ERA.

That success got me a shot with the San Diego Padres' Double A team in Wichita for the final two-and-a-half weeks of the 1994 season, a job I *thought* at the time would include a contract for the following season. Ironically, I turned *down* a chance to finish the season with the Indians, the team I was with at the end of the previous season, before taking the Padres' offer. I went with the Padres because of Reggie Waller, the assistant general manager, whom I had a long history with. Maybe that was a mistake. I'll never know.

I again thought my time in Double A would be brief—moving up to finish the season in Triple A would have given me a great shot at going to spring training with the Padres for the 1995 season. Didn't turn out like I'd planned.

I spent the entire brief stint in Wichita coming out of the bullpen, getting very limited opportunities. My final numbers: No decisions in just over 11 innings, and a 3.86 ERA. Would that be enough?

Shockingly, YES! But for all the wrong reasons.

The whole "replacement player" fiasco the following spring really soured me on baseball in America. I had no interest in being part of that mess or going back to Mexico. After the Pirates released me from their Triple A team in Calgary, I took Reggie's offer to go to Taiwan.

Eleven. The End

Ask yourself this: If you were me, and you still believed you were in "Phase Two" with a legitimate chance to pitch your way back to the big leagues, would you have given up on baseball at age 31? Me neither.

At the outset, I certainly didn't see Taiwan as a place I'd spend the next five seasons—the vast majority of the next five calendar *years*. I saw it as a stepping-stone ... perhaps to the Japanese League—which was becoming a pipeline back to the majors. Taiwan was a detour, not a destination. It was a better option than Mexico at this point. That much I was sure about.

The level of play in Taiwan—which was six years into fielding teams in the new Chinese Professional Baseball League when I arrived—was probably somewhere between Double A and Triple A. I just wanted to pitch and to be seen by scouts. It took one scout to like me to either get me to Japan or back into a big league team's plans. This is how you think in Phase Two.

Before I left, I heard the stories about how crazy different things were on *and* off the field. On the field, the style of play was still "small ball." There was a lot of bunting and slap hitters just trying to put the ball in play. What surprised me was that our Taiwanese players were ... soft. They're nice guys and I liked them, but they were soft. They needed band aids for little scrapes, and the trainer went through cold spray like crazy. When they were hit by a pitch, the game would stop. They'd writhe in pain, their faces grimacing, before the trainer sprinted out there and applied the cold spray. Sometimes it was funny to watch because you think to yourself, "that couldn't hurt that much." When a foreign player got hit by the same pitch, they'd just drop the bat, jog to first, and never even rub it. At times, they brought a stretcher onto the field to carry off the Taiwanese player. Magically, a little later, they were fine.

Don pitching in Taipei, Taiwan, 1996.

During one game, one of our players slid into third base and stayed down, rolling and writhing in pain. Our third base coach was checking him out and had our trainer hurry across the field. I saw his face. He was in agony, holding his knee, and we were thinking he must have really hurt himself—maybe torn ligaments or a fracture. The trainer and third base coach motioned for someone to bring the stretcher out, and they put him on it. They brought him into the dugout flat on his back in pain. I walked over, thinking I might see a bone sticking out of his leg. When the trainer pulled up his pant leg, there was no bone, no blood. All I saw was a skinned knee. He was writhing on the field, the game was delayed for him, and he was carried off the field on a stretcher ... for a skinned knee! Really. A little later, I asked him if that was it, a skinned knee? He told me, "Oh, but this stings so bad!"

Seriously.

What these guys lacked in toughness on the field they made up for off it. They were soft, but they could be hard-core whisky drinkers. At practices, you could smell the whisky coming out of their pores, and they smoked cigarettes like chimneys. They also chewed betelnut, this hard, juicy nut from a bush or tree. The Taiwan players put that stuff in their mouth and let it soak in, spitting out the juice. It's dark purple, and it stained their teeth and mouth. It's their version of our chewing tobacco. They bought their little plastic baggies of betelnut from tiny little stands off the side of the road, normally sold by young girls in their early 20s, wearing super-short shorts with small, low-cut tops. Sex sells, because practically every man chewed betelnut. Those stands were everywhere.

The atmosphere at games was amazing. Every night, the stands were full, and the crowd was raucous. You could feel the energy of the excitement from the fans. When our team was in the third base dugout, our fans sat on our side behind home plate, down past third base and the left field foul line, around the left field section of the bleachers, and into the middle of center field. The other team's fans sat from the middle of center field all the way around the right field and first base side to right behind home plate. The fans wore their team's colors and had several large banners and flags that they would wave throughout the game. They even had musical instruments they played throughout the game, especially big drums. There were plastic clubs they banged, and they sang chants for their teams throughout. Both sides went back and forth, waiting for their team to do something to give them the opportunity to out-cheer the other side.

I quickly found out that winning that night's game wasn't just important in the stands and in the standings—it was important to your wallet. Every time your team won, the entire team got paid a bonus, whether you played or not. If you didn't play, you'd get around $40 U.S. If you had three

Eleven. The End

A team autographing promotion for Fala, 1998.

hits, you could get around $125, and a home run got you even more. If you were the winning pitcher, you got around $150, and if you had a lot of strikeouts or threw a shutout, it went up from there. If your team lost, you got ... nothing, even if you had four hits in the game, or if you threw seven shutout innings, you lost. It was winner take all every night. I got $25 my first night there after I watched the game in street clothes.

Post-game interview with Don and a Chinese-speaking interpreter, also the team's general manager. Don was the game's MVP.

Yes, I definitely wasn't in America anymore.

When I got my first uniform, I noticed it had a name in Chinese writing on the back of the jersey: "Ow Gu Dzi Du." I asked our translator if those four characters meant "August." She said no, not exactly. I gave her a puzzled look. She told me Ow Gu Dzi Du meant the European King Augustus Caesar. They liked to give foreign players names that had some color to them. The writing was in Chinese characters, since they don't use letters. Most names are in two characters, but mine had four. It took me a week of practicing to learn to write my name in Chinese. I had to learn because the fans wanted autographs in Chinese.

My new team, the Jungo Bears, planned to use me as a closer, so I got my first crack at the role. You could pitch literally every night. This was old school baseball in the 1990s. The three-inning save was not yet out of fashion like it is today. In my first relief appearance, I came in to pitch in the seventh inning with a three-run lead. I tossed the final three innings and earning my first ever professional save.

I pitched again the next night—just one inning—and got my second save. By the middle of August, I had six saves, two wins, and an ERA of 1.44 ERA. Was America—or Japan—watching?

In late September, after I made 33 straight relief appearances, our manager, the legendary Taiwanese coach, Mr. Wu—who took over as manager at the midway point of the season—decided to use me

Chinese spelling of "Augustus Caesar" on the back of Don's baseball uniform in Taiwan.

Eleven. The End 179

as a starter. Fortunately, 20 of those 33 relief appearances were multiple innings, so I was ready. In my first start in mid–September, I went the full nine, scattering four hits without giving up a run. I got two more starts, losing one and winning the other. The team finished in last place. I finished my first season in the CPBL with a 4–5 record, 13 saves, and a 3.56 ERA. Would that get the attention of anyone back home?

Didn't happen. So I returned to Taiwan and played for the new owner of the Jungo Bears—who changed their name to the Sinon Bulls in mid-season—for 1996. I liked the name the Bulls, but the bad thing was our new team logo—an animated picture of a big fat cow, not a bull. The cow had big udders with a dumb, smiling face. The people of Taiwan love cute, animated characters.

Before the season, Mr. Wu and the coaches brought me and my teammate Daryl Smith together and asked for our input. One of us would be a starter, and the other a closer. I didn't want to be a closer again, but neither did Daryl. There was already enough pressure on every foreign-born player to be perfect every night. I quickly let them know I wanted to start, that I'd be more valuable to the team as a starter. Daryl gave in and agreed to be the closer. He ended up struggling in the role.

A few weeks later, Daryl came into the dugout very upset. He told us that he had just messed up ... bad. He was in the changing room when Dar, the general manager, came up to him and started giving him crap about his recent bad outings. Daryl admitted he was struggling, but Dar kept up the verbal assault until Daryl couldn't take it anymore. He told Dar that he'd had enough, but Dar said something that made Daryl snap. He punched the GM.

Don pitching for the Sinon Bulls, 1996.

Daryl expected the worst, and it happened after the game. He got released. The stress of having to be perfect when you are playing in a foreign country is very real.

The team got off to a terrible start with not much going right. There was one big similarity to baseball in America. When you're losing, it's the manager who takes the fall. There wasn't a better manager in Taiwan than Mr. Wu, but by the end of June, the first half of the season was over, and we were buried in last place. We lost games in a lot of ways. We got smoked; we lost close, low-scoring games; or we blew leads at the end when it looked like we had it won. We had a lot of losing streaks. One game summed it up: After the first two innings one night, we had a 9–0 lead. I knew there was still too much game left. Sure enough, the other team kept pecking away, closing the gap. We couldn't add on. We were ahead big, but we were the ones feeling the pressure. They got close, and we crumbled. They came all the way back and took the lead, and we ended up losing.

When the first half was over, Mr. Wu resigned. I liked Mr. Wu a lot. Usually, you blame the manager if the team isn't winning, but this was *not* Mr. Wu's fault. Regardless, he was gone.

We didn't fare any better under the new manager. We finished the season in last place again. I had a good season pitching for a bad team. We won 28 games overall; I was the winning pitcher in 14 of those games. I threw three shutouts ... and had a save. I pitched 13 complete games in 30 starts, which were CPBL records at the time.

I was *really* hoping to hear something from a team in Japan, but I never would.

Even though we had a new owner, negotiating a new contract for the following season (I was not giving up. Phase Two, remember?) wasn't any easier than the previous season. But there was a catch: This time, there

Don pitching for the Sinon Bulls, 1996.

Eleven. The End

was a rival league starting up. The Taiwan Major League, or TML. During the late part of the previous season, Tony and I had made an appointment with a guy named Dean, who was going to operate the new league. Even though I told him I was probably headed back to the Bulls, Dean made it clear that the new league wanted me too. I had some bargaining power. I used it. After I earned half of the team's victories that season, the Bulls made me an offer I could easily refuse.

But not at first.

Bulls GM Dar offered me a lot of money, much more than I expected. There were also a lot of incentive bonuses. He even said, "this is a lot of money I'm offering you." I was so shocked by the offer that I made him repeat it to make sure I heard it right. The meeting was so good and so positive. He told me to come back to the office tomorrow to finalize things and sign the contract.

Too good to be true? The next day I arrived at the office to sign the contract. Dar said, "I have bad news. Everything we had yesterday is now off the table." He told me what the new offer was—it was a lot less than it was the day before. What happened overnight? He said he was sorry and that this wasn't right, but the deal was taken away when the new manager, Coach Kim, saw it. He told the owner it was too much. I couldn't believe it. Why would any coach do that? It's not his money. Why would he interfere in a player's contract? What was he thinking? I just pitched 228 innings and won half of the team's wins; I was going to be his horse next season.

I told Dar that I wasn't accepting this new lowball offer.

I went home, still hoping I could find a team willing to give me a shot in the States. I had developed a new pitch—a hard slider, which no scouts outside of Taiwan had seen me throw before. I just needed a chance.

Once again, nothing available.

The new league made me a much better offer than I got from the Bulls. I signed with the TML for the 1997 season. I was still focused on getting back to the big leagues, possibly via Japan.

I was selected in the first round of the new league's draft, taken by the Kaohsiung team, called Kao-Ping Fala. It was going to be different, but the same. The way I looked at it, I gave the Bulls first shot, and they tossed up an air-ball.

In 1989, I was the Opening Day starting pitcher for the Milwaukee Brewers against the Cleveland Indians in old Municipal Stadium on the shore of Lake Erie. It was a cold, gray day, but there were 80,000 people in the stands. The atmosphere was electric. Now, eight years later, I was the Opening Day pitcher for Kao-Ping Fala against the Luka team in Chiayi in the brand-new Taiwan Major League. Just goes to show ya, you never know.

The game was a sellout, and the fans were crazy and as loud as ever. They already were taking to the new league. I was excited to pitch. I pitched okay, but our hitters came out swinging. I pitched a complete game, scattering 13 hits (is there such a thing as a 13-hitter?) and giving up six runs … but winning, 14–6, for my first win. I thought back to the season before, when I'd pitch two straight games and not get a single run of support. I was eager to see what this new team could do, especially after last-place finishes the previous two years.

I pitched much better games than that as the season wore on. We won four of my first five starts, and the season was off to a great beginning. But there's an ebb and flow to every baseball season, regardless of the continent. After the mid-season break, we slumped badly. We were falling to the bottom of the standings, just ahead of Agan. One night in Taipei, I pitched into the ninth inning and had a 2–1 lead. With two outs, our manager pulled me with two runners still on base. Our reliever only needed to get one out and we'd win the game. Instead, he let both runners score, and the Gida team walked off the win. I got the loss. That's how things were going.

I went a month without another W. Then we began to turn it back around. First a win, followed by a shutout. Things started to roll. The last three weeks of the season would see a tight race to make the playoffs. My final start of the regular season, I went eight innings, gave up just one run, and got the win. We finished the season with a 42–51 record and ended up in third place, a game and a half ahead of Agan, so we made the playoffs. I finished with a 10–12 record, 205 innings, 111 strikeouts, and a 3.51 ERA.

Those stats were good enough to get me a nice contract offer for the following season. Part of me wondered if Phase Two was truly over. But part of me knew that I was throwing the ball well enough that I could contribute to a team in the States. Obviously, no one from the other side of the Pacific Ocean was paying attention to Taiwan baseball. But was Japan? That was enough to get me to come back for a fourth season in 1998.

When I returned the following February, Taiwan was old hat for me. My Chinese was decent, I knew my way around, and I had a lot of friends and fans there. It was a second home of sorts. This would be my most memorable season in Taiwan, for many reasons.

Less than a week before our first game, our manager, Yamani, called a pitchers meeting. He told us that Ron Gerstein would be the Opening Day pitcher. This surprised me because I thought I would get that honor. I had earned it the season before. For the first two weeks of the season, we played only two games a week, at the end of the week. He added that Steve Wilson would pitch the second game. Again, I was surprised. This meant I wouldn't pitch in our first week of the season unless it was in relief. Then

Eleven. The End

Yamani added that Ron would come back and pitch the third game, saying he wanted to keep Ron sharp.

I was relegated to the fourth game, as the team's number three starter. So.... I wouldn't pitch until the end of the second week. Some pitchers would be making their third start by then.

I was pissed off. I had goals—like leading the league in all the main pitching categories. Not only would I make the big bonus money, but I needed to achieve these to get noticed by any Japanese teams and get the chance to play there … or even back in the States. Waiting gave other pitchers in the league a head start on me.

I used the decision as fuel. I intended to show Yamani that he'd made an error.

First outing went as planned. My arm was ready, my pitches were sharp, I had good control, and I dominated the game, throwing a complete-game, three-hit shutout.

My early season went well until something freaky happened. After I struck out the side one inning, Steve gave me a hard high-five. It connected *really* hard, and it tweaked my elbow. I finished a complete-game shutout, but the next day it was real sore and swollen right on that spot. It swelled so much that my elbow looked deformed, it stuck so far out. I couldn't bend my arm, and I couldn't touch my shoulder with my fingers.

I hoped that ice would do the trick, but when it was my day to throw a bullpen, I couldn't. I needed to rest it. I couldn't miss a start, because I was a foreign player, so I had to pitch, and pitch well, or else I'd get released. I went to the trainer and showed him my elbow, and he gave me some strong anti-inflammatory pills. You know, "Rub some dirt on it."

My stats up to this point: A 5–2 record, 36 strikeouts, and a 1.93 ERA. Would that be enough for them to keep me around if I had to go on the injured list? My elbow didn't get better with ice and anti-inflammatories. My next two starts weren't good.

A day later, I was heading out to do my running during batting practice. Our pitching coach approached me and said that he was going to run me today. I liked our pitching coach, a decent guy, kind of quiet. I think he may have been told by Yamani to do this. Maybe they felt like they were going to help me … or maybe it was a punishment for my previous two starts?

He took me out to the left field foul line. It was a very hot and humid day. He pulled out his stopwatch and said he would time me. I would run 40-yard sprints, and I had to make a certain time he set. He didn't say how many. I had to sprint out hard, then jog back, get set, and go again … and again … one after another with his stopwatch out, timing me. I ran a lot of these and got very tired, was sweating really hard too, but I said nothing. I wasn't going to let him beat me.

Finally, he said this was the last one. I pushed off to run this last one hard, but about halfway, I felt my hamstring blow out, and I went directly to the ground. I was lying there in pain, sweating profusely, breathing hard, and I couldn't move. The pitching coach and trainer got me to my feet, and I limped all the way to the dugout. The league doctor checked me out, and my hamstring was pulled. I wasn't going to pitch for at least four weeks.

My first thought was that they'd probably just release me rather than pay me for a month of not pitching.

I wondered if anyone on management's side felt guilty about this injury. It was their fault for putting me through the excessive wind sprints. They could see my elbow was swollen. I obviously wasn't faking anything. I always wondered what made them think all those wind sprints would fix my elbow.

I didn't hear anything about being released, and my new routine involved daily treatment. One good thing was being able to rest the elbow. I had to ice my hamstring every day continuously too, before games and practices. When I was at my apartment, I had to ice it too.

While I was not pitching, I was losing ground to the other pitchers in the major pitching statistical categories, which could earn you a very nice league bonus at the end of the season. I'd gotten myself right up there in the mix before I got hurt, and now I was falling behind.

I was improving and feeling better every day. I did hear some word of maybe getting released, but I think my hard work and improvement—and I think Yamani told the TML that he needed me—kept me in Taiwan. After nearly four weeks, my leg was better. Not 100 percent, but I told Yamani I was ready to pitch. He scheduled me to pitch against Luka. I wasn't totally sure if I could do it, but my first game back turned out well. I went 6 1/3 innings, gave up three runs, and got the win. That was just in time for the 11-day, mid-season league break and a trip home to Milwaukee.

At home, Tami had this stuff called OPC-3. It came in a powder that you mixed with water. She said this would get the swelling out of my elbow. I didn't believe it, but I had nothing to lose. I tried it, and in one day, the swelling went away. I was shocked, it really worked. I returned rested and ready to roll. By my third start back, my elbow was fine and my hamstring was right.

On the mound, I was getting into a good groove, just like at the beginning of the season. I noticed that my slider was electric, with a real hard, late, sharp break.

Not that anyone in America noticed.

By the end of August, we were in first place. I had a streak of six straight complete-game wins, which only ended when I took myself out

Eleven. The End

after eight innings of my seventh straight win with a big lead. The important part was that the streak reached 10 games, and I was leading the league with 16 wins. During the streak, I threw seven complete games with an ERA of 2.05.

With the season I was having, I hoped that the teams in Japan would notice. The rules in Japan in 1998 allowed each Japanese team to have two foreign players. Word was that they were going to allow for three foreign players per team in 1999. That gave me hope. With two weeks left in the regular season, I threw another complete-game win over Luka, my league-leading 18th win of the season. Two more starts. I could become a 20-game winner. We were still holding onto first place.

Didn't quite get there, but as we geared up for the playoffs, I got in one more outing to stay sharp. I pitched in relief and threw four scoreless innings, and as fate would have it, got credited with the win, my 19th. That's how well it was going for me. Despite not getting my first start until the second week of the season and missing nearly four weeks due to my hamstring injury, *and* pitching with an extremely swollen elbow, I led the league in wins (19), complete games (16), and shutouts (5), and I was fourth in ERA (2.56.). I had a great rookie season in Milwaukee in 1988, going 13–7 and finishing fourth in the American League Rookie of the Year voting. But I'm not sure that season was better than the one I had a decade later in Taiwan.

I earned what could accurately be called my 20th win of the season with a complete-game shutout in the playoffs. The 2–0 win put us up three games to two in the best-of-seven series. But … we lost the next two, and the series, to Gida. Our season was over. In the decisive game, I tried to come back and pitch in relief on two days' rest, but predictably, I didn't have much. We were trailing already, and I did my best to hold Gida down, but we ended up losing. It's really hard watching the other team celebrate on your field after losing a Game Seven.

That could have been an omen for my fifth and final season in Taiwan the following year.

Before going back to Milwaukee for the short off-season, I stayed for the season-ending awards banquet. It turned out to be a big night for me.

They honored the hitters first (of course), but when the host of the banquet got to the pitching categories, he started with the most wins and called out my name. I got to walk up to the stage, and they handed me an award made of solid jade. I spoke into the microphone—in English—saying what an honor it was to receive this award, and that I couldn't have gotten this without the help of my teammates.

When they got to the Pitcher of the Year Award, the host called out my name once again. I went back up and I received another solid jade trophy, and once again I said how honored I was to win this, and blah blah blah.

The TML gave out Gold Glove Awards for each position too, and I won that as well. I went back up, received another beautiful jade trophy, and when I spoke into the microphone said, "I don't know who to thank. I can't thank my teammates for this, I did this one all on my own, so…. I'll thank you me." I got a good laugh from the audience.

The last award of the night was the TML's Most Valuable Player Award. I had heard earlier that it was between me, Luis De Los Santos (my teammate), and another pitcher named Ben Burlingame. I was really honored when the host called out my name. I was the league MVP. I gave out all my thank-yous again. And I meant it. I ended up winning four awards, which made me a lot of bonus money … but mostly I hoped this could help me get to Japan.

When I got back to Milwaukee, I called up an old college teammate, Kevin Kohler, who was now an agent. He had tried to help me last off-season. I asked him if he could try to find me a Major League team, to let them know what kind of a season I just had, and said that I wanted to go to spring training with someone. I was hoping for at least a minor league invite, with at least a shot at Triple A and a chance from there. I felt like I had earned that. I always believed that if a player ever dominated a league, any league anywhere, from low A ball to any league around the world, that player should get an opportunity. If I didn't get a shot in the United States, then I should at least get a shot in Japan after the MVP season I just had.

Every year, the teams from Japan had taken top players from Taiwan. Kevin contacted the Major League teams, and they said they were impressed with my numbers from the past season, but at that time they didn't know what to think about the caliber of baseball in Taiwan. Kevin wasn't getting anywhere. Only one team was thinking about me, the Minnesota Twins. They didn't say no, just that they'd think about it. When they finally got back to Kevin, they decided to pass. The big reason was that I was now 35 years old.

Then it got worse. Big news from Japan: The country was hit by a huge financial crisis. The Japanese yen devalued badly. The financial markets tanked, and they were falling into a big recession. This was bad news for me for one big reason: It would now take more yen to pay American players in American dollars. The professional teams in Japan decided they were not only *not* going to add a third foreign player to each roster, but weren't even going to stay with two. They cut down to *one* foreign player per team. If they had kept it at two players, I might have gotten a chance, but now the Japanese teams weren't looking to add American players—they were looking to get rid of them.

Eleven. The End

The year I go off and kill it, I turn 35 and a financial crisis hits Japan at just the wrong time. I never heard a thing from Japan. I asked Kevin if he could reach out, but he had no contacts there. We did speak to an agent who did, but there was nothing for me. I lost out on *big* money—likely a base salary of $250,000 or more with performance bonuses that could have gotten me close to a million dollars. And if it went well, you could at least return to Japan with another nice contract … or maybe have a Major League team gives you a chance.

Now the only option I had left was to go back to Taiwan. I just had to suck it up and try to do it all over again.

As the Beatles sang, tomorrow never knows, right?

I probably should have expected that things wouldn't go so smoothly. It was a new season and a new team in a lot of ways. I got the Opening Day start I should have gotten the year before, but this wasn't last season. At all. In my first four starts, our offense produced exactly *one* run. Didn't win any of those games. I remember getting frustrated. Everyone was trying to stay positive, saying don't worry, it's just an early slump, we'll pull out of it, etc. Last year we were good, but right now we were bad. I'd gone from league MVP to losing my first *six* decisions.

I managed to string together three wins in a row, which helped ease the frustration level. But it didn't last. In the next nine games, I got exactly nine runs of support. The next time out, we won 15–1. Of course we did. All or nothing. That's baseball.

You know what else comes with baseball? Pressure. Lots of it. Most of it is self-imposed, but sometimes you get some piled on. A couple of days after I won a start, Yamani called me and fellow pitchers Bob Spears and Jose Salcedo into his office to have a meeting. He said the TML was going to make a move, and one of us was going to get released before the mid-season break. It depended on how each of us pitched in our next game. No pressure!

His plan: I would start against Gida and go maybe three or four innings, Bob would come in and pitch a few innings, and Jose would finish. They were putting extreme pressure on all three of us. They chose me because we were in last place, and I wasn't winning every game I pitched—and they were paying me a lot of money. For Bob and Jose, they weren't pitching very well. I was pitching well enough, but not getting any decent run support. In my last five starts, I'd given up one, two, three, one and one run. Why should I be on a cut line like this? And now if I blew this next game against Gida I was getting released?

I admit to being nervous to pitch in this do-or-die situation. Last season, I was the league MVP, and now I'm trying to keep from being released. I was supposed to pitch three or four innings and do really well.

I was confident and hoping not to have any bad luck. In the first inning, I put up a zero, but in the second inning I gave up a run. In my third inning, I put up another zero, and when I came into the dugout, I wasn't sure if I was done or not. When Yamani didn't say anything to me, I realized I had to pitch another inning. Just go one more scoreless and I'll be good. One run in four innings should do it. I went back out for the fourth and put up another zero.

As I came off the field, I said to myself, "I did it!" But when I got into the dugout, Yamani came up to me and said he wanted me to pitch another inning. I couldn't say no, even though I'd been told three innings, maybe four. Now I risked something happening in this fifth inning that would be used to release me. I went out for the fifth inning, and I put up another zero. When I reached the dugout, I was expecting Yamani to come up to me and tell me that I did a good job. Instead, he sent me back out for the sixth.

This time I reminded him that he told me before the game that I'd pitch three or four innings. He said, "One more inning!" I went out to pitch the sixth and held them scoreless again. When I came in, Yamani told me … to pitch one more inning again. This was getting to me emotionally. In the seventh, I was feeling the extra pressure, but I put up another zero. This time when I reached the dugout, Yamani shook my hand and told me good job, I was done. Now I could breathe. I had gone seven innings, given up just one run, and left the game winning, 3–1. Whew.

Jose came in to pitch the eighth inning. He was feeling it too, no doubt. He quickly gave up two runs to tie the game. This meant another no-decision … and lost bonus money. In the ninth inning, Jose gave up another run, and we ended up losing. I remember seeing Jose pleading with Yamani, saying he could do better and practically begging for another chance. Yamani finally yelled out loudly in English, "Enough!"

Now the plan was for Bob to start tomorrow's game and see what happened. Bob had prepared and was expecting to pitch in tonight's game, and he had to sleep another night worrying about tomorrow. The next day Bob started, knowing that if he was just okay, he'd probably be safe. He pitched about four innings and gave up four runs. Not great, but Bob did okay … definitely better than Jose.

Yamani called the three of us together. I'd pitched great and was pretty sure there was no way I was getting the axe … but anything could happen. I could see that Jose thought he was the one getting cut. Yamani surprised us. Bob was the one getting released. Jose looked totally relieved, while Bob looked very disappointed.

Nothing was going to save Yamani. Again, when the team goes bad, the manager pays the price. Yamani got fired with just three weeks left in the season. His replacement was an American I had close ties with, former

Brewers coach Dave Hilton. I thought this was going to be a cool thing for me ... until the next day, when Dave pulled me aside and told me I was being released by the TML.

That season with that team had burned me out. There were only about two weeks left in the regular season. We were a bad team in last place with no chance of making the playoffs. This was my last season in Taiwan regardless, and I didn't have the strength to want to come back again. I'd pitched pretty well without much support. For the year, I made 23 starts and had an ERA of 3.82, 10th-best in the TML. I had six complete games and one shut-out. Not the numbers I put up the year before, but definitely better than my 5–13 record.

I'd done a lot of good things in Taiwan over five years. I was a fan favorite, and I didn't deserve to go out like this. It came down to the fact that I was a foreign player making good money on a last-place team. It was hard to say goodbye to everyone, but I did. I knew I wasn't coming back.

When my plane took off and was making its way over the Pacific Ocean, I said to myself, "Ziajian, Taiwan. Xie Xie." (Goodbye, Taiwan. Thank you.)

I had a lot of time to reflect. I certainly didn't expect to be there for five baseball seasons. I counted. For the 53 months from May 1995 to October 1999, I was in Taiwan for 44, Australia one, and home for just eight. I made a lot of friends in Taiwan. The people there were always so good to me. You had to be tough to handle a very different culture and environment. I saw a lot of good ballplayers struggle. Things were just different, not done the way we do things in the United States. I'd been in someone else's country, and every day it seemed there was a problem to fix or an issue to resolve. Taking care of it in Chinese or broken English was always a challenge. Getting your utilities turned back on was a challenge. Being ready for my water to be turned off for the day was a challenge. Finding food was a challenge. There were a lot of challenges. Sometimes it was "mayo qwan chee." (No problem.) Other times, it definitely was.

The traffic. It was insane—and the more I watched it, the crazier it looked. It was "controlled chaos." Thousands of scooters everywhere. Entire families on one scooter at the same time. Taxis everywhere, making their own rules.

I saw dead people.

The average apartment in Taiwan typically didn't have a kitchen, so the people had to eat out all the time. The bathrooms were usually very small with a drain in the middle of the floor. The shower head came out, and you showered; the entire floor got wet, including the toilet. The floors were always tile. I don't know how, but they got dirty so quickly, probably due to the pollution, and you had to sweep the floor all the time.

Some stuff I would miss, like eating on plastic chairs on the sidewalk a few feet from the busy street with cars whizzing by me at 35 miles per hour. It was like the 1970s. People smoked cigarettes everywhere, inside of cars, cabs, airplanes, restaurants … in the dugouts during games … everywhere.

I don't have many bad things to say about the whole experience, except that I may have drunk too much and smoked too many cigarettes myself. I definitely didn't take great care of myself. I went to have my hearing checked out one time. The doctor put me through a lot of tests, listening to sounds through headphones, at high-frequency sounds, the whole bit. At the end of the testing, I asked him how my hearing was. "Slight hearing loss." He asked me some questions. First, "Do you stay up late?" I said, "Yes." Second, "Do you drink?" I said, "Yes." Third, "Do you smoke?" I said yes again. He told me I needed to stop drinking and smoking, go to bed earlier, and get more sleep. I replied, "If I give up all of those things, then what the hell do I even need my hearing for?"

I could tell by the expression on his face that he didn't get the joke.

Cecil Espy was right when he told me right at the start that I'd see the sun come up many times. We did go out a lot … but what else was there to do? We had a lot of down time. I spent a lot of time sitting alone in my apartment with my Sega Genesis.

Baseball was baseball. It was great to see people from different parts of the world love the game. I'll always remember my Taiwanese teammates, even though I can't remember most of their names … and the other foreign players who came from so many other countries. I enjoyed all my Japanese coaches and most of my Taiwanese coaches.

Being in Taiwan was an adventure. Some days were hard, but more were fun. The idea of simply laughing really did help.

When I got home, I came face to face with the reality that I was—and had been—in Phase Three all along. But what a Phase Three it was! Regardless of my success on the field, the reality was that I was too old now, past 35, for Major League teams to have any interest in me.

Then I remembered what Daryl Smith had told me, and I decided to put off a new career selling insurance for one more season.

In Italy, I got to play for fun more than money. Baseball was always fun. When you're between the lines, you aren't thinking about payday, you're thinking about winning. But unless you're a superstar making a gazillion dollars, money and job security are always in the back of your mind.

In Italy, things were very different. Yes, I was one of the best-paid foreign players. I'd earned that. But the pay was less than half of what I had made in Taiwan … and could have been made if I'd gone back for another

Eleven. The End

season there. But Italy allowed me to play on a very good team, experience historic Europe, and have a blast going out on top.

Foreign pitchers always pitched on Friday nights in the Italian Baseball League. I'd start once a week, and we almost always won. The caliber of play in Italy was roughly Double A. Even if I was slightly past my prime, I knew I could dominate in that league. And I did for the most part. I won my first three starts before losing a 1–0 game. Then came wins four, five, six, and seven in order.

After I got my eighth win, Tami and Logan were on hand to see me start a game. Usually when I'm pitching, I don't hear anything from the stands, but on this night, I could hear Logan cheering for me all night, saying, "Come on, Dad, you can do it." That meant everything to me. I pitched nine innings, but they took me out of the game tied, 1–1. Not a win on the scoreboard, but a win for life. A week later, Logan saw me throw a complete-game shutout. I gave him the ball afterwards.

There was no chance to win 20 games in the Italian League. Not enough games. But I got my ninth win at the end of the regular season, throwing a shutout. The playoffs were going to be a blast.

I started our first playoff game in Grosseto. In this best-of-five series, the first two games were played there, and after an off-day, the final three games in Rimini. The playoffs were exciting, and there were a lot more fans at the stadium. In the first game, I felt strong after a nice break. The American starter for Grosseto was Otis Green, whose 1.03 ERA was best in the league. I was doing my job against the Grosseto hitters, but Otis was mowing down our hitters too. I ended up throwing a complete game, but we lost, 2–1. It was a tough loss, but we were confident that we could still win this series.

We won the next two games, and I started Game 4 to try to clinch it. It was a rematch with Green. I threw another complete game … and I lost again, the score this time 4–1. Otis dominated, and we couldn't do anything against him. Now we had to play a decisive Game 5.

We needed all hands on deck for this one. But during batting practice, our Italian-American catcher, Nando Porzio, who caught most of the games during the season, found out he was not in the starting lineup. He had struggled at the plate to finish out the season, while our other catcher, Mateo Baldacci, had been hitting well and doing a good job behind the plate. Nando got so mad, he went and cleaned out his locker. He went up to Mike and Jimbo and told them that he quit, and he just left. He hung us all out, because without him we had only one catcher. If anything happened to Mateo, we were screwed. It was very selfish, all about him. One of the guys got his baseball bat and started to beat Nando's locker. Another player got his bat and beat the locker some more, then another guy, and another guy, and another guy until all of the players took a turn, and the locker was totally destroyed.

Jason Simontacchi went out and pitched another gem that saved the season. We beat Grosseto, and now we'd face Nettuno. There was beer in the locker room, and we began to celebrate. The celebration went on and on, then there was more beer, and some shots. Some of us had talked about getting up and leaving early the next morning for a quick trip to Switzerland and France. I wanted to celebrate a little, but I was like…. Okay, we won, but we haven't won the Championship Series yet. Still, the celebrating continued, and we never did make the trip to Switzerland or France.

I was set to pitch the first game of the seven-game championship series. We were home for the first two, and after an off-day, Games 3, 4, and 5 would be in Nettuno. Games 6 and 7, if necessary, would be back in Rimini.

Our stadium was packed again. Nettuno was a very good hitting team, but I was ready to go. Our guys came out swinging. I was on. I went eight innings, and when they took me out, we were winning, 10–1.

We won that one and the next two to take that commanding 3–0 series lead. Instead of it being a tight series with momentum up in the air, everything was going our way. They'd have to take four straight from us. I was scheduled to pitch Game 4.

I was pitching on three days' rest, but I was ready, and I wanted the ball. We were playing flawless baseball, getting great pitching, great defense, and timely hitting. We took an early lead, but in the middle of the game, Nettuno got a couple of runs off me to make it close. We came back and scored a couple more, which knocked the wind out of them.

Going into the bottom of the ninth inning, we had a 5–2 lead. The meat of their lineup was coming up. I was getting tired, but I was focused and going right at them. I got the first two outs, leaving us one out away. On a 0–1 pitch, I threw my best hard slider, and the batter hit it into the ground, a chopper to the left of our shortstop, Andrea Evangelisti. He made the play, then the throw. He made it look easy, the third and final out.

As soon as the first basemen squeezed the ball, I raised both of my hands up over my head. We had just swept Nettuno four straight. I was really proud of how well we played, how we all clutched up and played our best when it counted most. Everyone was jumping up and down on the field. It's a sudden jolt of euphoria when you win something like this. It's why you compete—to be part of that dogpile near the pitcher's mound after you win the championship. What an amazing feeling. On any continent.

I got two wins in the four-game sweep.

At the time, I didn't realize it, but this was my John Elway, Ray

Eleven. The End

Bourque, David Robinson, Peyton Manning moment. The last pitch I threw in a professional baseball game was the final out that clinched a championship and started a dogpile on the pitcher's mound. Exactly the way every player wants to go out. On top.

This was The End.

It almost wasn't. Earlier in the season, on a whim, I had decided to reach out to a guy named Paul Seiler, the President of the United States Baseball Federation. My baseball journey had begun when I was a member of the 1984 USA Olympic Baseball team. Could there be an encore?

Medal for winning the Italian Baseball League championship, August 2000.

Back when I first had contact with the Italian League, they raised the possibility of me playing with them in the 2000 Olympics. I was interested and even a little excited about it. But when we found out I couldn't (I did have relatives of Italian descent on my grandmother's side, but I didn't have an Italian last name. Her maiden name was Rigali, but that was not enough to get me qualified), I was actually relieved, because I didn't want to betray my country and play for another.

But as I continued to think about it, I still wanted to go. The more I thought about it, the more I wondered: why I couldn't still play with the United States team? The 2000 Olympics would be the first year countries could use professional players. Team USA wasn't going to use Major Leaguers since the Olympics were in the middle of the Major League season. They decided they'd go with minor leaguers.

Under those terms, I certainly qualified. I was still an active professional baseball player, even though I wasn't playing professionally in the minor leagues in the United States. Why did the USA roster have to come just from minor league rosters? If I was good enough, then I should have a fair shot at being on that team. Why not me?

I looked up the president of the USA Baseball Federation on the internet and found Mr. Seiler. I sent him an email telling him why I should be considered for the 2000 U.S. Olympic team.

First, I'm still an active American professional baseball player.

Second, I'm still pitching well, even though it is in Italy.

Third (and I thought this was a biggie), I have *17 years of professional experience.*

Fourth, I understand international baseball, having pitched in Mexico, Taiwan, Italy, Puerto Rico, Dominican Republic, and even Canada.

Fifth, I have experience of being in Australia (where the games would be held).

Sixth, I could be a veteran presence on a young team.

Seventh, I wouldn't expect to be the top starter, but I could make a good extra relief arm, again—being the experienced guy to relate to the younger players.

Eighth, I have Major League experience.

Ninth, I was in the Olympics before, Los Angeles 1984.

Finally, I told him it would make a great story—a player coming back 16 years later and playing in the Olympics again.

I pushed the "send" button. I wondered if he'd ever read it, and if so, would he even take me seriously? Would I get any response?

Less than a week later, I went back to a place called the Cyber Bar to check my emails. Over a carafe of white wine, I discovered that I had a message from the U.S. Baseball Federation. Paul Seiler replied and told me they *would* consider it. I wasn't getting a "no" right away. I thought maybe, just maybe.

"So you're telling me there's a chance...."

I was excited about this possibility, and I felt like I had a lot to offer Team USA. Again.

Later, I heard back from Mr. Seiler, and he told me that unfortunately, I would not be a part of the 2000 United States Olympic baseball team. He said that they did consider me, but they were going to stick with the minor league players. I had gotten my hopes up, and I was disappointed. It did feel good that they gave me consideration. I thought I made some good points, but I guess I had to look at their point of view. I *was* maybe a little too old at age 37. My good stats were from Italy, where the level of baseball wasn't as great as Triple A in the United States. Still, it would have been nice to play for the late, great Tommy Lasorda, the manager of that team. And that American team did win the Gold Medal in Sydney. Man, I wish I'd been there.

When that final out was made, and we won the Italian League title, Phase Three was finally over for me—a full eight years after it started. I realized I'd given baseball everything I had. No regrets that I "should have done this" or "if I'd only done that." I did my very best. That was good enough to set a couple of records, win an MVP Award in Taiwan and a championship ring, er, medal, in Italy.

Not too shabby.

Twelve

Glory Days

So now I was a recently retired professional athlete. It's been well documented that people in this group can suffer through difficult periods of adjustment, both personally and financially. Many guys ended up divorced, depressed, even down and out. I didn't want to go down any of those dark paths. But when I realized that professional baseball was finally over for me, my first thought was, "Okay. What do I do now?"

I didn't make crazy money playing baseball, not enough so I could retire and never have to work again. We had a nice house in a great middle-class neighborhood, but that was it. I had to start earning money another way.

The idea of becoming a minor league coach wasn't appealing. I'd been gone for what seemed like a lifetime—I'd been at home in the USA for just eight months ... in five years. I had to start the next phase of my life now, starting a new career at age 37. The whole idea was to be home with my family full-time. But it would be an adjustment for sure.

Did I want to coach, though? I had an offer to join the coaching staff at Menomonee Falls High School. During my brief off-seasons, I'd made friends with Dave Weber, the head coach. He called and asked if I'd be interested in coaching high school baseball in his program. I thought about it, and I told him, yes.... I might be. At the time I was about to give the insurance business a go, so I wasn't sure about the timing. Since he needed to know right away, I couldn't commit for that 2001 season. But now the thought was in my head.

I knew what kind of coach I'd want to be ... and not be. I had plenty of examples. I thought back to some of the coaches and managers I had during my career that I really liked and respected. Guys like Carlos Alfonso, Tom Trebelhorn and others in the Brewers' system. My high school coach, Bob Zamora, and college coaches Paul Deese and Mike Weathers were really outstanding too. Maybe I could do for some other kid what they did for me. If I could take the traits I admired most in them, I could do good things for young players. In Taiwan, I played for the

Twelve. Glory Days

legendary Mr. Wu, whom I greatly admired. Mr. Wu had been the coach of the Chinese Taipei team in the 1984 Olympics when I played against him. He was an outstanding manager too. I wanted to be like that.

But there's also value in knowing what not to do. I had a few examples of that, too.

I played for a guy named Terry Bevington in Triple A. Perpetually pissed off—blaming the pitching staff for everything that went wrong. Yet he won games. In fact, he won the American Association championship one year—and he was so miserable he got let go anyway.

One time in Des Moines, Iowa, we had a particularly lousy day on the mound and in the field. After the game, we sat in a silent clubhouse, getting ready to shower, when Bev announced that everybody had to put their uniforms back on, that we were going back out onto the field to practice hitting the cutoff man. We were the visiting team, mind you, but Bev still had the stadium workers turn the lights back on. Back on the field we went. He had the pitchers run the bases while he hit one ball after another to the fence, where every player had to chase down the ball and hit the cutoff man, while the pitchers sprinted around the bases over and over and over again.

It was bullshit. He treated us like little kids, and it went on for a long time. Bev did get in trouble for doing this. It cost a lot of money to turn those lights back on, which I think he had to pay for. I don't think the Brewers' minor league director liked this outburst much either. He was let go at the end of the year.

Across the Pacific, I also had to deal with a guy everyone called "Coach Adam," and he was, plain and simple … a dick. He was a new Taiwanese coach. My second season in Taiwan, we went to Brisbane, Australia, for spring training for a month. Coach Adam was new to the team, and at first, he seemed like another okay guy.

Wrong.

We quickly found out that Coach Adam was our "hard ass" coach and would flex his authority. One morning, we were at the field doing our stretching. The foreign guys were doing the normal amount of chatting and telling stories while we stretched. This has gone on with every team I've ever played on from high school through the big leagues. It's standard practice. But for some reason, Coach Adam wouldn't have any of that.

He came up to us and rudely told us we had to be quiet! I wondered: what was this guy's problem? There was no reason why we had to be quiet, and we weren't being that loud anyway.

The next day, same thing. Two of my teammates were talking to each other, and I was just sitting there listening when I saw Coach Adam walking quickly directly at us. He grabbed one guy's arm and shoved him away from us, then came back and, without saying a word, grabbed my arm roughly and started yanking me in another direction, treating me like I was some little kid in front of the team.

I was instantly pissed off. I wasn't going to let this little pencil-necked asshole do this to me. I wasn't even talking. I stopped my feet and with my other hand, I grabbed his arm, and I threw him hard back away from me. He staggered hard and almost fell. I yelled at him, "never ever grab me again like that!" He had a look of surprise on his face. I thought I was going to get in trouble, maybe get released, but our manager, Mr. Wu, never said anything to me. I wasn't going to let anyone treat me like that.

Don't ever be like Coach Adam.

Is that what coaching turned you into?

When I finally did enter the high school coaching ranks, I wanted to take the best of guys like Treb and Mr. Wu with me instead.

But before I ever got there, I had to see if selling insurance would be my second career. Before I left for Italy, I told one insurance company I would give them a call when I returned. I followed up on that and went to the Joe Manone Insurance Company. Joe had me come into their meetings and listen in on what they were doing. If this was good with me, then they would begin training me. Joe told me, "Either you will love it, or you will hate it."

He was right about that.

I went through the training and then out on appointments on my own. We were considered a union insurance company because we serviced the local unions in the area. I had to call union members up from a card they filled out that gave them free extra accident coverage. I told them I was confirming their coverage, but now I wanted to set up an appointment to deliver them the coverage and to see if

Don throwing a pitch, with a still action effect.

Twelve. Glory Days

they could use more of our insurance products. The people only wanted the free stuff, they didn't want an insurance man coming to their home to sell them some more. I ended up not liking this business, and after about three months of giving this a try, I hated it. I ended up dreading going to work. I told Joe thanks for giving me the opportunity and the training, but this wasn't for me. He told me no problem and said the door was always open if I ever wanted to come back.

The coaching bug had already bitten me, I just didn't realize it. Since 1990, when I was home, I had given pitching lessons. I still do. After I returned from Italy, I went right back to that. I found out I really enjoy working with kids of all ages. I want to show kids the basic mechanics of pitching. I want them to enjoy being a pitcher, and I want them to have fun doing it and not to get hurt. I believe the kids will have more fun when they throw more strikes. By this point, I've given literally thousands of lessons all over the region. I've even given pitching lessons to men in their 60s. One guy wanted lessons from me because he just joined an over-60 baseball league and was asked to pitch, but he didn't want to hurt himself. I've made extra money doing this, but I enjoy it because it has kept me connected to baseball.

Now that I was home to stay, I was able to watch Logan play baseball. He started in Little League, and I had a blast watching him, just like he did when watching me a few years earlier. I remembered when he was in the stands with all the crazy Taiwanese fans, banging those noise makers together and laughing. I had some very good games when Logan was there to watch.

Now he was having fun—and playing well—with me watching.

After a couple of years, he tried out for the Menomonee Falls "Select" baseball team, the Falcons. This was more competitive baseball than Little League. There were more games, traveling to tournaments, the whole bit. This was for the kids who wanted to play more. I didn't want to coach this team, I just wanted to be the dad and watch the games. I told the coaches that this was their team, but if they wanted to ask me questions or ask me to help out at the practices, that I would. I figured if I coached high school, I would get my chance to coach Logan then.

It was fun watching my son play, since he was a good infielder and had a knack for pitching. He always said his position was the infield, not pitcher. I think he wanted his own identity.

Logan also played flag football—a neighbor and I coached ... very poorly. He had his son on the team too. In two years, we won only three games. Logan also played select basketball and played on his middle school team. It didn't matter the sport. I always enjoyed watching him play all through his school years.

Maybe it was watching Logan, or maybe the kid in me never did grow up. But for some reason, after surviving a long, cold Wisconsin winter, in the spring of 2001—less than a year after I threw my final pitch in Italy—I had the itch to play more baseball. Remember, this would be the first spring ... ever ... in my life that I wasn't at least preparing to play competitively. I had to think about that for a minute. Wow.

I remembered the "Land O Lakes" baseball league. I played in this league for a bit back in 1992 after I was released by the San Francisco Giants in spring training. I played for five weeks until I got a minor league deal with the Detroit Tigers organization. I talked to a guy I knew who was playing in the league. He told me the name of the manager of the Land O Lakes team in Menomonee Falls, Tony Logue. Since I lived in Menomonee Falls, they had "my rights."

In 2001, there were over 40 teams in the four divisions. This wasn't a joke. It was a competitive adult baseball league. I called Tony, told him who I was, and asked if I could play for his team. He instantly said yes, but I told him there were two circumstances that we had to be clear with: First, I wanted to hit for myself. I'd help the team best by pitching, but if a DH had to hit for me as a pitcher, then I didn't want to pitch. I'd rather play another position. If this wasn't okay, I'd look for another team. He said sure, no problem. Second, my son's baseball games had to come first. If his game was at the same time as our game, I'd miss ours to watch his. Tony agreed again. I told him that I had missed a lot of things in Logan's life being away playing baseball, and I wasn't missing anything else.

I began playing again in this league in 2001, and

Don as a member of the Fala team in 1998.

Twelve. Glory Days

I played right up until 2019. In 2018, I led the league in innings pitched. In 2020, I moved to the 55-and-over league, having decided it was time I played with the kids my own age. Back in 2011, I played on the same team with Logan, who had finished playing his senior year of high school ball. We might not have quite been the Griffeys, but we did pretty darn good together. As the years went by, I became teammates with a lot of the kids I'd coached in high school, Logan being one of them. For several seasons, I was teammates with my son, playing competitive baseball. It doesn't get more special than that.

The coaching thing worked out too. Dave Weber hired me to be the Junior Varsity Head Coach at Menomonee Falls High in 2002, and I got my first chance to run my own team.

I decided to be the JV coach because I wanted to run my own team and call the shots. It would also allow me to see Logan's baseball games when he was still young. I've been coaching the JV since 2002. In 2024, I coached my 600th game, and I picked up my 497th win. I enjoy teaching and working with young men learning the game of baseball, and I love the competition.

In 2009, Logan was a sophomore, and he played for me on the JV team—another major highlight in my coaching career. In 2010 and 2011, Logan played on the varsity.

While I continued to be the JV coach, they asked me—since I'd be attending the games anyway—if I wanted to help out with the varsity team too. I ended up doing double duty, which made for long days in the hot summer sun … but I was with Logan in the dugout, which made everything worth it.

This wasn't the big leagues, and no one was asking for autographs … in any language. But it's just as special as my playing days. Since 2001, Menomonee Falls has made it to the Wisconsin State Tournament ten times and lost the state championship game twice. But we were the State Champions "Back to Back" in 2015 and 2016. Winning those state championships are two of my greatest memories from my baseball career. There's nothing better than the feeling of winning a championship, at any level in any role! I still have my championship ring from Charlotte in 1993 and from the Italian Championship in 2000 ("il scudetto") Those dogpiles on the pitcher's mound after you've won it all never ever ever get old.

People have asked me why I don't coach a varsity team. Simple, really. I enjoy the role I'm in. My job was to support the varsity coach—first Dave Weber, then Pat Hansen, and now Tim Gotzler—within their programs. I do what it takes to help them, to support their ideas, much like the bench coach's job at the Major League level. It's the manager's job, his philosophy, etc. The assistant coaches have their specific jobs to do to support the manager, but if things go wrong, it's on the manager, the manager gets fired. I remember seeing this when I was pitching for the Brewers. Tom Trebelhorn was the manager, and the late, great Andy Etchebarren was his bench coach. Andy's job was to support whatever Treb needed. He gave ideas and talked things out with Treb when asked. I'm sure Andy may have wanted to do some things in a different way, but his job was to support Treb's agenda. If Andy wanted to do things his way, then he needed to become a manager of his own team. Sure, there have been times over the years that I may have done some things differently than the varsity coach did, but this was his program. If I wanted to do things my way, then I would need to get my own program as a varsity coach at another school.

I love coaching high school baseball. I hope I can do it for the rest of my life.

I had other coaching opportunities come my way. The first one was in 1997, while I was still playing professionally in Taiwan. The Brewers called to see if I'd be interested in being a minor league pitching coach. I told them I was still pitching professionally—and of course I asked if they would sign me as a pitcher now, and a coach later. I still wanted to keep pitching. I asked if I could call them back whenever I decided to retire. They said, "sure." That never happened.

Out of the blue in 2001, Tim Ireland, the (crazy) old Gida coach from Taiwan, called and said he'd gotten a managing job in the independent professional Western League, and wanted to know if I'd like to be his pitching coach. I was flattered that he asked me, but I had to turn him down. I had just finished playing in Italy, and I was home now with my wife and son. I didn't want to move across the country and not see them. Plus the pay was way too low … and of course Tim was a crazy man. I'm sure I would have been in a number of bar fights with him if I had accepted.

I've had some other local high schools contact me about running their program as the varsity coach. I've had people tell me they could help me get a job as a coach in the district where they lived. Each time, there was a conflict—I was coaching Logan and in a good place at Menomonee Falls High. Other times, the travel distance was too far from where I was teaching during the school day. New Berlin, Germantown High, and others asked, but I was happy where I was at doing what I was doing.

My former teammate, Hall of Famer Robin Yount, and former Brewers executive Dean Rennicke offered me the pitching coach gig with the summer collegiate team Robin owned in Wisconsin, the Lakeshore Chinooks. I had to turn that down too. Not enough hours in the week.

I did come close to landing a head coaching gig at a small college near my home, the Milwaukee School of Engineering. I would have given up high school coaching for that gig. It's a small Division III school. I had a former high school player going there at the time. I applied online, and a couple of days later I got a phone call from the Athletic Director. One of the first things he asked me was whether I was serious about coaching at their school. I told him I was very serious. He said he didn't want to waste time if we weren't on the same page for the salary. He told me what they could offer and asked if that could work for me. I told him yes.

We talked on the phone for 45 minutes. I was excited because he kept saying "we" will do this and "we" will do that, never saying "if" you're here. At the end of the conversation, an in-person interview was arranged, and I was excited and looking forward to it. The day came, and I arrived at the school for the interview. The way the AD talked, it sounded like that interview was just a formality.

I felt like the job was mine. They should call soon to get this thing going. When I didn't get a call going into the weekend, I got a little nervous. On Monday, my phone rang. It was the AD. I was glad to hear his voice. I was expecting him to say congratulations and let's get things going. Instead, he said, "Hey Don, I want to thank you for applying for the baseball job at MSOE and considering us." I knew right there I didn't get it. He said, "but we decided to go with someone else. I wanted to call you and let you know first before we notify the media."

I asked him why I wasn't chosen. He didn't seem to be expecting me to ask. He said he had concerns that I could do a budget and recruit. That was a bogus answer. There was a budget already in place for that season, and for the next season, I could have made some changes if needed moving forward. As far as recruiting, I think my name alone and my Major League background would have helped me out. I had access to a national database on players through people I knew with the Perfect Game organization. I had a lot of people I knew locally that could help.

I guess the bad business side of baseball had to bite me on the ass one final time.

I still had my high school coaching gig, but high school coaching is not a way to make a living. After my first year of coaching, I tried to figure out what kind of day job I could do. Over the years, I always wanted to finish my college degree. Because I had signed my professional baseball contract after my junior year, I still had one year to complete to be a college graduate. I put together the ideas of getting a job, finishing college, and continuing to coach baseball. Tami and I decided I'd go back to college and get a teaching degree. I could be a teacher and a baseball coach. I enrolled at Carroll College.

It felt strange enrolling in college again. I had just the one year of undergrad work to do, but in order to get my teaching degree, I had to complete three full school years. I came in as one of those "nontraditional" students, a full-time undergrad at age 39. I would be taking classes with 18-to-22-year-old students. It was back to school.

Things had changed in the 18 years between classes. At Chapman, I never saw anybody wearing a backpack. Now everybody was wearing them to carry their books and other supplies. I grabbed one of Logan's old ones. The degree I was going for was in Secondary Education. This license would allow me to teach social studies from grades 6 through 12.

It felt like everyone was staring at me as I walked through campus wearing a backpack. Maybe they were just looking around. I got used to it. I remember being in an early Monday morning class, and I heard one of the young students telling another that he couldn't believe that he made it to this class because he was still so hung over from the weekend. I'd been there a couple decades earlier. Now, I thought to myself, I feel great, I got plenty of sleep. I had to get into the routine of being a college student again … but I did. My first semester, I made the Dean's List.

I didn't have a full-time job, but I continued to do pitching lessons. The tuition at Carroll College was pretty steep. It was taking a bite out of our savings account. I needed to keep bringing in some money. The baseball coach at Carroll offered me a job on his staff, but I had to turn that down because I didn't have the time and still had my JV team.

Eventually, after participating in a baseball camp with former Brewers teammate Jim Gantner and Bad Ronald Nedset, we came up with the idea of doing an annual camp in Menomonee Falls. These have become a big hit. The "Gantner/August Baseball Camps" were held every year from 2002 to 2019. It was very gratifying to see all the support we got for this.

I've done other similar camps with the Major League Baseball Alumni Association, working with former Brewers teammates and MLB alums. One who was a special blast to work with was George Foster, the Leuzinger High School grad. Back in California, I went to Leuzinger my first two years of high school and was there the year George hit 52 homers and was the NL MVP for the Cincinnati Reds. We were able to talk about our old neighborhoods and the teachers at Leuzinger when we were both students there.

Over the years, I got to see and hang out with former teammates and big league stars like Hall of Famers Phil Niekro, Robin Yount, Rollie Fingers, Carlton Fisk, Paul Molitor, and Fergie Jenkins. It's a blast sharing stories with Gantner, Jerry Augustine, Gorman Thomas, Pete Ladd, Paul Wagner, Tom Tellman, Charlie Moore, Greg Vaughn, Larry Hisle, Willie Mueller (who also had the role of The Duke in the baseball movie *Major League*), and Cecil Cooper. Even though I didn't play with a lot of these guys, we've become lifelong baseball friends and look forward to seeing each other every year. We have watched each other age, and some guys have passed away, like Johnny Logan and Davey Nelson. It's always good to see the new guys, either much older or guys I played with and against from my era, or younger guys. We have those shared experiences from our time in the Majors ... and they're always curious to hear my stories from around the world.

As for college, I made the Dean's List every semester, and I graduated after the Spring semester of 2005. I got to wear my cap and gown and walk across the stage to receive my diploma. Oprah Winfrey happened to be in the audience ... she was there for someone else.

After three years of college, I had my teaching license. I was licensed to teach history, geography, sociology, and broad field social studies. I did end up getting a job in the Menomonee Falls School District as a permanent building sub at Riverside Elementary School. I showed up every day, and whenever a teacher was absent, I was there to sub that class. If no teacher was absent, then I helped out in the office.

As a newbie in the school district, I had to put up with the same kinds of institutional politics that I thought I was leaving behind in the business of baseball. I helped the district through a tough patch when another teacher had personal issues, and when that was resolved, I was supposed to return to the junior high. However, because of budget problems, I went back to the junior high as a building sub, with no benefits and the sub salary. That really sucked. I bailed them out in a crisis, and when things were back to normal, they dumped on me. A lot like professional baseball.

This pattern repeated itself for several years. I bounced around, looking for jobs in other school districts, not able to find good opportunities. I accepted a "60%" job in our Menomonee Falls school district, but I kept being let go for budget reasons (just like in Mexico).

While I was going through all this, Logan was thriving. He was a baseball standout in high school—where I got to coach him for that short time. He went on to the University of Wisconsin, where he played on the Badgers' Club Baseball team. (UW is the only Big Ten school without a varsity baseball program.) While he was there, Tami and I got to watch him play a lot. One of the games we saw in person was at the end of his sophomore year. It was a regional championship qualifier, with the winner advancing to the Division Two club baseball World Series. Logan got the start on the mound and fired a no-hitter. When he moved up to the Division One UW team, his team participated in the D1 World Series in Tampa. Tami, Eileen and I listened to the game against Delaware on the internet.

Now I was finding out what my family had gone through while following my games from afar all those years. I felt helpless. We were so nervous as Logan came in from the bullpen in the fifth inning. He worked through an early jam and then settled in. He had some good, quick innings. In the seventh, the Badgers scored four runs to tie the game. The game would stay tied and go into extra innings, and Logan stayed in the game. I was a wreck. UW ended up winning the game in the 13th with Logan pitching the last 7 1/3 innings in relief with no runs on one hit.

There was a post-game radio show. Logan was the Player of the Game, and he was interviewed. It was about 3:00 a.m., but we stayed up the whole time, so excited to listen to Logan talk on the radio about his performance.

The script had officially been flipped.

Logan graduated in the spring of 2015 with his business degree.

Over the years, I've done various things for the Brewers, public relations and promotional work—like being a part of Brewers Fan Fest and other team events. I've even done some broadcasting for local cable high school and college games, and a few Brewers games on Fox Sports North. I really enjoy that. I've made some new friends in the Brewers' organization like Rick Schlesinger, Tyler Barnes, and Jeff Levering. I enjoy being a small part of it.

As for that teaching degree, I think I found my calling. After leaving the Menomonee Falls school district, I subbed for a couple of years. In 2015, I was asked by the Germantown School District if I would be a full-time special education aide at Kennedy Middle School. I agreed. The only bad thing about this job is that it is considered a part-time job, six-and-a-half hours a day, therefore no benefits, most particularly no health insurance. Otherwise, this is a very rewarding gig. I worked with 6th through 8th grade students who have learning disabilities; now I'm at the high school. Some students just need extra help, and some have behavioral issues that affect their learning.

There were a couple of boys who made me earn my money every day my first year, but it's so rewarding when you make a connection and help them. I had other students who had Autism, Down's Syndrome, and other physical and mental disabilities. I have gained experience working with kids with disabilities. You become very close with these kids, they also learn to trust you, and they love you. I get close with them because I like to joke around and tease them.

They like that, being treated like a typical kid and student. I have continued doing this job through the present 2024–2025 school year.

I obviously still watch baseball at the professional level with great interest. I understand that baseball has continued to change over the decades. I still love watching, even with my little gripes about the modern game. I despise how pitching is used today. The starting pitcher doesn't go out to pitch the entire game. Even when the starting pitcher is dominating, he gets taken out for a reliever. Starters are often taken out in the fourth and fifth innings, even when they're winning. The automatic relief pitcher roles—the seventh inning man, then the eighth inning man, and then the closer for a one inning (or less) of relief to save the game. Not a fan of this approach.

From my point of view, it takes just one of these guys to blow it. I believe in using the "hot hand" to pitch. Today in the big leagues, even if a guy strikes out the side in "his" inning, he gets taken out for the next guy, who sometimes comes in cold and blows it that day. I don't use a relief pitcher unless relief is needed. Also, I hate the 100-pitch count. When a pitcher gets near that 100-pitch count, changes automatically have to be made. It's all about "the book." I don't like a game to be run by "the book" or the analytic statistics. I do agree with using stats to help you make a decision, but don't let every decision be based on statistics alone over human heart and feeling. You can do something unexpected. It's too easy to play it safe "by the book," and if it doesn't work, a manager can just say he went with the statistics.

Teams should bunt when the whole left side of the field is wide open. The power swinging versus the power pitching dominates. Nobody hits the ball to the right side to move a runner over anymore. There's no bunting because analytics say it gives away an out when a home run drives the runners in from any base. Same thing about base stealing. The book says why risk the out of stealing, when a home run scores a runner from first just as easily? They're all playing for the home run now.

As for pitchers, it's like the Pittsburgh Pirates coach told me. You're not a prospect unless you throw 95 miles per hour. For my money, I want to see pitchers pitch, carve a hitter up by changing speeds and locations with more than just the power fastball.

I truly believe the game will change again and move back in the other direction soon enough.

Bottom line is that nothing has made me love the game any less. If you love something, you want only the best for it. When I'm critical, it's because I care so much.

I still get fan mail—including baseball cards I'm asked to sign. I try to take care of all the requests. It's nice to be remembered. It's crazy where fans send these cards. They find any address they can connect to me and mail stuff there. They used to send them to your home stadium, but after you're done playing, they have to find another address.

So now, my baseball cards—everything from my Topps 1984 Olympic team card to my Major League cards—get sent to my mom's house in Mission Viejo, California; to my brother Brett's house, where his ex-wife still lives (and she forwards them to me on occasion); my mother-in-law's house in Menomonee Falls; the middle school and high school where I've taught and coached; and of course the house where Tami and I live now. Not sure how they find these addresses, but they do.

Besides signing things, people ask me questions. Most of them ask things like: who were my best friends on the team, who were the toughest batters I pitched against, what were my favorite stadiums to pitch in, etc., etc. It's fun to relive the good old times when writing back. It never ends, and I don't mind. I actually enjoy it. It's great that people still remember.

Over the years, a lot of people have talked baseball with me, and I told them a lot of my stories. Continuously over the years, people seriously told me that I should write a book with these funny, weird, and interesting stories. I never took them seriously. I felt like people who didn't know me wouldn't be interested or wouldn't think my stories were interesting.

I'd just laugh it off. I didn't have the urge or want to put the time in to do it.

Until now.

After being roughly 15 years removed from my playing days, I decided that I'd do it. In March of 2015, I began putting my thoughts down on paper (or at least a computer screen). I wanted this book to show what life and baseball was like for an American playing in foreign countries. It's a long process, and it's hard to expose yourself—things I think are funny and good, maybe other people may not. Could be embarrassing.

In the end, what I want to get across is just this: "What a life!" What a ride I was able to experience. I owe everything to baseball. It's my life, passion, and soul, it's what I am. I want to be involved in baseball until the day I die.

There are way too many people I'd love to thank for their invaluable help along the way: Family, friends, coaches, teammates, and many more. I can't list them all. I just want those people to know how much they've meant along the way, too.

I heard a story about a man who was over 80 years old still playing in an over-60 baseball league. He felt a little tired at the end of an inning, took himself out of the game, and went over to sit at the end of the bench. A few minutes later, somebody noticed that he was slumped over, and they saw him fall off the end of that bench. He died of a heart attack right there in the dugout. His son was telling the story. He said that his father died happy. He was wearing his baseball uniform at the baseball field.

If I get to choose, that's how I'd like to make my final out.

Epilogue
With a Little Help from My Friends

No athlete who reaches the highest level of his profession ever gets there alone. My journey wouldn't have even gotten off the ground without people like my parents and my youth coaches, of course. Guys like Coach Bob Zamora at Capistrano Valley High School and Coaches Paul Deese and Mike Weathers at Chapman College deserve mounds of credit for helping me reach my potential. I want to acknowledge them and some more of these guys before we close this book.

There were my professional coaches, like Tony Muser, Carlos Alfonso, Tom Trebelhorn, Chuck Hartenstein, Charlie Manuel, Eddie Watt and more. All helped me along the way as I progressed through the ranks.

But the journey through professional baseball—especially when you're deciding to play in a foreign country—also includes teammates who are truly important to your success on the field, and your survival off of it.

At home, I was lucky enough to be teammates and friends with guys like Mike Hogan, Chuck Jackson, Rob Mallicoat, Mark Knudson, Mark Ciardi, John Henry Johnson, Bryan Clutterbuck, Tom Filer, Dan Plesac, Mike Birkbeck, George Canale, and Mark Lee, to name just a few. These are guys I would be friends with for the rest of my life. It's not a coincidence that all of them except Jackson and Canale were fellow pitchers.

When I started "Phase Three" of my career, I started to lean on other guys for support and guidance—guys who had been in these foreign environments before me. You needed guys to show you the new/old ropes, because after being in the big leagues for four years, going back to bus rides and budget motels takes a lot of adjustment.

At the start, I made a friend in teammate Don Vesling, a left-handed pitcher who was the only guy on my Double A London, Ontario team who was as old as I was. Don let me live with him, drive to the ballpark with him, and even took me along for a night of bar-hopping on the team bus. We got to be close in a short period of time before the ugly side of the business reared its head. A few weeks into my assignment in Canada, our manager, Mark DeJohns, and pitching coach, Jeff Jones, called me into their office. I thought they were going to tell me that I was moving up to Triple A. Instead, they told me the minor league director had told them to ask me a question: The team was going to release a pitcher from our team, and they wanted me to know that if I was unhappy here, they would let me go and I could go find another team. If I wanted to stay, they were going to release Vesling. It was bullshit that they put that on me, but I wanted to continue my career. I told them I wanted to stay, so they called Don in and released him.

Even in the dead of summer, the minor leagues can be a very, *very* cold place.

In Triple A, I was also lucky enough to cross paths with guys like Karl Allaire, Jeff Kaiser, and Dave Johnson. When I started traveling to foreign lands, I found more guys I could turn to for help getting adjusted. Jeff Parry and Mackey Sasser helped me in Puerto Rico. I really appreciated them.

In Mexico, I leaned on Roy Salinas, Chris Bennett, and Phil Harrison. Roy was the go-to guy. His parents were born in Mexico, but he was American. Roy was bilingual, which was huge at the start of my time there. Meanwhile Phil, a fellow Californian, had a little trouble adjusting to Mexico. He went AWOL, but he came back ... and we became good friends. But eventually being in Mexico got to him, and he got released. I was bummed.

I met pitcher Tom McCarthy at the end of the 1993 season when we were teammates in Charlotte. Later, Tom joined our team during my second stint in Mexico. Tom and I got along great. He was a fun guy, and we hung out a lot on the road in Charlotte. He was one of my better friends on that team. When Tom got to Puebla, he and I roomed together with Marty Clary, before Marty's son died tragically in the accident at our apartment building.

Mike Browning was another pitcher I became close with—although we had our stressful moments. We got to be close friends and confidants. I was with Mike when he found out his mother had died back home. We shared a lot. But a few times while walking with Mike, I got so irritated with him. Once he was telling me about something, and I didn't understand what he was talking about. When I told him that, he got all pissed off and told me I was an idiot for not knowing what he was trying to say. Kind of like brothers fighting, I guess. But if either one of us needed help, we were always there for each other.

As important as American teammates—guys who were already familiar with the surroundings—were in Mexico, they were ten times that important in Taiwan. I don't know how I would have survived that first season on the island if I didn't have guys like Tony Metoyer, Ron Jones, and Cecil Espy already there and waiting for me. Tony and I had played together in the Astros' organization when I first signed, and I'd played against Cecil when he was with the Texas Rangers. In fact, I once threw a pitch pretty much right under Cecil's chin in a game in Arlington, Texas. I wasn't sure if he still remembered that the first night I joined the team when he came by my hotel room in Taiwan.

Remember, these are all very competitive guys. Nobody came to Taiwan for a vacation. This was work for us. And we had to keep that competitive frame of mind all the time. Even when we were just hanging out, those competitive streaks would show through. One night soon after I arrived in Taiwan, we were at Tony's apartment and out came the dominoes game. I hadn't played dominoes in a long time, but it didn't take me long to get in the swing. These guys got *into it!* They slammed down their dominoes and got in your face when they made a good play. It wasn't a quiet game by any means.

One night while we were playing, Cecil brought up the knockdown pitch. "Hey, Don, do you remember the time when I was with the Rangers when you dropped me with that knock-down pitch?" I paused, then said, "Yes, I remember." He replied, "I was so pissed at you, I wanted to kill you." I told him I remembered him looking crazy mad when he got to third base while I was backing up, and how he was cursing at me. I also told him he seemed to be okay when I ran into him at a bar after the game. He said he was still pissed off but didn't want to say or do anything in a public place. Then he added, "That was a great knockdown!" The other guys enjoyed listening to the story.

Tony was the guy who had been in Taiwan the longest—seven years—so he knew the ropes the best. I learned everything from Tony—how to get around, how to speak to cab drivers, order food, find essential stores, do my banking, read the sports pages, find fun things to do … all of it. He introduced me to a lot of people who became valuable friends over the course of the next five years. I owe him a lot.

I crossed paths with a lot of former teammates who had also picked Taiwan as a place to continue their baseball careers. Chris Bennett, my roommate from Mexico, showed up. So did my former Astros organization roommates, Rob Mallicoat and Chuck Jackson. I also ran into former Astros teammate Julio Solano in Charlotte, Mexico, *and* Taiwan. It's a small baseball world, after all.

After playing my first two seasons in the Chinese Professional Baseball League, I moved over to the Taiwan Major League and met new American teammates like Corey Powell and Ron Gerstein. Corey and his wife, Glory (fellow SoCal natives), and Ron and his wife, Tisa, became close friends and helped me a lot ... especially when Tami and Logan came to visit. I really appreciated what they did for us.

One day, Corey got locked out of his apartment, and nobody was there. He came by my apartment, which was right next door on the 28th floor. He came to hang out and wait for someone to return. After a while, he got antsy and thought he could go out on my balcony and somehow go across the four-foot gap between our balconies. This didn't sound like a good idea to me. We were 28 floors up, and this four-foot gap between our balconies didn't have a safety net. He asked me to hold onto him as he crossed over. I didn't want to do this, but I held him as he crossed. If he had slipped, there was no way I could have held him, since he weighed around 230 pounds. He made it across, but for weeks after that I had nightmares every so often of him slipping and me watching him fall the 28 floors to the sidewalk below. Sort of like the dumb thing I did when we were hanging out on the roof of our high-rise apartment where I walked on the ledge 33 stories up.

I met another American teammate, outfielder Brad Strauss, who played the previous year for Gida and Luka. He was one of the top hitters in the TML, and we ended up roommates. One night while Tami and Logan were visiting and I was staying in, the rest of the guys went out on the town. We were asleep when all of a sudden, I heard someone pounding on the front door ... hard. Bam! Bam! Bam! I woke up thinking, what the hell's going on? It was about 3 a.m. After more pounding, I heard Corey yelling, "Brad, open up the door, you motherfucker, open up! I want to kick your fuckin' ass!" I heard Brad say, "No.... I'm not gonna open the door." Corey banged on the door some more. This noise also woke up Tami and Logan. I'm sure it woke everyone living on my floor. After a while, Corey finally left. He was really pissed about something. The next day I found out why.

The night before, they'd all been out drinking and playing pool. Brad was not a good drinker. His personality changed. He would begin to talk a lot of crap and get obnoxious. Evidently, Corey had gotten tired of Brad's mouth. Something happened, and Corey snapped. He punched Brad in the head, and the rest of the guys had to grab and hold Corey so he wouldn't kill Brad. Holding Corey gave Brad the opportunity to get out of the bar, and he came back to our apartment. Corey followed, which led to the pounding on the door. Unfortunately, when Corey punched Brad, he hurt his hand. When he went to the doctor the next morning, he found out it was broken. Now our home run hitter and best outfielder was out. What could we tell the team?

As fate would have it, in the game the previous night, Corey had to dive for a ball in the outfield. He told our manager, Yamani, and the TML

Don (left) and teammate Corey Powell in 1999.

officials that he hurt his hand on that dive. All of us backed up his story and never said anything about the fight at the bar. The next day, when Corey had cooled down, Brad apologized, and everyone told Corey to let it go. Corey was originally told he would miss over a month of the season, but he only missed about three weeks, thankfully.

Like I said about Mike Browning, teammates are like brothers … and brothers fight. Then they get over it and move on.

We even had an American coach I got to be friends with. His name was Mark Budaska, and he was our hitting coach. He earned my respect when he took a stand for us with a medical clinic that wanted to take a not-so-safe shortcut in doing blood work on us.

We were at the end of the process of getting complete physicals, and the whole while, we had been laughing and joking around with the nurses. Then they ushered us into a room that wasn't at all clean or sanitary. The table that we were supposed to sit at looked like a large card table. It was dirty, and it had other people's blood still on it. It wasn't just a drop or two, it had two big spots of blood the size of 50-cent pieces. They asked three of us to sit down first and give our blood. When we saw the blood on the table, we were shocked and not sure what to do. The nurses took used syringes that were already sitting on the table and were getting them ready to be reused. The mood changed quickly from everyone being relaxed to everyone being very serious.

One of the guys spoke up and said, "This isn't right." We asked the nurses if they could clean the blood off the table and get new syringes for each of us. They said, "No, everything is fine." We asked them if those were used syringes, and they said, "yes, but it's okay." We quickly said, "No, it's not!" They were refusing to get new syringes. It appeared to be a cost-saving thing. Finally, Mark stood up and announced, "If they don't clean up that blood and get new syringes, we are leaving, I'll take the blame!" Now the nurses were mad at us, and they went and got the doctor. When the doctor arrived, Mark told him the same thing. The doctor started saying the same thing as the nurses. They didn't believe that we would leave, but when we all got up and started to go out the door, they finally changed their tone. They cleaned the blood and got new syringes for all of us. It was amazing. They were so mad at us, like we were the "arrogant Americans" and had done something wrong. It was awkward for the rest of the time. There was a lot of silence; you could feel the tension as each of us took our turn to give blood. When we were done, we left the clinic. I was proud of Mark for standing up for us, and being willing to take the blame. He earned all our respect that day.

Not all my American teammates found success in Taiwan. That didn't mean we weren't friends, of course. Bob Spears came to Taiwan having played Independent League baseball after pitching at Ohio State. I could see that he was kind of freaked out and overwhelmed in Taiwan. While he was adjusting off the field, on the field he was given the Taiwanese name "Babeer." He didn't like it much. He said that we all had cool Chinese names—like mine meant Augustus Caesar the European King. Corey's Chinese name was Chung Shwin, which meant "The General." Bob said his name had no meaning and sounded stupid. Since he let us know that he didn't like his name, we of course teased him about it all the time. Bob was let go after a short time with the team, and he and I flew back to the States on the same plane during our mid-season break. I was going home for a visit. We had a layover in Los Angeles, and I could tell Bob was bummed out that Taiwan didn't work out for him. Too bad. He was a good dude.

All this was happening around the time I first met Steve Wilson, the left-handed pitcher from Canada who would become my favorite baseball roommate ever. We did everything together while we were teammates, and even after Steve retired, he stayed in Taiwan, and we still got to spend time together. He helped me through some tough times, and we'll always be friends.

I was very surprised and saddened when I found out that Steve had decided to hang up his spikes after the TML released him. For two seasons, Steve pitched very well for us. He was my home roommate in 1997 and my road roommate for both 1997 and 1998. I had so much fun hanging with him. He was always game to do things.

I said goodbye to all these great people when I went home for the final time. Haven't seen any of them since. I still hope to someday.

Then there was Italy and all the adventures Europe had in store. I had some great teammates there too, guys who helped me adjust to a very different foreign country. For starters, practically every player on the team spoke English, which was nice. Our manager, Mike Romano, was a good guy from New York City who had played on the 1984 Italian Olympic team. We spent some time reminiscing about those days—and it rekindled my interest in perhaps playing in the 2000 Olympics—a quest that didn't quite work out. He and pitching coach Jim "Jimbo" Dickson made playing in Italy easy for me.

In Italy, I became teammates with Jim Vatcher, a former San Diego Padres player I'd also played against—and hung out with—in Taiwan. Vatch had played with Rimini the season before and knew all the ropes. He was an outstanding defensive outfielder who's now a prominent baseball outfield coach and trainer in SoCal. It was great being his teammate.

Tista Perri was a pitcher from Northern California I really leaned on when I first got there. He helped me learn how to grocery shop and generally just get along in Rimini and there was Eric Pini and Brian Thomas. Jason Simmontacchi, another pitcher from Mountain View, California, had a great season for us. I was impressed with his stuff—he threw hard, in the low 90s, and had a hard, sharp breaking ball. Jason pitched in the Major Leagues with the St. Louis Cardinals a few years later. Around the same time, I found out I was not going to be part of Team USA in the 2000 Olympics, we found out that Jason would be part of the Italian team. I was so happy for him. He really deserved it.

I never intended to spend more than one season in Italy, so leaving after winning the championship meant saying goodbye to a lot of great teammates. Just like the guys I played with in America, Mexico, and Taiwan, they all helped create some great memories for me, and I will always be grateful for the help and support they gave me.

Index

Adair, Rick 107
Adriatic Sea 153, 166
Agan 99, 182
Akins Sid 12, 13
Akron, Ohio 106
Alaska 2, 8, 24, 135, 169
Alaska Baseball League 154
Alaska Psychiatric Institute 135
Albany, New York 57
Alfaro, Flavio 12
Alfonso, Carlos 17, 20, 196, 209
Allaire, Karl 210
Alondra Park 6
Alps 158
Altar of the Fatherland 162
American Association 197
American Institute in Taiwan (AIT) 126
American League East 170
American League Rookie of the Year 19, 185
American Zone 53
Anaheim, California 11
Anaheim Stadium 9, 104
Anchorage, Alaska 100, 101, 154
Anderson, Sparky 5
Anzio, Italy 154, 155
Argentina 71
Arizona 141, 142
Arizona Fall Instructional League 15
Arizona State University 8
Arkansas 107
Arlington, Texas 211
Arno River 167, 168
Asia 152
Astro Dome 11
Atlanta Braves 92, 109, 110, 112, 118
August, Brett 6, 10, 207
August, Gary 6
August, Lance 6, 10, 28, 47, 56, 103–105, 148, 153, 155–158, 161, 162, 164, 167
August, Logan 26, 53, 69, 77, 90, 91, 93, 94, 97–103, 122, 144, 153, 164–169, 171, 182, 191, 199–202, 204–206, 212
August, Sharon 6, 16
August, Steve 6, 10
August, Tami 25, 29, 33, 34, 47, 49, 53, 68, 69, 77, 85, 90, 91, 93, 96–102, 109, 119, 122, 138, 139, 144, 145, 152, 153, 164–169, 171, 184, 191, 203, 205, 208, 212
Augustine, Jerry 204
Augustus Caesar the European King 178, 214
Australia 21, 35, 83, 146, 189, 194
Austria 158, 159
Avery, Steve 110

Badgers 206
Baker Dusty 136
Baldacci, Mateo 191
Baller, Jay 112
Baltimore, Maryland 152
Baltimore Orioles 111, 170
Bando, Sal 20, 170
Bankhead, Scott 12–14
Barker, Len 26
Barnes, Tyler 206
Barquistimeto, Venezuela 120
Baseball Hall of Fame 24, 107
Battle of Puebla 122
The Beatles 66, 187
Ben (Australian kid) 146
Bennett, Chris 24, 37, 59, 74, 136–138, 210, 211
Berchtesgaden, Germany 159
Berra, Yogi 16
Berry, Chuck 106, 119, 138, 172, 174
Bevington, Terry 197
Big Ten 205
Binghamton, New York 171
Birkbeck, Mike 172, 209
Black Eagles 132
Bologna, Italy 153, 164, 165
Bonifay, Cam 109, 112–114

218 Index

Boone, Bob 18
Borque, Ray 193
Bosnia 158
Boston Red Sox 19
Brewers Fan Fest 206
Brisbane, Australia 146, 197
Brock, Greg 170
Browning, Mike 94, 210, 213
Budaska, Mark 85, 150, 213, 214
Buddhist Temple 51
Burba, Dave 20
Burlingame, Ben 186
Byrd, Paul 22

Caffrey, Bob 11
Cairo, Sergio 128, 129
Calgary, Canada 49, 110, 115, 116, 118, 141, 142, 174
Cal State Fullerton 8, 9
California 28, 37, 148, 204
California Angels 9, 18, 20
California vs Oklahoma High School All-Star Game 7
Calvo, Bernie 59, 60
Campeche, Mexico 39, 41, 59, 78, 94, 106, 174
Canada 12, 21, 36, 57, 106, 146, 194, 210, 215
Canale, George 112, 209
Cape Cod All-Stars 11
Capistrano Valley High School 6, 7, 209
Caribbean 35, 36
Carlos (cabbie in Puebla) 91
Carmen, Mexico 41
Carroll College 203, 204
Cashman Park 104
Castillo, Marty 8
Castle Sant'angelo 162
Castro, Bill 41
Castro, Fidel 102
Champion, Keith 107
Chan 50
Chapman College 8, 9, 17, 135, 204, 209
Charlotte, North Carolina 22, 23, 25, 41, 92, 107, 112, 138, 139, 201, 210, 211
Chiayi, Taiwan 84, 181
Chicago, Illinois 77
Chicago Cubs 146
Chicago White Sox 19, 114, 115
Chichen Itza 40
Chin Yi Ping 144, 145
China 27, 30, 49, 124–126
China Airlines 95
Chinese New Year 101, 102
Chinese Professional Baseball League (CPBL) 30, 49, 66, 81, 82, 117, 125, 127, 131, 132, 144, 145, 179, 180, 211
Chinese Taipei 5, 12, 13, 101

Chinese Taipei Olympic Baseball Team 197
Chris (pub owner, Germany) 160, 161
Ciardi, Mark 209
Cincinnati Reds 154, 204
Cinco de Mayo 122, 123
Clark, Will 12, 13
Clary, Ginger 92–94
Clary, Marty 92–94, 210
Clary, Weston 92–94
Cleveland, Ohio 19, 107
Cleveland Indians 22, 23, 25, 26, 42, 106, 138, 139, 170, 172–174, 181
Cleveland Municipal Stadium 181
Club Baseball World Series Division 1 205
Club Baseball World Series Division 2 205
Clutterbuck, Bryan 209
Coach Adam 197, 198
Coach Kim 181
The Colosseum 162, 163, 165, 167
Columbus, Georgia 16
Columbus, Ohio 172
Columbus Clippers 172
Cook Inlet Bucs 8
Cooper, Cecil 204
Cooperstown, New York 22–25, 107
Costco 87
Craig, Roger 20
The Creation of Adam 163
Crim, Chuck 170
Cuba 102
Cyber Bar 194
Czech Republic 156

Da Pan 148
Dachau, Germany 160
Dachau Concentration Camp 160
Dalton, Harry 17, 20, 170
Dante (Rimini concession man) 155, 156, 164
Dar (Sinon Bulls GM) 177, 179, 181
Darwin, Danny 16
Davis, Chili 18
Dean 181
Dean's List 204, 205
Dedeaux, Rod 5, 13–15
Deese, Paul 8, 136, 196, 209
DeJohns, Mark 210
De La Cruz, Hector 128, 129
DeLeon, Elcilio 126
De Los Santos, Luis 186
Denver, Colorado 19, 170
Denver Zephyrs 20
Des Moines, Iowa 197
Detroit, Michigan 49, 100
Detroit Tigers 25, 26, 57, 170, 171, 200

Index

Dickson, Jim (Jimbo) 154, 155, 158, 159, 161, 191, 215
Dodger Stadium 5, 12, 13, 104
Doi San 148, 149
Dominican Republic 12, 13, 21, 41–43, 46–49, 54, 60, 73, 75–78, 80, 91, 121, 173, 194
Dominican Winter League 173, 174
The Doors 19, 61
Dorado, Puerto Rico 36
Double Day Field 22, 25
Downing, Brian 18
Dublin, Ireland 161
Dunne, Mike 12, 13, 15
Duomo 168, 169

Eagle Pass, Texas 59
Eagles 132
Eagle's Nest 159
earthquakes 32–34
elephants 128, 130
Elway, John 192
Espy, Cecil 28, 79, 190, 210
Etchebarren, Andy 202
Europe 156, 158, 160, 161, 191, 215
European Cup (baseball) 156, 157
European Cup (soccer) 156
Evangelisti, Andrea 192

Fala 177, 200
Fehr, Donald 113
Fermin, Felix 121
Fernando 42–44, 47, 48
Filer, Tom 209
Fingers, Rollie 204
Fisk, Carlton 204
Florence, Italy 167, 168
Florence Cathedral 168
Flores, Jesse 7, 9, 21
Florida 111, 113, 141
Flynt, Will 117, 119
Foster, George 204
Fountain of Trevi 162
Fox Sports North 206
France 192
Freddy 44–47
Frohwirth, Todd 112, 115

Galleria dell' Academia 168
Gantner, Jim 204
Gantner/August Baseball Camp 204
Garland, Wayne 118
Garmisch-Partenkirchen, Germany 160, 161
German people 45
German soldiers 155, 168
Germantown High School 202

Germantown School District 206
Germany 89, 153, 156, 159, 160
Gerstein, Ron 53, 54, 102, 182, 183, 211
Gerstein, Tisa 53, 102, 211
Ghost Money 96
Ghost Month 96
Gida 149, 150, 182, 185, 187, 202, 212
Glavine, Tom 110
Gotzler, Tim 201
Graffiti's 104
Green, Gary 12
Green, Otis 191
Griffey, Ken, Jr. 201
Griffey, Ken, Sr. 201
Grizzly Adams 97
Grosseto, Italy 162, 191, 192
Guinness 89, 161
Gwynn, Chris 6, 12, 15
Gwynn, Tony 6

Hall of Fame Game 22, 107
Haney, Larry 18
Hansen, Pat 201
Harrison, Phil 24, 37, 74, 136–138, 210
Hart, John 173
Hartenstein, Chuck 209
Hi Corbett Field 17
Higuera, Teddy 19
Hilton, Dave 189
Hisle, Larry 204
Hitler, Adolf 159
Hogan, Mike 209
Holland 153, 156, 157
Hollywood, California 5
Hooters 86
Hoover, John 12, 13, 15
Horn, Sam 23, 112
Houston, Texas 11
Houston Astros 9, 10, 15–17, 20, 25, 28, 49, 109, 136, 171, 211
Houston Colt .45s 154
Hsinchu, Taiwan 80

Inglewood, California 6
Innsbruck, Austria 160
Iran 126
Ireland 89
Ireland, Tim 149–152, 202
Irish Pub (Garmisch) 160
Irvine High School 7
Italian Baseball League 153–156, 191, 193, 194
Italian Olympic Baseball Team; 1984 215; 2000 215
Italy 1, 12, 21, 35, 71, 87–90, 105, 152, 155, 156, 158, 159, 164, 170, 190, 191, 194, 195, 198–200, 202, 205

Jackie 131
Jackson, Chuck 17, 209, 211
Jackson, Mike 20
Japan 11, 12, 15, 61, 144, 151, 178, 181–183, 185–187
Jenkins, Fergie 204
Jensen, John 139, 140
Johnson, Dave 210
Johnson, John Henry 209
Jones, Jeff 210
Jones, Randy 8
Jones, Ron 64–66, 210
Jordan (Taiwan) 143, 144
Jordan, Michael 114, 115, 143
Jose (landlord) 92, 93
Joyner, Wally 18, 113, 114
Judy (Taiwan) 147, 148
Jungo Bears 143, 144, 178, 179
Jurassic Night Club 143

Kaiser, Jeff 210
Kansas 107
Kansas City A's 154
Kansas City Royals 152
Kao-Ping Fala 181
Kaohsiung, Taiwan 28, 33, 34, 51, 55, 82, 85, 87, 103, 125, 143, 181
Kaohsiung Harbor 149
Kennedy Middle School 206
Kenting, Taiwan 99, 100
Kevin (translator) 70
King Dome 120
Kissimmee, Florida 15
Knepper, Bob 16
Knudson, Mark 17, 18, 113, 209
Kohler, Kevin 186, 187
Korea 5, 11–13, 25, 69
KTV 63, 66, 129, 133, 143
Kuo, Chin-hsing 132

Ladd, Pete 204
Lake Erie 181
Lakeshore Chinooks 202
Land O Lakes Baseball League 200
Lanier, Hal 16
Laredo, Mexico 40
Laredo, Texas 140
Larkin, Barry 12
Las Vegas, Nevada 47, 104, 107
Lasorda, Tommy 23, 194
Lawndale, California 6
LAX 103
Leaning Tower of Pisa 162
Lee, Mark 111, 209
Leon, Max 60
Leuzinger High School 6, 7, 204
Levering, Jeff 206

Libres, Mexico 73, 74
Licey 173
Linehan, Mary 71, 72, 153, 154
Linehan, Tim 71, 72, 153, 154
Lions 101, 131
Little League 199
Little League World Series 61
Logan, Johnny 205
Logue, Tony 200
London, England 169
London, Ontario, Canada 26, 57, 171, 209
Long Beach State University 8
Lono, Joel 154
Los Angeles, California 14, 36, 101, 103, 105, 214
Los Angeles Coliseum 12, 14, 15
Los Angeles Dodgers 5, 6, 14, 22, 23, 146
Louisville, Kentucky 10
Lu Ming Su 150
Lucas, Gary 8
Luka 181, 184, 185, 212

Machado, Julio 120, 121
Mack, Shane 12, 13
Maddux, Greg 110, 119
Major League (movie) 204
Major League Baseball Alumni Players Association 204
Mallicoat, Rob 209, 211
Manning, Peyton 193
Manno, Bruce 17
Manone, Joe 198, 199
Manuel, Charlie 172, 209
Marco (Kenting Thai restaurant owner) 100
Marsh, Tom 48
Marzano, John 12, 13
Mattingly, Dennis 8
Mayans 40
Maysey, Matt 112, 141
McCarthy, Tom 92, 210
McDonald's 79, 87, 88, 166
McDowell, Oddibe 6, 12–14
McGwire, Mark 5, 12, 24
Meacham, Bobby 116–118
Menomonee Falls, Wisconsin 200, 207
Menomonee Falls Falcons 199
Menomonee Falls High School 196, 201, 202
Menomonee Falls Lakers 200
Menomonee Falls School District 205, 206
Mercedes, Luis 112, 140, 141
Metoyer, Tony 28, 29, 66, 68, 82, 127, 128, 143, 145, 181, 211
Mexican League 36, 39, 48, 73, 107, 110, 174

Index

Mexico 1, 21, 23, 35–37, 41, 49, 58–61, 73, 75, 77, 78, 80, 82, 90–92, 106, 107, 116, 117, 119, 122, 123, 136, 138, 139, 151, 172, 174, 194, 205, 210, 211, 215
Mexico City, Mexico 39, 91, 123, 124, 139
Mexico City Tigres 59
Michelangelo 163, 168
Micronesia 136
Miller, Dyar 173
Milwaukee, Wisconsin 1, 19, 27, 33, 41, 44, 47–49, 56, 71, 90, 101, 103, 112, 119, 120, 138, 170, 184–186
Milwaukee Brewers 2, 14, 16–18, 20, 23, 25, 108, 109, 111, 112, 117, 120, 149, 170–174, 181, 196, 202, 206
Milwaukee County Stadium 18, 19, 170
Minnesota Twins 7, 9, 21, 186
Mirabella, Paul 18
Mission Viejo, California 6, 101, 207
Mitchell, Kevin 20
MLB Network 2
Modena, Italy 157
Molitor, Paul 18
Montana's Bar 146
Monterrey, Mexico 40
Moore, Charlie 204
Morton, Kevin 52, 53
Mountain View, California 215
MSOE (Milwaukee School of Engineering) 202, 203
Mueller, Willie 204; The Duke 204
Munich, Germany 160
Muser, Tony 20, 209
Mutual of Omaha's Wild Kingdom 98

Narr, Don 103
Narr, Eileen 90, 91, 97, 122, 164, 166, 167, 205
National League Central 170
Nedset, Ronnie 204
Nelson, Davey 205
Nelson, Fred 20
Netherlands 153, 156, 157
Nettuno, Italy 154, 155, 191, 192
New Berlin Eisenhower High School 202
New York City 25, 125, 215
New York Mets 17
New York Yankees 6, 170
Newark, Doug 136
Nicaragua 12
Niekro, Joe 16
Niekro, Phil 204
USS *Nimitz* Fleet 126
Nixon, President Richard 125
Norfolk, Virginia 138
Normandy, France 154

North Carolina State University Hall of Fame 2
Northern California 215

Oakland A's 136
Ogea, Chad 22
Ohio State University 214
Oliver's 87, 165, 166
Olympic Baseball Card 12, 207
Olympic Village 11, 12
Olympics 1, 5, 11, 15, 24, 101, 136, 194; 1972 Innsbruck 160; 1984 Los Angeles 12, 14, 15, 156; 2000 Sydney 193; 2000 United States 194, 215
Opening Day 107, 108, 115, 181; TML 1997 Chiayi 181; TML 1998 182; TML 1999 187
Orange County High School Baseball All-Star Game 7
Oregon 154
Ortiz, David 65
Orza, Gene 113

Pacific Coast League 16, 117
Pacific Ocean 29, 101, 103, 182, 197
Pacillo, Pat 6, 12, 13, 15
Pancho Villa 40
Parma, Italy 154, 156, 164
Parry, Jeff 210
Peña, Arturo 121
Peña, Tony 42, 91, 92, 121
People's Republic of China 125
Perfect Game 203
Perri, Tista 215
Pettibone, Jay 8
Philippines 29, 146
Phoenix, Arizona 17, 21, 136
Piazza, Mike 23
Piazza del Popolo 162
Piazza della Signoria 167, 168
Pico, Jeff 77
Pig and Whistle 143
Pingtung, Taiwan 27
Pini, Eric 88, 157
Pisa, Italy 162
Pittsburgh Pirates 48, 49, 61, 109–11, 115, 116, 118, 140, 143, 174, 207
Players Association 109, 111, 113, 115, 116, 119
Plesac, Dan 1, 18, 209
Ponte della Paslia 154
Ponte Sant'angelo 162
Ponte Vecchio 167
Porzio, Nando 191
Powell, Corey 33, 54, 55, 67, 68, 84–86, 102, 104, 105, 150, 211–213
Powell, Glory 33, 102, 211
Procuratie Vecchi 15

Puebla, Mexico 36, 38, 40, 41, 58, 74, 77, 78, 91, 92, 106, 122, 124, 137–139, 172, 174
Puerto Plata, Dominican Republic 41, 43, 44, 75, 76
Puerto Rico 21, 27, 28, 36, 49, 58, 73, 90, 107, 112, 116, 172, 194, 210
Puikunas, Ed 135, 136

Ramirez, Manny 22, 42
Ray, Johnny 18
Reagan, President Ronald 12, 24
Rennicke, Dean 202
Replacement Players 108–112, 114–117, 151, 174
Republic of China 49, 125
Reynolds, Craig 16
Richmond, Virginia 110, 172
Rigali, Rosalind 193
Rimini, Italy 71, 87, 152–156, 158, 161, 162, 164–167, 191, 215
Riverside Elementary School 205
Robinson, David 193
Robinson, Ron 20
Rodriguez, Boi 116
Rogers Center 1
Roman Forum 162, 167
Romano, Mike 157, 191, 215
Rome, Italy 162, 167
Rookie of the Year 99
Rosen, Al 20
Ryan, Nolan 16, 18

St. Claire, Randy 112
St. Louis Cardinals 215
Saint Peter's Basilica 162
Saint Peter's Square 162, 167
Salcedo, Jose 187, 188
Salinas, Roy 37, 59, 210
Salzburg, Austria 159
Sambito, Joe 16
San Diego Padres 49, 106, 108, 117, 170, 174, 215
San Diego State University 7
San Francisco Giants 20–22, 25, 117, 118, 170, 200
San Jose, California 7
San Juan, Puerto Rico 36
San Marino 21, 155, 156, 166
Santiago, Dominican Republic 41, 42, 44, 45, 47, 69, 76, 91, 121
Santo Domingo, Dominican Republic 47, 123
Sarasota, Florida 115
Sasser, Mackey 112, 115, 210
Schlesinger, Rick 206
Schofield, Dick 18

Scolinos, John 13
Scott, Mike 16
Scottsdale, Arizona 117, 140, 170
Il Scudetto 20
Seattle Mariners 20, 120
Sega Genesis: Operation Pacific 54, 190
Seiler, Paul 193, 194
Shea Stadium 25
Sheffield, Gary 170
Silver Medal 25
Simmons, Nelson 112
Simontacchi, Jason 156, 157, 191, 215
Sinon Bulls 133, 179–181
Sistine Chapel 162, 163, 167
Sky Dome 1
Slovenia 158
Smith, Daryl 126, 152, 179, 180, 190
Smith, Joe 141–143
Smoltz, John 110
Snyder, Cory 5, 6, 12, 13, 15, 23
Solano, Julio 211
Southern California 27, 32, 58, 73, 211
Southern California vs Northern California High School All-Star Game 7
Southern League 16
Soviet Union 151
Spain 156
Spanish Steps 162, 167
Spears, Bob 187, 188, 214
Spittal, Austria 159
Stanford University 7
State Champions Back to Back 201
Statue of David 168
Steve the Homer True 111
Stoney 129, 131, 133
Strait of Taiwan 27, 126
Straus, Brad 54, 100, 212, 213
Subway 86
Surhoff, B.J. 12, 14, 15, 17
Sveum, Dale 112, 117
Swift, Billy 12, 20
Swift, Taylor 65
Switzerland 192
Sydney, Australia 194
Syracuse, New York 172

Tai Chi 98
Taichung, Taiwan 27, 30, 34, 50, 52, 66, 101, 102, 128, 145
Tainan, Taiwan 101, 132, 147, 148
Taipei, Taiwan 27, 34, 35, 48, 49, 52, 53, 64, 66, 79, 80, 84–86, 95, 96, 151, 175
Taiwan 12, 21, 27, 28, 30–35, 49–51, 53, 56, 61, 63, 64, 66, 69, 71, 73, 78, 79, 82, 84, 86, 88–90, 94–97, 100–104, 106, 117–119, 124, 125, 150–153, 155, 164, 174, 176,

Index

179–182, 184–187, 189, 190, 194–197, 202, 210, 211, 214, 215
Taiwan Major League (TML) 132, 133, 146, 148, 149, 181, 184, 187, 189, 211, 212, 214
"Take Me Out to the Ballgame" 99
The Talking Heads 25
Tampa, Florida 113, 205
Team USA 1, 5, 10–14, 193, 194
Tellman, Tom 204
Texas 37
Texas Chicken 79
Texas Rangers 146, 211
TGI Fridays 79
Thomas, Brian 157
Thomas, Gorman 204
Thome, Jim 22
TML Gold Glove Award Pitcher 185
TML Most Pitching Wins Award 185
TML Most Valuable Player Award 185–187, 195
Tokyo, Japan 49, 100
Toledo, Ohio 26, 172
Toledo Mud Hens 171
Tony Romas 79
Toronto, Canada 20
Torreon, Mexico 123
Trebelhorn, Tom 18–20, 170, 196, 202. 209
Tucson, Arizona 16, 117
Turkey 32, 34
Typhoon Herb 29, 30
Typhoon Huaning 29
Typhoon Zeb 30

UCLA 8
Ueberroth, Peter 15
Ukraine 156
United States 43, 59, 61, 68, 81, 87, 106, 116, 118, 121, 126, 137, 140, 151, 178, 180–183, 186, 189, 193, 194, 196
United States Baseball Federation 193, 194
United States Olympic Team 2, 193
University of Arizona 9
University of Delaware 205
University of Georgia 102
University of Southern California 8

University of Wisconsin Club Baseball Team 205
University of Wisconsin–Madison 205
Untruth Game 129, 130
US/NATO Military Base 161
Utica, New York 23, 25

Vancouver, Canada 17, 109, 146
Vasquez, Edicta 120
Vatcher, Jim 215
Vatican 162, 167
Vaughn, Greg 204
Velden, Austria 159
Venice, Italy 71, 154, 158
Vesling, Don 209, 210
Vukovich, Pete 109, 110, 112, 114, 118

Wagner, Paul 204
Walker, Chico 18
Waller, Reggie 10, 49, 106–108, 117, 119, 174
Watt, Eddie 17, 209
Wauwatosa, Wisconsin 124
Weathers, Mike 8, 10, 196, 209
Weber, Dave 196, 201
Wendy's 79
Western League 202
WIAA Baseball State Tournament 201
Wichita, Kansas 107, 108, 117, 174
Wichita State University 9
Wilson, Jeffrey 49, 145
Wilson, Steve 85, 146–148, 183, 214
Winfrey, Oprah 205
Witt, Bobby 6, 12, 13, 15
Wood, Bill 16, 17
World Series 6, 107; 1994 48, 106
World War I 159
World War II 154, 168
Wu, Mr. 101, 102, 178–180, 197, 198

Young, John 8
Yount, Robin 18, 202, 204
Yucatan 40

Zamora, Bob 6–8, 10, 196, 209
Zulia Eagles 120